The New Investor Relations
Expert Perspectives on the State of the Art

Edited by Benjamin Mark Cole

"**This compendium by various experts adds significantly to the body of knowledge** related to contemporary investor relations issues."

LOUIS M. THOMPSON, JR.
President & CEO, National Investor Relations Institute

"Executives of today's public companies find themselves in two businesses: their business, and the investor relations business. **This book is a useful tool for success** in that second business."

FREDRIC M. ROBERTS
Former chairman, National Association of Securities Dealers (NASD)
President and founder, FM Roberts & Co.

"**This compendium of guidance is required reading for all those involved with public companies,** whether they be blue chip or microcap. Fifteen experts offer practical advice for dealing with the new world of shareholder relations. These practitioners provide practical investor relations lessons on critical topics including IPOs, crisis management, stock buybacks, M&A, the Internet, investments, private placements, the press, rating agencies, and even chat rooms."

THOMAS FOREST FARB
General Partner and Chief Financial Officer, Summit Partners

"At last, here is a **commonsense guide** to an endeavor celebrated little for common sense."

MICHAEL J. KOSS
President and CEO, Koss Corporation

The New Investor Relations

BLOOMBERG PROFESSIONAL LIBRARY

The New Investor Relations

Expert Perspectives
on the State of the Art

EDITED BY
BENJAMIN MARK COLE

Bloomberg PRESS

PRINCETON

Chapter 14, "IR and the Credit-Ratings Process," by Clifford M. Griep, is published in this volume by permission of Standard & Poor's Ratings Service, a division of The McGraw-Hill Companies, Inc.

This publication contains the authors' opinions and is designed to provide accurate and authoritative information. It is sold with the understanding that the authors, publisher, and Bloomberg L.P. are not engaged in rendering legal, accounting, investment-planning, or other professional advice. The reader should seek the services of a qualified professional for such advice; the authors, publisher, and Bloomberg L.P. cannot be held responsible for any loss incurred as a result of specific investments or planning decisions made by the reader.

First edition published 2004
1 3 5 7 9 10 8 6 4 2

Library of Congress Cataloging-in-Publication Data

The new investor relations : expert perspectives on the state of the art / edited by Benjamin Mark Cole. -- 1st ed.
     p. cm.
Includes index.
   ISBN 1-57660-135-8 (alk. paper)
 1. Corporations--Investor relations--United States. I. Cole, Benjamin Mark

   HD2744.N49 2004
   659. 2'85--dc21   2003012993

Acquired and edited by KATHLEEN A. PETERSON
Book design by BARBARA DIEZ GOLDENBERG

To Rah, who has just entered the world

Contents

PART 1: UNDERPINNINGS OF THE NEW ORDER

PART 2: IR IMPLICATIONS
FOR SELECTED FINANCING SCENARIOS

PART 3: IR TACTICS IN PROXY WARS AND OTHER CRISIS SCENARIOS

9 Crisis Investor Relations   139

Michael S. Sitrick, Sitrick and Company, Inc.

10 The Art of Winning Proxy Wars   149

Based on interviews with *John C. Wilcox*
Georgeson Shareholder Communications Inc.

PART 4: SPECIAL CASE PERSPECTIVES

14 IR and the Credit-Ratings Process — 209

Clifford M. Griep, Standard & Poor's

15 The Information Investment Managers Want From Public Companies — 221

Christopher N. Orndorff, CFA
Payden & Rygel Investment Co.

About the Contributors

Donald Allen is founding partner of The Allen Group, an investor relations consulting firm based in Laguna Hills, California. Prior to forming the consultancy, Allen worked for several public companies as director of corporate communications and investor relations. He most recently held that post with Quest Software, FileNET Corp., and Wonderware Corp. He began working in IR in 1970 at Digital Equipment Corp. following a stint in public relations and financial communications at Xerox Corp. He began his career as a journalist with United Press International. Allen holds a B.A. degree from the University at Albany, has studied in the M.B.A. program at the University of Southern California, and has completed the Advanced Investor Relations Program at the Goizueta Business School at Emory University. Allen serves on the Board of Directors of the National Investor Relations Institute (NIRI), based in Vienna, Virginia, is a member of NIRI's Senior Roundtable, and serves as the NIRI board's representative to the Canadian Investor Relations Institute (CIRI). He is also President of the Orange County (California) chapter of NIRI, serves on the Board of Directors, and is a member and former director of the Orange County chapter of the Public Relations Society of America. *(Chapter 1)*

Neil G. Berkman is president of Berkman Associates, a Los Angeles–based investor relations firm he founded in 1988. He notes that many of his firm's clients, companies of all sizes in a variety of industries around the country, have implemented stock repurchase programs. Previously, he established and managed the Los Angeles office of a New York–based investor relations firm. From 1977 to 1981, Berkman was senior economist at the Federal Reserve Bank of Boston, where he conducted research on topics in macroeconomics and monetary policy, and published numerous articles in the *New England Economic Review*, as well as the *Journal of Money, Credit and Banking;* the *Market Chronicle;* and other publications. He received a Ph.D. in economics from the University of California, Berkeley, and an M.A. and B.A. in economics from UCLA.   **(Chapter 5)**

Alexander L. Cappello is the chairman and chief executive officer of the Cappello Group, Inc., a boutique global merchant bank specializing in the private placement of capital and merger/acquisition/strategic advisory services for public companies with market capitalizations from $250 million to $20 billion. Thompson Financial Securities Data ranked Cappello Capital Corp. the number five managing underwriter of privately placed convertible preferred stock in the period 1994–1998, which included a number two ranking behind J.P. Morgan in 1996. Cappello is a member of the Young Presidents' Organization (YPO) and in 2003–2004 has served as chairman of its international board. He is a founding charter member and past chairman of both the Santa Monica Bay and Bel Air chapters of YPO in California and a founder of the Lisbon, Portugal; Moscow, Russia; and Malibu, California chapters of YPO. Cappello received a Bachelor of Science degree with honors from the Marshall School of Business at University of Southern California. He has been a guest lecturer at the USC, UCLA, and Harvard business schools.   **(Chapter 7)**

Kenneth R. Cone is a senior vice president at Lexecon, an economics consulting firm. Cone's areas of expertise include financial economics, valuation, and the operation of securities and commodities markets as well as damage calculations related to securities cases. He has testified as an expert witness in cases related to securities markets and valuation in state and federal courts and before arbitration panels. Cone has consulted on and directed studies of trading and securities-related issues in a broad variety of markets and industries, including equity markets, bond markets, currency markets, option and derivative markets, and markets for commodities and raw materials such as copper and oil. In addition, he has published articles in the fields of securities markets and securities damage calculations in scholarly journals including *The Journal of Law and Economics, The Business Lawyer,* and *The Journal of Health Economics.* Before joining Lexecon in 1991, Cone served as senior vice president for strategic planning at the Chicago Mercantile Exchange. Prior to his employment at the CME, he was a management consultant at Booz Allen and Hamilton and an assistant professor at the University of Chicago's Graduate School of Business.   *(Chapter 11)*

Daniel R. Fischel is chairman and president of Lexecon, an economics consulting firm. Fischel's areas of expertise include securities, corporation law, regulation of financial markets, and the application of the economics of corporate finance to problems in these areas. He has been cited by state and federal courts at all levels including the United States Supreme Court. Fischel has given expert testimony on numerous occasions in federal courts, before arbitration panels, and in regulatory proceedings in the areas of securities, commodities, corporation law, regulation of financial markets, and the application of the economics of corporate finance. For the past few years, he has been the principal damages witness for the United States Department of Justice in a series of breach of contract cases involving over $100 billion, commonly called the Winstar cases. His article "Use of Modern Finance Theory in Securities Fraud Cases Involving Actively Traded Securities," Business Law 1 (1982), is considered the seminal article describing the application of financial economics to securities fraud litigation. Fischel is coauthor of *The Economic Structure of Corporate Law* with Frank H. Easterbrook and author of *Payback: The Conspiracy to Destroy Michael Milken and His Financial Revolution*. He is the Jack N. Pritzker Distinguished Visiting Professor of Law at Northwestern University and the Lee and Brena Freeman Professor of Law and Business at the University of Chicago. Fischel is also the chairman, president, and chief executive officer of Nextera Enterprises, Inc.   *(Chapter 11)*

Bryce Goodwin is a communications professional with expertise in a wide range of financial communications disciplines including media relations, mergers and acquisitions, litigation, corporate positioning, investor relations, and crisis communications. Goodwin joined Edelman Financial in March 2000 and is also a member of the firm's Corporate Governance Advisors practice, a group, led by former SEC Chairman Richard Breeden, that provides companies with guidance on issues related to corporate governance. Goodwin graduated from Georgetown

University with Honors, earning a B.S. in foreign service. He also earned a Certificate of Political Science with Honors from l'Institut d'Études Politiques in Lyon, France, and has studied at La Universidad Católica de Ecuador in Quito, Ecuador.   *(Chapter 2)*

Clifford M. Griep is executive managing director and chief credit officer of Standard & Poor's. As CCO, Griep chairs the firm's Analytical Policy Board and serves as the ratings group chief rating officer. The Analytical Policy Board directs the rating firm's criteria and rating methodologies and is comprised of senior regional credit officers, general counsel, and the heads of criteria and ratings policy for each of the global practices.

Griep joined Standard & Poor's in 1981. Prior to his current position, he headed Standard & Poor's Global Financial Institutions ratings unit and before that, its Global Structured Finance unit. He is an active contributor to Standard & Poor's publications and a frequent speaker on credit market developments. Griep is a former president of the Fixed Income Analysts Society. He received an M.B.A. in Money and Financial Markets from Columbia Graduate School of Business and a B.A. in English Literature from Rutgers University.   *(Chapter 14)*

Heather Harper is a senior vice president at Edelman, the world's largest independent public relations firm, and leads an investor relations account team within the firm's financial communications practice. While at Edelman, Harper has handled engagements involving communications for corporate governance issues, financial crises, transactions, and shareholder litigation as well as marketing clients to the investment community. Recently she advised pharmaceutical company Elan on crisis communications, CIT Group on its IPO and spin-off from troubled Tyco International, and utility company Aquila on restructuring issues. Harper worked with Belgium-based Delhaize Group on its cross-border purchase of minority interests in its U.S. subsidiary. Additionally, her team's work has included investor relations for small- and mid-cap companies in the biotechnology, telecommunications, and professional services industries. Her team's programs for clients have won industry recognition including *PR Week*'s 2003 "Campaign of the Year" and best investor relations program awards as well as a Silver Anvil from Public Relations Society of America and a

Golden World award from International Public Relations Association for best investor relations programs. Harper earned a bachelor's degree in economics and French from Denison University and an M.B.A. in finance from New York University's Stern School of Business.

(Chapter 2)

John F. Hartigan is the managing partner of the Los Angeles office of Morgan, Lewis & Bockius LLP and chairs the firm's Securities Practice. He advises clients, including some of the nation's largest financial institutions, in the areas of securities law, mergers and acquisitions, and corporate finance. Named one of the top mergers and acquisition attorneys and one of the fifty most powerful attorneys in Los Angeles, Hartigan, who was with the SEC for more than eight years and served as assistant director of the Division of Enforcement, is a frequent lecturer, panelist, and author on topics relating to securities law, mergers and acquisitions, corporate finance, SEC enforcement, and broker-dealers. Active in professional organizations, Hartigan has served as vice chair and a member of the Executive Committee of the Business Law Section of the State Bar Association of California, and chaired the Education Committee of the Business Section of the State Bar Association of California. He is currently and has been the chair of the Securities Regulation Seminar cosponsored by the SEC. He has also served on the Executive Committee of the Business and Corporations Section of the Los Angeles County Bar Association and chaired that Broker-Dealer Committee. Hartigan received a bachelor's degree in finance from the University of Illinois and his law degree from the Georgetown University Law Center, where he was case and notes editor and a member of the executive board of *The Tax Lawyer*.   *(Chapter 6)*

Scott P. Hilsen is a partner at the Atlanta office of Alston & Bird LLP in the Securities Litigation Group. His practice includes securities class actions, derivative suits, broker/dealer matters, and corporate investigations. Hilsen is a frequent speaker at various CLE seminars on securities litigation issues. He recently played a major role on a trial team that won a $50 million jury verdict in a securities-related case that involved claims for breach of contract, business fraud, and tortious interference. He received his J.D., cum laude, from Georgia State University, where he was managing editor of the *Georgia State University Law Review*. While in law school, Hilsen clerked for Justice Leah Sears of the Georgia Supreme Court. He received an M.B.A. from Georgia State University and a B.A. from the University of Florida.   **(Chapter 3)**

John R. Lefebvre, Jr. has twenty-five years of experience in the securities industry, having been trained by Merrill Lynch in the late 1970s. His Colorado-based firm, Shareholder Relations, has performed investor relations work for more than seventy clients in twenty different industries since 1988. Shareholder Relations runs cost-effective, pragmatic investor relations campaigns designed to raise investor awareness and broaden the shareholder base and has advised clients on matters as diverse as investor relations, corporate development, and corporate finance. The website of *The Harvard Business Review* said that *Investor Relations for the Emerging Company* (a guidebook coauthored with Ralph Rieves) was "a must read for anyone even thinking of going public."   **(Chapter 13)**

Thomas E. McLain is a partner in the Los Angeles office of Sidley Austin Brown & Wood LLP. McLain's practice concentrates on international business and technology transactions. He advises both international and domestic entities in joint ventures, private equity investments, strategic acquisitions and investments, privatizations, and restructurings. Significant transactions include negotiating the rights to build Tokyo Disneyland, establishing the joint venture to build and operate Osaka Universal Studios, and representing the Koran Asset Management Corporation to sell portfolios of nonperforming real estate loans and to restructure the foreign assets of Daewoo Corporation. McLain is a trustee and member of the Executive Committee of the Asia Society and chairman of The Asia Society Southern California Center, a member of the Board of Directors and Executive Committee of the Library Foundation of Los Angeles, and a member of the Steering Committee for the Japan-American Young Leaders Project of the U.S.-Japan Foundation. He has served as a commissioner of the Japan-U.S. Friendship Commission and the United States-Japan Conference on Cultural and Educational Interchange, as a director of the U.S.-Japan Bridging Foundation, and as member of the Board of Visitors of the Terry Sanford Institute of Public Policy at Duke University. He has taught courses on the Japanese legal system at the University of Southern California Law Center, and has been a featured speaker at numerous conferences. McClain received his A.B. degree, with highest honors, from Duke University and his J.D. degree, also with highest honors, from Duke University School of Law. *(Chapter 12)*

Christopher N. Orndorff, CFA, is managing principal at Payden & Rygel, where he oversees the firm's equity strategy group, high yield credit group, and investment grade corporate credit group. He is one of six members of Payden & Rygel's investment policy committee. Before joining Payden & Rygel, he was a vice president at Northern Trust Company, where he managed domestic and global institutional portfolios. Orndorff has published several articles on global investing as well as being a contributor or coauthor of three investment books. He has spoken at many investment forums, including the AIMR Investing Worldwide Conference. He is frequently quoted in the press, including CNBC. He is a member of the Investment Counsel Association of America, Inc. (ICAA), the Los Angeles Society of Financial Analysts, and the Association of Investment Management and Research (AIMR). He also serves as a trustee of the Children's Bureau of Southern California Foundation and as a trustee of Westridge School. A Chartered Financial Analyst, Orndorff holds a master's degree in Business Administration with an emphasis on finance and international business from the University of Chicago and a bachelor's degree in finance from Miami (Ohio) University. *(Chapter 15)*

Gregory J. Pelnar is a vice president at Lexecon, the economics consulting firm, where he is responsible for researching and summarizing "the state of economic knowledge" on issues of concern to clients. His research is integral in the formulation of opinions of Lexecon's experts and their criticisms of opposing experts. In addition, Pelnar has assisted with the research, editing, and proofreading of two books, Dennis W. Carlton and Jeffrey M. Perloff's *Modern Industrial Organization* and Daniel R. Fischel's *Payback: The Conspiracy to Destroy Michael Milken and His Financial Revolution*. Pelnar has an M.A. in economics from the University of Chicago. He is a member of Phi Beta Kappa. *(Chapter 11)*

Hollis Rafkin-Sax has been a leading professional in the financial and public relations industry for more than twenty years. She is currently the global managing director of Edelman's financial practice. As a longtime strategic communications adviser, Rafkin-Sax specializes in corporate positioning, M&A, investor communications, crisis situations, and financial restructurings and reorganizations. She also created and leads Edelman's Corporate Governance Advisors, which is chaired by former SEC Chairman Richard C. Breeden. Edelman's CGA is an industry first, blending communications consulting, regulatory, and board-level expertise; capital markets experience; and strong investment community and media relationships. This group deals with critical corporate governance and corporate credibility issues as well as board composition and financial transparency and reporting. Rafkin-Sax is a graduate of Bowdoin College in Brunswick, Maine. She was elected to the Bowdoin College Board of Governors in 1988 and served two terms as a Trustee of the College. Rafkin-Sax did graduate work at the London School of Economics in international relations and defense issues and completed the Karl Landeggar Mid-Management Training Program in International Business-Government Relations at Georgetown's School of Foreign Service. She also serves on the advisory board of the Make-A-Wish Foundation.   *(Chapter 2)*

Ralph A. Rieves is managing director of the Emerging Companies Research Institute (ECRI), a division of Farragut, Jones & Lawrence. ECRI advises recently listed companies about current research in the areas of financial reporting, compliance, capital markets, and institutional investors' portfolio strategies. He was managing editor of the *Journal of Investment Consulting* and was previously the executive editor for capital markets publishing for Dow Jones–Irwin books and Irwin Professional books. Rieves is the recipient of the book industry's Bowker LMP Award for distinguished achievement. He is the coauthor, with John Lefebvre, of *Investor Relations for the Emerging Company* (John Wiley & Sons, 2002).   *(Chapter 13)*

David J. Ross is a senior vice president at Lexecon, the economics consulting firm, where he specializes in finance, labor economics, and the economic analysis of the law. He has testified and authored expert reports regarding such issues as causation, materiality, damages, and valuation in cases involving allegations of breach of contract, illegal insider trading, investment neglect, misappropriation of business opportunities, stock manipulation, unsuitable trading, securities fraud, and improper tax-avoidance schemes. He has consulted and directed studies on a wide variety of industries, including banking and communications. Ross is the author of several academic articles on topics in finance and the economic analysis of the law in such scholarly journals as *The Journal of Law and Economics, Harvard Law Review,* and *The Journal of Derivatives.*

(Chapter 11)

Theodore J. (Tod) Sawicki is a partner in the Securities Litigation Group in the Atlanta office of Alston & Bird LLP and focuses his practice on the litigation and arbitration of securities and business disputes as well as class action litigation. Sawicki has successfully represented a number of companies, financial services firms, executives, and professionals in a wide range of litigation matters. In addition, Sawicki is one of the Securities Litigation Group's specialists in broker-dealer and investment advisory litigation, arbitration, regulatory counseling, and representation. In September 1997, Sawicki spent two weeks in Croatia as part of a Financial Services Volunteer Corps independent expert assessment team evaluating shareholder rights following that country's privatization effort. In March 1999, at the request of the Financial Services Volunteer Corps, he provided commentary and proposed revisions to the Varazdin, Croatia OTC Market Surveillance and Enforcement Rules. Sawicki received his B.A. degree, cum laude, from Duke University and his J.D. degree from Emory University School of Law, where he was notes and comments editor of the *Emory Law Journal.* Upon graduation from law school, he served as a law clerk to The Honorable John H. Moore, II, United States District Judge for the Middle District of Florida. He is a member of the State Bar of Georgia and the Florida Bar. *(Chapter 3)*

Douglas M. Sherk is the founder and CEO of San Francisco–based EVC Group, LLC, a consultancy dedicated to creating communications programs that generate enhanced valuation for companies with market capitalizations below $1 billion. With nearly twenty-five years of experience, Sherk is considered one of the thought leaders and innovators in business communications. During his career, he has personally developed investor relations strategies for more than fifty initial public offerings and created a proprietary program for companies planning to go public called IPO Prep. Sherk holds a bachelor of science degree from the S.I. Newhouse School of Public Communications, Syracuse University, where he was best known as being basketball coach Jim Boeheim's first manager. A frequent speaker on business communications and investor relations issues, Sherk currently teaches a graduate course on investor relations at Golden Gate University, San Francisco. He is a member of the National Investor Relations Institute. He also serves as treasurer of the Black Adoption Placement and Research Center and is a past board member of the Omega Boys Club.   *(Chapter 8)*

Yoshiki Shimada is a partner in the New York office of Sidley Austin Brown & Wood LLP. He has more than seventeen years of experience as a corporate attorney and has advised on capital market transactions, joint ventures, and cross-border entertainment transactions. Shimada currently serves as special securities counsel to a major Japanese securities exchange and major Japanese publicly reporting companies in connection with their filings with the U.S. Securities and Exchange Commission. As adviser to Japan's leading theatrical company (Shiki Theatrical Company), he has negotiated cross-border production/licensing agreements with major Broadway producers, including Walt Disney Theatrical Productions, to bring *Beauty and The Beast* and *The Lion King* musical productions to Japan. He also represented a major Fukuoka real estate developer during its joint venture negotiations with AMC Entertainment. Shimada has published articles on corporate governance practices in Japan and the United States in *Gaiko Forum, International Legal Strategy, International Securitization & Structured Finance Report, International Financial Law Review, Harvard International Law Journal, Harvard Asia Quarterly, Virginia Journal of International Law, International Legal Strategy,* and *Columbia International Law Journal.* He is admitted to the bars of the State of New York and the District of Columbia. Shimada received his A.B. (Phi Beta Kappa) from Cornell University and his J.D. from Harvard Law School.   *(Chapter 12)*

David Silver, APR, is president of Silver Public Relations, a financial public relations and investor relations firm based in Los Angeles. His firm provides strategic counseling and advice on financial public relations, litigation public relations, crisis communications, and investor relations issues for Wall Street companies and national law firms. Silver has degrees from UCLA and the University of Southern California, is accredited APR by the Public Relations Society of America, and is a graduate of the Investor Relations certificate program at the University of California, Irvine, which has been developed in collaboration with the National Investor Relations Institute in Washington, D.C.   *(Chapter 4)*

Michael S. Sitrick is chairman and chief executive officer of Sitrick and Company. A nationally recognized expert in the strategic use of communications, Sitrick has been the subject of numerous articles and profiles focusing on the results he has achieved for clients. Since founding the firm, he has provided advice and counsel to more than 500 companies, including some of the nation's largest corporations—and some of its highest-profile individuals—both on routine and extremely sensitive matters. Prior to forming the firm, Sitrick served as senior vice president of communications for Wickes Companies, Inc., where he was the architect of Wickes' Chapter 11 communications programs and director of the company's communications efforts through a series of takeover attempts and defenses, litigation issues, a major product liability problem, and numerous other critical matters. Before joining Wickes, Sitrick headed communications and government affairs for National Can Corporation; was a group supervisor for the Chicago public relations firm Selz, Seabolt and Associates; and served as Assistant Director of Public Information in the Richard J. Daley administration in Chicago. He also worked as a reporter for such publications as the *Washington Star* and the *Baltimore News American*. Sitrick has lectured on public relations and crisis management before numerous professional groups and forums as well as at the graduate schools of UCLA, USC, and Dartmouth, and the Journalism Fellows Program at the University of Michigan. He is the coauthor of *Spin: How to Turn the Power of the Press to Your Advantage* (Regnery Publishing, 1998) and a contributing author to *Workouts and Turnarounds II* (John Wiley & Sons, 1999).   *(Chapter 9)*

John C. Wilcox is vice chairman of Georgeson Shareholder Communications Inc. During his thirty years with the firm, Wilcox has specialized in corporate governance and has consulted with many corporations on defensive and offensive tactics in proxy contests and tender offers. He is a member of the American Society of Corporate Secretaries and its Securities Law Committee, a member of the National Investor Relations Institute, a member of the Issuer Affairs Committee of The National Association of Securities Dealers, a member of the Board of Governors of the International Corporate Governance Network and chairman of its Committee on Cross-Border Voting Practices, and serves on the Board of Trustees of Woodrow Wilson National Fellowship Foundation and Bennington College. Wilcox has written articles on securities regulation, takeovers, corporate governance, investor relations, and globalization of the securities markets. His articles have appeared in the *Financial Times,* the *New York Times, The New York Law Journal, The American Lawyer, Insights, Pensions & Investments,* and other publications. He has appeared as an expert witness in court cases involving shareholder matters and has testified before Congress and regulatory agencies on matters relating to securities regulation. Wilcox received a B.A. from Harvard College, where he was a member of Phi Beta Kappa; an M.A. from the University of California, Berkeley, where he studied as a Woodrow Wilson Fellow; a J.D. from Harvard Law School; and an LL.M. degree from New York University Graduate School of Law. He is a member of the American and New York Bar Associations.   **(Chapter 10)**

Acknowledgments

I WISH TO ACKNOWLEDGE the expertise and talents of the contributing authors of the book, each of whom made a special effort to bring this evolving field—investor relations—into focus.

I also wish to thank Kathleen Peterson and Tracy Tait at Bloomberg Press for their guidance in bringing this entire book together. Anyone who has edited a book involving a small platoon of writers will know of the great demands placed on editorial and logistical skills.

Introduction

THE LANDSCAPE FOR WALL STREET and publicly held American corporations in the past several years has changed more than at any time since the Great Depression, and with that, the operating environment for investor relations professionals. Arguably, only the early years of the Great Depression, with the seminal Securities Act of 1933 and the Securities and Exchange Act of 1934, resulted in greater alterations for public companies than the reforms and changes in sentiment resulting from the post-1990s meltdown on Wall Street.

Yet as important as relatively recent legal and regulatory changes are—such as Regulation Fair Disclosure (Regulation FD) or the Sarbanes-Oxley Act—Wall Street and publicly held companies were already entering an environment much different from that existing just a generation ago. A most notable advent has been the proliferation of financial media, especially electronic services. Few Americans need to be reminded of the ubiquity of cable television, which rendered "narrow casting" economically feasible. Amid the flood of new shows were the all-financial stations, which now routinely air in newsrooms and trading houses across the nation, seemingly incessantly. And the Internet, with its marvelous ability to immediately present and then archive news stories, press releases, and data, and its "chat rooms" about company stocks—and rumor-mongering online traders—was virtually unknown only a decade ago. Now, every company must consider the effectiveness of its website, at the minimum.

There has also been a floodtide of new business publications, as well as a beefed-up *Wall Street Journal,* and a new national daily, *Investor's Business Daily.* Many major daily papers have expanded their business coverage. One could contend, with just a little hyperbole, that it is difficult to live in any major city in America and not be aware of the trading range of the Dow Jones Industrial Average.

Public companies today address a radically larger, and in many ways a better-informed, press corps than ever before. One could even argue that the phenomenon of the "corporate crisis" is as much fueled by the avalanche of media coverage as by bona fide corporate misdeeds. A generation ago, would accounting scandals have attracted nearly the attention they receive today or have elicited calls for systemic reforms?

The same might be said for the perhaps quixotic campaign of New York State Attorney General Eliot Spitzer and the Securities and Exchange Commission (SEC), to reform brokerage analyst research. Such research has been compromised for decades, some would say ever since brokerage houses could both underwrite securities and then advise investors to buy them. Why the reforms now? There was, after all, a prolonged and ugly bear market after the 1960s boom years on Wall Street, but no reforms or even talk of a regulatory shake-up. To be sure, the transgressions of the 1990s seemed to epitomize all that was wrong with Wall Street, and on a grander scale than ever before. But surely, media coverage played a role in the actions of Spitzer and the SEC.

In addition, Wall Street and corporate America have been pressed by other tectonic shifts in the economic and business scenes, which have been building for years. These include the following factors, notably:

♦ The number and size of mutual funds have exploded in the last two decades, representing an enormous financial stake for many American households—and that much more reason for legislators to scrutinize Wall Street and push regulators to be more aggressive. Moreover, a generation or two ago, pension funds hewed closely to bonds, but they now invest heavily in equities as well, while millions of Americans hold equities in 401(k) plans. A few brave foundations, declaring themselves "permanent investors," even went so far in the late 1990s as to invest only in equities, which historically have outperformed bonds.

Consequently, how the enormous baby boom population of America—those born after World War II through 1968—will fare in retirement is tied to Wall Street, a daunting thought.

One can guess that in the years ahead, the intertwined fortunes of stocks and wanna-be retirees will lead to a gathering level of interest and concern about Wall Street, corporate governance, and accounting standards, as has already begun.

♦ Like so many other business sectors, Wall Street has been globalized during the past twenty years. Many foreign corporations now seek listing on U.S. exchanges, and many foreign companies often wish to buy U.S. companies. Oftentimes, such entities will have to learn to comply with the increasingly rigorous U.S. regulatory mandates and accounting standards.

♦ Though recently cooling, the last decade saw an unprecedented upsurge in mergers of public companies, a trend one can expect to revive a bit when economic conditions allow—although the M&A salad days may be over for good: Too many mergers have not panned out, a fact that will force public companies to concentrate on generating returns for shareholders through improved operations, organic profits, or even share buybacks.

♦ New funding mechanisms have emerged, including much more sophisticated financing for mergers and acquisitions (which helped the M&A boom of the 1990s), and more recently, private investments in public equity, or PIPEs.

♦ Wall Street has become increasingly litigious, with seemingly every stock plunge or accounting scandal bringing an onslaught of lawsuits.

♦ Proxy wars are likely to become more common, due to ever more forceful shareholder activism. Mergers or expansion campaigns that appear to be empire building and not in the interests of shareholders are more likely to be challenged.

Given all of the above developments, I have selected a retinue of investor relations or Wall Street professionals to present their expert opinions on the current status of investor relations, or IR. The roll call is as follows:

Don Allen, IR practitioner and board member of the National Investor Relations Institute bats lead-off, in Part 1, "Underpinnings of the New Order." Allen, together with IR authorities Heather

Harper, Hollis Rafkin-Sax, and Bryce Goodwin of Edelman Financial Communications Worldwide, present chapters on what might be called "the state of the art" in the nuts-and-bolts practice of IR. As one will discover from reading their chapters, good IR these days involves as much good corporate governance and compliance with regulation as it does timely and accurate disclosure. These two chapters are also a superb introduction to the craft of IR.

Meanwhile, litigation seems to have become a permanent fixture of American corporate life, so that IR professionals today do well to bone up on their obligations in this arena. Theodore J. Sawicki and Scott P. Hilsen of law firm Alston & Bird have authored Chapter 3 with that intent. They also admonish IR professionals that to provide investor relations today—the era of cable financial shows and the ever-active Internet—is to be "on call, 24/7." The Sarbanes-Oxley Act, remind Sawicki and Hilsen, puts corporate executives directly in the path of financial steamrollers, should they be found wanting for accurate and timely disclosure. It becomes the job of IR professionals to keep disclosures both timely and accurate, but also universal (i.e, made available to everybody in the market simultaneously, as much as practicable).

Rounding out the book's opening section is Chapter 4, "The IR-PR Nexus, by author David Silver, president of Silver Public Relations, who presents a fascinating review of the public relations and investor relations trades, including a historical glimpse into the emerging crafts and how they evolved—and why the two businesses evolved separately. Silver argues powerfully that the separation is no longer practical nor appropriate in today's marketplace.

Part 2 of *The New Investor Relations* peers closely into the IR challenges implicit in a variety of financial scenarios facing corporations today. Stock buybacks are already an increasingly popular method to reward shareholders, and IR authority Neil Berkman offers advice in Chapter 5, in terms of both strategy and impact on investor relations, for the right way to present such plans to shareholders. As Yogi Berra once said, "Making predictions is really hard, especially about the future," but one guess is that more public companies will turn to buybacks in the years ahead.

The mergers game is a bit sullied as an avenue to growth, and market average price-earnings multiples are not likely to double, and then double again, as they did in the 1980s and 1990s. Yet even though the pace of corporate mergers has slowed, another wave is likely in the offing because if asset values were to fall any further, buy-out artists or corporations would look to expand operations—or, conversely, if the economy were to perk up, so would the merger trade. Low interest rates and cheap money also bode well for the merger game. Every IR professional needs to be armed and ready to handle a merger scenario, and Chapter 6 by John Hartigan, of the national law firm Morgan, Lewis & Bockius, reminds IR teams of their obligations and opportunities in and around mergers.

In recent years, the financing vehicle known as private investment in public equity (PIPE) has become a relatively prominent method of raising capital on Wall Street, yet its IR requirements are unique, and nearly the opposite of those called for in an initial public offering. Boutique investment banker and private placement expert Alex Cappello in Chapter 6 counsels public companies on the right way to broach this topic with investors.

And let's not forget initial public offerings (IPOs), even if Wall Street has, for now, done so. Someday, the IPO will make a come-back, and corporate communications guru Doug Sherk, of the EVC Group LLC, in Chapter 7 offers cogent suggestions to would-be public companies on how to avoid a post-IPO meltdown. Having excellent internal lines of communication set up in advance (especially for business data) and relating those facts to the market in a timely way are two key elements of successful IPO investor relations, argues Sherk.

With "crisis du jour" all too often defining the climate for publicly held companies today, Part 3's lead-off chapter on Crisis IR, by author Michael Sitrick, is not only pertinent but also essential reading for many managers. In something of a departure for the IR community, Sitrick counsels not just responding to rumors but, rather, actively engaging them and the journalists reporting on them. To hide in the shell like a turtle is to allow others to define the news landscape, argues Sitrick, in this guideline-filled chapter. Although Sitrick's maxims are designed for full-on crisis modes, many of his arguments and action plans make sense for less serious corporate troubles as well. By the way, Sitrick is the consummate voice of experience—it was he who handled key PR and IR communiques behind the scenes in America's biggest corporate bankruptcy ever, the 2002 WorldCom filing.

Of late there have been some rip-roaring proxy wars on Wall Street, as the days of genteel boards of directors and timid shareholders retreat further into the past. Although proxy wars are hardly common, shareholders are likely to grow increasingly restless in years ahead in their search for returns. Many large investors, such as the pension fund for California state employees (the California Public Employees Retirement System, or CalPERS), have announced that they are forced to be "permanent" investors in most large-cap stocks, and thus must be more aggressive in preserving shareholder value against the predations of wayward managements. John Wilcox, of the leading proxy solicitation firm Georgeson Shareholder, warns that proxy fights are inherently destabilizing and should be fended off early, when possible. Wilcox, in Chapter 10, argues that the best defense can be a good offense, and that means communicating with shareholders often and knowing who they are.

Following Wilcox's presentation, we have a fascinating chapter highlighting the shareholder opposition in the renowned Hewlett-Packard proxy battle of 2002, authored by principals Kenneth R. Cone, Daniel R. Fischel, Gregory J. Pelnar, and David J. Ross, of the economics consulting firm Lexecon. This remarkable proxy tussle was precipitated by Hewlett-Packard's decision to merge with Compaq Computer. Even though proxy fights may become more commonplace, these authors warn corporate revolutionaries that the swimming is upstream. Too many shareholders do not have the time to study thoroughly the issues and so defer to management, and if not management, then to the Rockville, Maryland–based Institutional Shareholders Services, the consulting firm. But ISS does not—and does not even pretend to—examine the business merits of proxy questions, but only whether management is following proper corporate governance practices. The Lexecon chapter makes for a thought-provoking look at proxy votes and the role of ISS.

In the late 1990s, we saw many foreign companies becoming listed on American exchanges, in search of credibility and attendant higher valuations. Like so much on Wall Street, that trend has turned a bit quiescent for now, but nothing is permanent on the Street. Moreover, there is talk of a tidal wave of Asian companies seeking U.S. listings as the behemoth economy of China expands. Sidley Austin Brown & Wood's Tom McLain and Yoshiki Shimada explain the requirements of doing business in a style acceptable for a U.S. listing, which may compel foreign entities into some serious reformulations of business practices. At times, something so elemental as enforceable contracts with suppliers is missing in foreign companies, warn Shimada and McLain. Any IR professional helping an offshore company seek a U.S. listing should read this chapter, which introduces the book's Part 4, "Special Case Perspectives."

Next up in this section of the book, Ralph Rieves, author and IR consultant, with his colleague John R. Lefebvre Jr., contributes a chapter on IR for emerging public companies, filled with guidance both sage and timely, in light of recent events. Although readers, by this point in the chapter lineup, may feel a bit beat about the head with admonitions to be honest and frank, Rieves and Lefebvre point up that emerging companies, too, must walk the walk if they want to survive on Wall Street (and stay out of the courtroom or worse).

And though sometimes overlooked in this context, dealing with the bond-rating agencies is also a critical part of IR, but it requires a much different approach than that generally applicable in the equities market. A fact perhaps not widely known, the credit-rating agencies are privy to much information that is effectively "classified" and would not otherwise be disclosed, except to all market participants. In fact, there is a special clause in Regulation FD that allows the recognized rating agencies to have access to otherwise nonpublic information, writes Chris Griep, of Standard & Poor's, in Chapter 14. The credit-rating agencies, like so much of Wall Street, have come under fire of late, for not raising red flags early enough on such huge debacles as WorldCom. One can assume a "get-tough" stance from ratings agencies going forward, and nothing in this, the penultimate chapter of the book, suggests otherwise. IR professionals are going to have to play ball with the ratings agencies, and on their terms.

Finally (and maybe it should have been first), this volume includes a chapter from a money manager, presenting a fresh consumer view on what constitutes good investor relations. It is a chapter well worth reading: After all, notwithstanding that the experts assembled here have weighed in at length, with invaluable guidance on effective IR practice, bear in mind that the real "buyers" of IR today are largely institutions, be they pension funds, insurance companies, money managers, or mutual funds. All the expert advice in the world won't help a company if this brand of consumer is not impressed. Chris Orndorff, managing principal and head of equities at Payden & Rygel, a money shop with $45 billion under management, explains what he wants from good IR, and it's a lot less polish and lot more candor than perhaps many public companies are attempting.

ANY PUBLIC COMPANY has obligations to shareholders and the larger capital markets to be as open as possible at all times, and to share information in a timely manner. In the long run, this has the happy coincidence of benefiting a company's shareholders: The more a market trusts a public company, the higher the valuation, or price-earnings ratio, that stock will have (all other things being equal). Conversely, errant, misleading IR will hurt shareholders and, in some small way, help to decrease the public's faith in capital markets.

The deceptive course—from outright cooking the books to any corporate shenanigans that skirt accurate and timely disclosure—may temporarily enrich or seemingly offer short-term solutions, but could incur financial and even criminal penalties for those involved. Moreover, with the advent of the Internet, one's career at public companies has a very long tail. It is very easy for future employers or business partners to review all regulatory actions and news articles ever written about a particular individual or company. Questionable or illegal behavior can be revisited every time somebody plugs a company's name into a search engine on the Web.

Without question there are guidelines and words of wisdom in abundance in the chapters of *The New Investor Relations: Expert Perspectives on the State of the Art*—and some of it may indeed be critical advice for an IR professional facing a crisis. However, it would also be accurate to say that much of this book boils down to one simple phrase: "Tell it like it is."

BENJAMIN MARK COLE

The New Investor Relations

PART 1

Underpinnings *of the* New Order

1 Fundamentals of Investor Relations

DONALD ALLEN

The Allen Group

To MOST CORPORATE EXECUTIVES, the term *investor relations* (IR) conjures up images of financial communications with a public company's shareholder base. The present-day practice of IR, however, encompasses far more than communicating with one's shareholders. Investor relations is a proactive and strategic executive function that combines elements of finance, communications, and marketing to provide the investment community with an accurate portrayal of both a company's current performance and its future prospects. IR incorporates multiple program elements that work in concert to market the company and its stock and to help increase shareholder value in the long term—while operating within the prescribed framework set by the Securities and Exchange Commission (SEC), the Financial Accounting Standards Board (FASB), and other agencies. Given that good investor relations can also help enhance a stock's price-earnings ratio, a solid IR program should be considered a fiduciary responsibility of management.

The basics of investor relations include the following practices:

- Developing and maintaining a corporate disclosure policy, including an internal "process" for timely disclosure of material information
- Managing required financial reporting to shareholders, regulatory agencies, stock exchanges, and other key audiences

3

◆ Creating targeted outreach programs designed to increase market awareness and understanding of a company
◆ Building and maintaining relationships with the investment
community

An effective IR program emphasizes not only prospects, but also
accountability, good corporate governance, and transparency. Such a
program can help build credibility for your company and obtain better market valuations. It can help lower your cost of capital. And it
can help your company achieve the capital growth that investors seek.
Properly planned and executed, the IR function serves both the company and the investment community. It's a two-way conduit between
the public markets and the corporation, providing information of
value to both investors and management. For the investor, the information that's communicated helps drive investment decisions. For
the company, investor feedback can help management adjust business
strategies and facilitate creation of long-term shareholder value.

What's the Point?

It's axiomatic that when companies perform well, their stock prices
go up. When companies don't meet expectations, share prices go
down. This means that companies must provide a consistent flow of
good, reliable, and transparent information so that investors can evaluate future performance with confidence. And since perception is
often reality, it's important to manage expectations as well. Working
in tandem with corporate communications, a good investor relations
program will manage five vital steps in creating a strategic program
and enhancing its tactical success:

1. **Define the company image** and then support that image with
information that positions the company as a positive and iden-
tifiable investment opportunity. Although it may be trouble-
some, sometimes public companies discover that by thinking
about their image and what they can offer to the Street they
have to change their substance—perhaps spinning off divisions
that blur the company's focus. In this sense, good IR can help
shape a company. For example, it may be enough to be a good

real estate investment trust—but to empower investors (and thus gain their favor) would it be better to be a REIT with a certain type of portfolio, such as apartments only? Or a REIT that emphasizes not only dividends but also dividend growth?

2. **Conduct market research** to identify investors who have invested in opportunities before and thus might do so again.

3. **Determine the best vehicles to communicate** the information to targeted investors and the financial media.

4. **Implement the program** that broadly defines your company image on Wall Street.

5. **Measure results** and adjust the program accordingly.

Background on Corporate Disclosure

The first public company in the United States, reportedly, was the Boston Manufacturing Company, which was founded in 1814 in Waltham, Massachusetts. The company was a textile maker, and in order to fund expansion of higher volume production, its founder sold stock to ten associates. Happily enough, the ten investors all received substantial returns on their investments during the next several years, and thus was born a new business model that has flourished for close to two centuries. The novel idea of stock ownership was enticing to investors, especially in the unfettered environment reflecting the near-absence of government or stock exchange oversight prior to and during the early decades of the twentieth century. Spasms of speculation—and it was rank speculation, given the lack of financial information available to investors—resulted in the Roaring Twenties and subsequent Crash of 1929.

The federal government's response to this market crisis and the resulting Great Depression of the 1930s was to create the Securities Acts of 1933 and 1934, which established the Securities and Exchange Commission (SEC), the government agency that regulates and supervises stock market activities in the United States. These acts, and subsequent case law during the past seventy years, have defined what information companies must disclose to investors and how they must disclose it.

Understanding Disclosure and Materiality

The 1933 and 1934 acts define two types of disclosure: structured and unstructured. *Structured disclosure* refers to explicit information about a company's operating results and must be provided in a precise manner, as stipulated in required SEC documents such as Form 10-K (annual financial report), Form 10-Q (quarterly financial report), Form 8-K (event reporting), and other documents such as registration statements, prospectuses, proxy statements, and the management discussion and analysis (MD&A) section of the annual report to shareholders. The intent of setting such reporting standards for all public companies was to provide a structure that allows investors to easily compare corporate reporting and, in theory, better evaluate a company's performance relative to its peers and to other industries.

Unstructured disclosure describes information that companies may disclose at will, within certain broad guidelines. These implicit disclosure obligations are defined under the general antifraud provisions of the 1933 Securities Act, Rule 10b5, and include media such as annual reports, letters to shareholders, press releases, advertisements, speeches, investor meeting presentations, conference calls, and telephone conversations with investors or analysts.

Because hard and fast rules are not specified under the act, unstructured disclosure can have untoward results, especially if some investors learn material facts that others don't, or some investors contend they were misled. Two major factors affect this type of unstructured disclosure: the definition of "material" information and what constitutes an "insider." In general, *material information* is knowledge that would cause an ordinary person to make a decision to buy, sell, or hold a stock. It's basically any information that might change someone's evaluation of your stock—either upward (to buy), downward (to sell), or reinforcing an opinion to hold the stock.

An *insider* is someone who is deemed to have material information prior to its public disclosure and who thus cannot trade based on that information—and cannot pass the information along to anyone else to trade on it. There are several famous cases of insider trading. For example, in a classic case involving IBM's acquisition of Lotus

Development Corp. in 1995, more than thirty people in Westchester County, New York, were charged with insider trading because a secretary who was simply copying legal documents told her husband of the pending acquisition. The news spread like wildfire through the community. A more recent case is the alleged insider trading in ImClone stock in 2002, which snared famous names such as Martha Stewart. Routinely, however, insiders usually are corporate management and employees, outside IR consultants, attorneys, accountants, investment bankers, or even suppliers such as printers working on stock offering documents.

The issues of materiality and disclosure of quantitative information aren't unusually complex. When considering whether information is material, use the Five Minute Rule suggested by Louis Thompson, president and CEO of the National Investor Relations Institute (NIRI). According to Thompson: "If it takes more than five minutes to discuss whether something is material or not, it's material. Disclose it." Nobody has ever gone to jail for too much accurate disclosure of a company's financial or business matters to the broad investing public. And it is hard to fight the perception that nondisclosure may be in management's interests, but not that of shareholders.

Quite often, the question of materiality arises from qualitative data about a company's operations and anticipated results. This type of information, usually nonfinancial in nature, is protected by provisions of the Private Securities Litigation Reform Act of 1995. This law provides a so-called safe harbor for forward-looking statements and makes it somewhat more difficult for lawyers to file suits on behalf of shareholders claiming to have lost money because of something the company did or didn't say.

Creating and Maintaining a Disclosure Policy

Given the importance of ensuring consistent, nonselective disclosure of material information, it's important that companies have a disclosure policy that makes clear who is allowed to speak for the company, how they may do so, and what guidelines they must follow. NIRI lists the basic elements for a suggested corporate disclosure policy in its publication *Standards of Practice Handbook for Investor Relations.* Here are their suggestions:

❑ Designate a disclosure policy committee, which should include legal counsel, the CFO or treasurer, the chief investor relations officer (IRO), and chief corporate communications officer.

❑ Designate authorized spokespersons and make a corporate commitment to keep these spokespersons fully apprised of company developments. Both the financial media and professional investment community quickly size up IR or PR representatives as either knowledgeable spokespersons or mere company stooges.

❑ Instruct all employees who are not authorized to speak for the company to forward any calls or inquiries to the authorized spokespersons.

❑ Have a policy on reviewing analysts' reports on the company. If your policy is to review reports, restrict comments to correcting errors in fact and don't comment on forecasts. Provide corrections only in writing.

❑ Implement a policy on commenting on analyst earnings estimates. Most companies don't officially comment on estimates, but try to provide a steady and consistent flow of information to help analysts arrive at their own good estimates.

❑ Have a policy on responding to rumors. A simple "Our corporate policy, at this time, is that we don't comment on rumors" will sometimes suffice, so long as the company itself is not the source of the rumor, but it can backfire with the financial media and even the professional investing community. Obviously, some rumors are persistent, or they may appear grounded in fact due to particular circumstances. If a rumor is a rumor, say so forthrightly. If a rumor is partially accurate clarify the situation by truthful disclosure. If a rumor is affecting the price of a stock, then it has become a material event, certainly in investors' minds. It's a judgment call, but it's always smart to err on the side of good disclosure.

❑ Have a policy on providing forward-looking information. Follow the provisions of the Safe Harbor Act in providing qualitative information while not inviting lawsuits.

❑ Have a policy on providing fair distribution of and access to corporate information.

❑ Have a policy on the conduct of analyst meetings, conference calls, and webcasts.

❏ Have a policy regarding media participation in analyst meetings and conference calls. Most companies prohibit media from participating, but the use of live webcasts of conference calls makes it easier to provide information to the media.

Regulation Fair Disclosure (Reg FD)

The SEC issued new disclosure requirements in October 2000, in the form of Regulation Fair Disclosure, or Reg FD, as it's popularly known. This regulation was aimed specifically at leveling the playing field between institutional investors (the professionals) and individual shareholders (the amateurs). In the past, companies all too often favored analysts or institutional investors by conveying information to professionals that wasn't officially available to the broader investing public until after the fact. In effect, the institutions were used as an information conduit to the retail market. This gave certain institutions an unfair advantage. Rightly so, it is now required to disclose material information to all investors simultaneously as much as technologically feasible so that no investor has an advantage over any other investor.

In practice, Reg FD applies only to a company's communications with market professionals and investors. It does not include the press, customers, or suppliers. Reg FD also covers only communications by senior management, investor relations staff, and others who regularly communicate with investors and market professionals.

The regulation specifically does not apply to communications with certain people:

♦ Any person who owes a duty of trust or confidence with the company, such as accountants or attorneys.

♦ Any person who expressly agrees to maintain the information in confidence (by signing a nondisclosure agreement, for example) such as investment bankers or potential merger partners.

♦ Any entity whose primary business is the issuance of credit ratings, such as Standard & Poor's or Dun & Bradstreet.

♦ Any person contacted in connection with a registered offering, such as during a "quiet period," since it's assumed that documents related to that registered offering will provide sufficiently broad disclosure.

How does a company accomplish broad, nonexclusive disclosure under Reg FD? There are three primary ways:

1. Via distribution of a press release using a news wire service, and simultaneous posting of information on the company's website.
2. Via a Form 8-K filing with the SEC. Form 8-K is the "current report" that is used to report any material events or corporate changes, which previously have not been reported and which are important to investors or security holders.
3. Via a conference call (by telephone and/or Internet webcasting), with properly broad notice to potential audiences.

Simply posting news on a company's website is not considered broad public disclosure. Good disclosure requires that people be notified that the information is there, which is why distributing a news release, holding a conference call, and/or filing a Form 8-K are considered proper solutions.

What should a company do if it discovers it has unintentionally made a selective disclosure of material information? The company is required to promptly make a public disclosure of that information. This must be done as soon as is reasonably practical, but no later than twenty-four hours following discovery by any "senior official." This may even require an update to previous guidance in some cases.

The SEC has said that its top enforcement priority concerns selective disclosure of anticipated earnings. It specifically warns that private discussions with analysts seeking guidance will involve a high degree of risk. A company will be in violation of Reg FD if it communicates selectively to an analyst that earnings will be higher, lower, or the same as what analysts have been forecasting. In other words, management can no longer communicate with analysts with a "nod or a wink" when it comes to commenting on anticipated financial results.

The Softer Side of Corporate Reporting

Any analyst or investor can read all about a company's financial performance in the required reporting that's done via SEC filings. This structured reporting is what a company has to do to meet its legal requirements. In theory, this is all anyone would need to know about

FIGURE 1-1   **Reg D Disclosure Requirements**

♦ Corporate information must be disclosed broadly to all audiences simultaneously.
♦ Selective disclosure of material information is prohibited.
♦ What is "material" often can be unclear, so when in doubt, disclose.
♦ Selective earnings guidance will be the element most likely to trigger SEC enforcement action.

a company. But theory is very different from practice, and potential investors usually want to know considerably more about a company than just what's happened in the past.

In addition, formal financial reporting documents such as Forms 10-K (the annual report) and 10-Q (the quarterly report) are required to include information about potential risk factors. These risk disclosures, even when disclosed in dull boilerplate, can cast a dark light on even the best prospects. The SEC also is exerting greater pressure for the management discussion and analysis (MD&A) section of the annual report to anticipate scenarios in which revenues do not hit targets, and what that would mean in terms of capital availability—in short, in what scenario would the company run out of money?

To offset the negative, even "doomsday" impact of some of this reporting, many IR programs create documents and presentations that are based on the SEC disclosure documents, but that don't include the risk factors or the harsher portions of the MD&A. Such presentations allow for more than mere reporting on activities. They can provide a forward look at where a company is headed and how management plans to get there.

This approach often involves discussions about nonmaterial information that can help analysts and institutional investors create the "mosaic" from which they form an opinion about a company's future. Just as a mosaic involves the creation of a large image from many small pieces of tile, the mosaic theory allows analysts and investors to create the big picture of operations from many small tidbits of information that, by themselves, wouldn't be considered material.

For example, there are many professional investors who believe that predicting the future is close to impossible, so they back companies that have excellent management in place, come what may. To reach such investors, management can be made accessible, at which point managers should communicate their drive for profitable performance, while honoring all corporate governance and disclosure standards. Indeed, proactively assuring Wall Street that, due to existing conservative accounting practices, there will not likely be downward earnings re-statements can be a wise course (in substance, as well as in terms of IR).

Within SEC guidelines, there is considerable latitude to use nonfinancial information to help "market" a company and its stock. This can take the form of news releases, annual reports, company profiles, investor relations Web pages, fact books, speeches at financial conferences, and even shareholder information packets. It's all a matter of defining who you are as a company and what type of investment opportunity you therefore represent to potential investors. Once these elements are defined, do targeted research to find those investor types and begin communicating with them. It's a classic marketing situation—only now you're marketing your company, not just your products. Your target audiences hopefully will want to hear all about you and they'll want to get to know your top management and build relationships with them in the process.

The Art of the Message

Message development focuses mainly on why a company is a good investment prospect. As noted, a lot of important company facts have nothing to do with financial information. To go beyond merely reporting the results of operations, however, consider the investors' perspective and develop answers to the basic questions they will ask. Be prepared to tell them why they should invest in your company. If they're already shareholders, explain why they should continue to hold the company's stock or perhaps buy more. And provide analysts, money managers, brokers, and specialized financial media with information so that they can recommend the stock to their customers and back up the recommendation with solid information.

To prepare a good message, explain corporate strategies and programs, competitive strengths and advantages, the company's management and employee base, and its corporate ability to use all these factors to enhance your performance (such as increases in revenues and net income, improvements in margins, or generation of excess cash). Note, for example, that in the future, there may be a reduction or elimination of federal taxes on dividends, which have been an important and longstanding component of total long-term returns on Wall Street. Should the law change, a good IR program explaining dividend policy should be developed and implemented. In the meantime, the issue of stock buybacks needs to be addressed.

The following are examples of some of the factors to consider incorporating in your message:

❑ Build on your reputation for (and the reality of) delivering customer service that is truly better than your competitors' and take advantage of your good brand name, if you have one. If you are number one or number two in your market, promote that—many investors seem to gravitate to companies that are the largest within their industry or segment. If you are lower on the food chain, perhaps explain that you intend to take over a top position, or mine a more-lucrative corner of the market the "big boys" cannot get to as well.

❑ Explain "franchise" technology that allows you to innovate, create new products, maintain good product quality, and push the envelope in your particular business or technology. Though sometimes Wall Street forgets, the reality is that a service or good that is replicable is not a franchise. Competition will inevitably drive down profits; explain why you have a defensible niche.

❑ Explain production efficiencies (which make you a low-cost supplier). If you are not the low-cost supplier, explain why you are relatively a low-cost supplier (for example, if your service is twice what the competition offers, but only 50 percent more expensive). If you have customers who are fans of your product or service, make them available to researchers.

❏ Show how your margins give you cost or price advantages and, therefore, higher profitability and cash generation.

❏ Show the advantages of your strong marketing and sales organizations.

❏ Explain your corporate culture and how it's helped to build a smart management team as well as an extraordinary family of employees. Included in this idea of culture should be that the company follows strict ethical and corporate governance standards. This minimizes the risk of a "time bomb" in the form of earnings restatements or a sudden exodus of top management. Investors increasingly want to know that management is ethical.

❏ Show how you not only have the ability to generate strong internal, organic growth but also have the management capabilities to make heavily screened acquisitions that can help the business grow and round out your market offerings through external additions of new technologies, products, or other elements. However, be aware that the M&A growth story is a tattered one, as the vast majority of M&A campaigns flop. Talk along the lines of a few, very heavily scrutinized acquisitions, or that (if market values fall low enough) you are buying on the cheap, well below replacement cost.

❏ Show that the administration knows how to manage money, so you're able to fund future operations as well as earn income on invested cash. A permanently funded stock buyback program can be a component of this money management expertise. Such a program also shows shareholders you care about them, not just about building a bigger empire. The name of the game is increasing earnings per share, not expanding executive profiles and compensation.

❏ Show that your company knows how to find new applications for its existing technology and products.

❏ Show that you can enter new markets to capitalize on existing or related skills.

❏ Show that you're globally oriented, positioned to take advantage of world markets and greater growth opportunities.

This type of information is the foundation on which you'll create multiple media opportunities for reaching prospective investors. Such information will find its way into everything you publish and say.

Whether you're making a corporate presentation or preparing a new printed document, these factors should be divided among three primary message categories:

1. Financial and operating information, which is a requirement for proper disclosure
2. Corporate vision, mission, strategies, direction, and programs, which provide a contextual framework for the numbers you report
3. Industry context, which places your company relative to others in your industry so that potential investors will better understand your future prospects

One note of caution, however: Be careful when communicating vision and mission information and make sure that your goals are attainable. One CEO with whom I worked a few years ago said it best when he repeatedly admonished middle management: "The difference between vision and hallucination is delivery."

Always remember that performance is what ultimately counts, so don't set yourself or your company up for failure by communicating goals that aren't achievable. That can hurt you in the long run.

Targeting the Right Audiences

Once you've determined what sort of investment opportunity your company represents and have created the basic messaging to convey that positioning, you then need to research what potential investors—both institutional and individual—might be interested in your stock. There are several financial industry suppliers that provide everything from printed directories to comprehensive databases of institutions on the sell side (brokerages and investment bankers) and buy side (pension funds, mutual funds, banks, insurance companies, foundations, endowments, and so forth). By querying these databases (or poring over the directories, which is much more time-consuming) you can sort the thousands of professional investors according to their investment interests—and identify those whose investment styles match up with your company's characteristics.

Institutional investors can be classified in several broad categories:

Momentum investors. Momentum investors seek out stocks that are moving up in price. They don't really care what a company does, but are interested only in upward price movement. Once that upward momentum wanes or a stock's price falls, they sell and are gone. They won't be at all interested in your company's message.

Growth investors. Growth investors look for solid companies that operate in industries where steady growth is expected. This focus emphasizes good upward stock price movement for the long term, and if a company is growing within a growth industry, it's obviously more attractive. Growth investors commonly look at industry sectors first, and then scout out company opportunities within them.

Value investors. Value investors tend to look for companies that are undiscovered or that have gone through a bad period and are about to recover. Such conditions would also indicate upward price potential in a stock; therefore, a company may be more attractive from this perspective. Value investors often seek out company opportunities first, with industry sector as a secondary issue.

Both growth and value investors find appealing a company strategy of sustained stock buybacks. Buybacks increase earnings per share (creating the same effect of a growth stock). At the same time, your company could be considered undervalued, which is why you are buying back the stock. (For a detailed discussion of stock buybacks, see Chapter 5.)

Since the corporate scandals that began in 2001 and have continued to occur on a regular basis, many investors once again are looking for income stocks, i.e., those that pay dividends and therefore may be expected to supply a steady income stream into the future. Historically, companies that have paid dividends or have had low earnings growth rates (such as public utilities or heavy industry) have usually been viewed as stodgy. They paid dividends in order to attract investor interest because they weren't in high-growth sectors. However, some of today's leading technology companies, whose growth rates are slowing, are now considering paying dividends instead of retaining cash, as a means of proving they're a good investment that will generate cash flow.

In addition to attracting institutional investors, you may want to establish a parallel program to generate interest among retail investors.

This can best be done by tailoring a program through organizations such as the National Association of Investors Corporation (NAIC), the World Federation of Investors, or the Value Investors' Club. Organizations such as these offer many avenues to reach individual investors through membership in investment clubs. You can also use "advertorial" tools in several well-known financial industry trade journals that are designed to equip retail stockbrokers with information about your company as a means for promoting your stock.

Additionally, a public relations effort to "sell" your company to the mainstream financial media is another way to reach retail investors. It is remarkable how many high-net-worth individuals say they get investment ideas from reading newspapers and watching the business news television shows. If you have a particularly charismatic chairman or CEO, consider promoting his or her image to the public. The classic example of this is Berkshire Hathaway's Warren Buffett—there are investors who put money with his company simply because they have faith in Buffett. Moreover, a chairman or CEO who is quoted frequently in the media gains credibility—a big plus with retail investors.

Although it may seem obvious, it is remarkable how many CEOs fail to show that they put shareholders first during media interviews, often allowing ego to show large. Before media interviews, CEOs should be coached to have several talking points they emphasize, and certain catchphrases they repeat, one of which should be "I work for my shareholders, and I answer to them." Or, in answer to a question, a sentence can be led with the phrase, "It is in my shareholder's interests to..."

There are several facets to the IR research effort that are beneficial for targeting appropriate investor types for both communications activities and relationship building. First, monitor your existing shareholder demographics, to see who already owns your stock. It's easier to retain your existing holders than to attract new ones. Develop a balance among momentum, growth, and value investors over time so that you maintain good trading activity in your stock but aren't too volatile with wild price swings that have no bearing on reality. Over time you'll likely want to enhance the mix of institutional and individual retail holdings. A key part of this effort is to identify key opinion leaders among analysts and investment managers. You may also want to extend your domestic IR programs globally to key international financial markets, in particular Europe, Asia, and Latin America.

Outreach to the Investor

When it comes to communicating with a company's various audiences, you'll need to develop several tactical elements in tandem. Primary among these is the preparation and distribution of corporate news releases. This can include disclosure of your quarterly and annual financial results as well as other corporate news (such as acquisitions, joint ventures, and executive changes) that would be material and of interest to investors. The goal, of course, is to ensure full and fair disclosure in all communications activities. Earning a reputation for clear and forthright communications practices can be of great assistance in managing expectations in the investment community.

A related communications effort is the setup and conduct of conference calls with analysts and investors. This is especially important under Regulation FD. The simplest way to conduct these is to use a telephone conference call service through which professional investors can listen to your management's discussion of periodic results and can ask questions for clarification. A simultaneous live feed of the call can be broadcast on your Internet website (using any of several webcasting companies) so that retail investors and the financial media can listen to your presentation. This webcast version can then be archived for some period of time on your IR Web pages for listening by those people who couldn't attend the original call. Notify your potential audience via e-mail and fax of the call details and repeat those details in your quarterly news release.

One note about preparation for conference calls: It's important that you script remarks so that you not only don't omit any details that should be included, but also so you don't disclose any information beyond what's being reported.

The growth of the Internet and its positioning as one more key communications channel for reaching people has brought marvelous new capabilities to any company's IR program. A major effort should be the setup of a well-planned, well-designed, and content-rich corporate IR website. Such sites are now the first place any investor goes to obtain basic information about your company, and some of the cost of developing an IR website will be offset by significant reductions in telephone and mail expenses for communicating with investors. IR contact phone numbers should be displayed frequently and prominently, perhaps even on the home page. Work closely with good Web producers to create a complete set of pages with appropriate information that can be used for research on your company as well as for broad distribution of information as it becomes available. People should be able to easily subscribe to a publish-on-demand system for quickly and automatically obtaining the latest news about your company.

This isn't to say, however, that the Internet will replace traditional printed materials such as annual reports, investor profiles, fact sheets, corporate backgrounders, or capabilities brochures. Indeed, if you're serious about marketing your company and your stock, you'll still need to produce these materials. Nearly every investor has a computer today, yet many still prefer hunkering down with research materials in a comfortable den, or while commuting.

Note that in regard to printed materials, the SEC recently has recommended transparency standards in several areas. This includes a meaningful, clear, and communicative MD&A section of the 10-K and annual reports. In addition, in October 2002 NIRI promulgated a set of "best practices" recommendations to improve earnings releases. While they tend to parallel what any good company should have been doing all along, the NIRI recommendations have been adopted as an SEC guideline.

Among these practices are the following:

❏ Include both a complete income statement and a complete balance sheet with your earnings announcements.

❏ Put GAAP earnings up front, preceding any pro forma results and be sure to reconcile the two.

❏ Include key MD&A information in the earnings announcement.

Legislative changes affecting corporate disclosure have come about with the passage of the Sarbanes-Oxley Act, which took effect for all public companies in 2002. The act contains several sections concerning corporate responsibility, disclosure, and new penalties for improper conduct. Among its provisions are the following:

♦ Certification of periodic financial reports including signature by the CEO and CFO
♦ A ban on loans to executive officers and directors
♦ Shortening of the timing for reporting executive stock transactions to two business days after the transaction has been executed
♦ New standards on director independence
♦ New standards for board audit committees, especially the independence of such committees, and the qualifications of committee members
♦ Elimination of certain executive compensation upon restatement of financials
♦ New whistleblower protection for employees
♦ Management assessment of internal accounting controls
♦ Codes of Ethics for senior financial officers

Within the area of disclosure requirements, the Sarbanes-Oxley Act requires:

♦ Full disclosure of off-balance sheet transactions
♦ Pro forma financial information reconciliation with GAAP results
♦ Plain-English disclosure on a "rapid and current basis" of any additional information concerning material changes in the financial condition or operations

Because there is more to this legislation than can be covered in summary form, consult with your board of directors, general counsel, executive management, and IRO about compliance with the Sarbanes-Oxley Act. Case law and SEC rule and interpretation will help clarify and expand the impact of this act over time.

Need for Flexibility and Adaptability

Perhaps the greatest attribute you can develop in your investor relations program is to be flexible and adaptable over time. Good IR is a moving target, and although you should do your best to operate within the perimeters of the regulations promulgated by the SEC and FASB, not all of your communications efforts will be planned in advance. There will be times when you'll need to implement crisis communications activities—such as responding to financial or market crises related to your information programs or providing a response about the implications of unplanned corporate events such as product defects, recalls, plant disasters, or labor issues. For this reason, it's important that any major IR program includes good "inbound" communications to company management. No one can work well in a vacuum, so everything that executives do must be done relative to the environment in which they operate. Management doesn't decide a company's value, shareholders do.

Some IR shops annually poll their largest ten or twenty shareholders with standard questionnaires, to find out how management and the company are viewed. Often they discover that a certain planned venture or corporate executive is not well received. That's why feedback to management is more important than ever. It's essential to have an IR person or staff personnel who can maintain good contact with the investment community and advise management on what should be done, rather than the other way around. That communications loop must be closed in order to achieve the most successful investor relations program possible.

2 | IR for Blue-Chip Companies: The New Look

HEATHER HARPER
HOLLIS RAFKIN-SAX
BRYCE GOODWIN
Edelman Financial Communications

F RAUD, INDICTMENTS, GREED, and deceit have destroyed the comfortable feelings of trust that traditionally formed the foundation of relationships between investors and blue-chip companies. As trust has been fractured and operating performance has generally weakened, market volatility has grown and valuations have plummeted. In this environment, investor relations officers face the daunting task of rebuilding and strengthening relationships with a highly skeptical investment community.

Such difficulties are only the most recent in a series of business challenges that blue-chip market leaders face. New threats to established business models emerge regularly, including the dot-com wars of the 1990s, the corporate raiders of the 1980s, and the economic and social turmoil of the 1970s. Today, leaders of blue-chip companies also face challenges that stem from internal sources.

Because of the spectacular failures of some high-profile companies, even firms with the most sterling reputations for integrity are being questioned about governance issues, accounting policies and procedures, management practices, and protection of stakeholder interests. This skepticism has resulted in a conflict of perception that is based on highly subjective issues rather than the easily quantifiable performance measures and breakdown in share values on which the market has focused in the past. Gone are the days when a blue-chip company's market leadership, presence, and historical performance insulated it from the effects of criticism and questions in the markets. Success or failure now rests with the willingness of blue-chip companies to conduct introspective, honest assessments of their own weaknesses and take meaningful action if needed.

Communication has become a key resource for fighting and winning this battle over perception and reputation. Once companies better understand their strengths, weaknesses, and any needed corrective actions, key leaders—such as investor relations officers, senior managers, and board members—can embark on a communications effort to preserve, build, or restore investor confidence. Above all, these initiatives must be used to foster understanding of policies and philosophies embraced by the organization and its management, rather than to create perceptions that are misaligned with the internal values of the firm and its people.

In addition to accomplishing the objectives relevant to the individual business, blue-chip companies carry the burden of market leadership. Leadership in today's markets requires reaching beyond minimum standards and the narrowest legal interpretations of new regulations, and adhering to the spirit of rules intended to promote fair, timely, and transparent sharing of information.

Where Are the Blue Chips Hiding?

Before considering what blue-chip companies must do to succeed fully in managing relationships with today's investors, we must first understand the definition of a "blue chip" and examine the companies that make up the category today.

Blue-chip companies have traditionally been defined as companies meeting three primary criteria:
- ♦ **Returns** that have been consistently positive and delivered over time
- ♦ **Risk** that is lower than the market average
- ♦ **Reputation** for quality and ethical leadership

These factors have allowed blue-chip companies to benefit from a Teflon coating. They have enjoyed almost unquestioned public confidence and built reservoirs of goodwill that can insulate them from the effects of momentary spikes in negative public opinion.

Historically, companies that came to be considered blue chips seemed to hold the distinction almost indefinitely. However, actions at companies such as Enron and WorldCom showed that breeches of trust can and will revoke membership in the blue-chip club. Similarly, the rise of entrepreneurs and the Internet in the late 1990s presented challenges to established business models, taking its toll on the ranks of companies once considered invincible blue-chip performers.

As a result of these recent business dynamics, we have seen a radical transformation in the leading blue chip sectors. For example, numerous companies in the quintessential blue-chip industry—utilities—plunged into deregulated markets and speculative trading to compete with the faster growing companies of the 1990s. In the process, these firms fundamentally altered not just their business models but also their basic investment thesis in an attempt to remain attractive to investors. At the same time, Microsoft—just a fledgling start-up in 1975—now has a market capitalization of more than $250 billion, is paying a dividend, and ranks high on many investors' lists of dependable new economy blue chips.

In facing these market changes, it is certain that previously unquestioned industry leaders can no longer take their position for granted. Now, more than ever before, market leaders and emerging companies that seek to join the blue chips as peers have to actively and effectively communicate their accomplishments in the areas of returns, risk, and reputation that truly define the blue-chip category. With accounting scandals and widespread allegations of aggressive bookkeeping, investors are questioning quality of returns as well as actual reported figures. As the market scrutinizes earnings quality and the Securities and Exchange Commission (SEC) helps weed out cases of misleading financial reporting, the other two factors that define the blue-chip category—low risk and first-rate reputation—are becoming an even higher priority for investors. Addressing these areas of investor interest in an effective way is an increasingly sophisticated and complex task, considering the dynamics in the market, proliferation of media and information sources, new securities regulations, and the changing role of securities analysts.

Before taking into account how investor relations professionals address market issues and use communications most effectively, it is important to have an updated and thorough understanding of the audiences that financial communications programs must reach and successfully influence.

A Buyer's Market

Above all, blue-chip companies must understand and accept the new power dynamic in the market. Investors in today's market are more in control than ever before, voting with their dollars on the credibility and worth of public companies—and making judgments quickly. Corporate issuers are on the defensive in this buyer's market and must adapt to new investor demands rather than remain complacent with old practices.

This new realism in the investment community follows the bursting of the market bubble and public revelations about corporate and executive misconduct. Current skepticism and intense scrutiny from fund managers is in sharp contrast to the irrational expectations at the height of the bubble. Experienced hedge fund managers such as Soros Fund Management's Stanley Druckenmiller, Tiger Management's Julian Robertson, and Vinik Asset Management's Jeffrey Vinik exited the markets at that time because they found it hard to justify valuations and deliver competitive returns.

Executives of market-leading companies are beginning to set examples of how to address this new environment by adapting their reporting, governance policies, and communications practices. General Electric in particular is among a handful of blue-chip companies taking proactive steps to adapt to new demands of the market. In addition to splitting the company into four separate reporting divisions in summer 2002 to improve transparency, the company holds and webcasts quarterly earnings conference calls. And in the fall of 2002, GE made public new guidelines on executive stock ownership and corporate governance.

General Electric and other blue chips will certainly have to continue responding to concerns about corporate governance, disclosure, and accounting practices that are at the top of investors' minds throughout the market. In addition to addressing these issues and meeting the more traditional needs of institutional—and sometimes individual—investors, blue-chip companies must consider the motivations and demands of two other types of players that have become increasingly influential in today's markets.

Return of the Balance Sheet

Nearly forgotten at the height of the equity bubble in the late 1990s, fixed-income investors and analysts are making a comeback. These analysts often have been some of the first observers to spot the early warning signs of a corporate decline and have in many cases issued critical reports that countered the prevailing sentiment in the equity market. Now, as a larger number of investors are raising balance sheet questions and considering liquidity and solvency issues more closely, fixed-income teams and ratings agency analysts are getting more time and attention from investor relations officers at blue-chip firms.

For example, following its return to the public markets as an independent company, finance company CIT Group established a new investor relations department that includes a dedicated point of contact for fixed-income investors staffed by a professional who had spent years working in the company's treasury department. This approach was lauded by investors in a perception study conducted by the company.

Even for companies with limited need to access the debt markets, investor relations professionals should understand the best practices in fixed-income communications and consider them as models. At a minimum, a thorough, regular review of balance sheet and cash flow statements with the finance staff will prepare investor relations officers for questions and help them gain an early warning on issues that could become of interest to equity investors in the near future.

Playing Defense

While making plans for marketing to desired investors, blue-chip companies must also have a defensive communications strategy in place. Blue-chip companies are not immune to the tactics of shareholder activists, short sellers, and momentum players, especially in a fragile market when corporate credibility is at an all-time low.

Shareholder activists have recently caused a great deal of concern for blue-chip companies. Shareholder litigation continues to increase and is a primary tool of activists, who use the media to bolster their causes. Blue-chip companies can expect these suits following any sharp drop in a firm's share price.

In addition to ongoing litigation activity, a new type of activist is emerging in the form of more aggressive hedge funds and financial advisers who claim to represent groups of well-known institutional investors holding a large portion of a company's outstanding shares. Corporate governance issues have been a primary focus for these activists who use public pressure and threats of control battles to push for management reforms, changes to board composition, separation of chairman and CEO roles, and other actions. In recent high-profile cases, Disney and Aetna both came under attack over governance issues.

Investor Relations Today

In the middle of these unsettled markets, the investor relations function sits as a link between investors and management teams. The role, scope, and influence of this function vary greatly from company to company, as do the skills required of the professionals staffing the departments. The diversity in approach to investor relations results in part from the hybrid nature of the function. The National Investor Relations Institute (NIRI) defines investor relations as "a strategic management responsibility using the disciplines of finance, communication and marketing...."[1] This definition highlights the need for the combination of both financial analysis and marketing skills in one function and in investor relations officers themselves. In difficult markets where rebuilding credibility is often a primary objective, blue-chip companies must have investor relations officers who are experts in both areas. Only by drawing on a solid base of financial knowledge and using proven communications techniques will investor relations officers be able to effectively convey their companies' strengths in the three "Rs"—return, risk, and reputation—that define a blue-chip company.

Ultimately, the most important duty of a corporate investor relations officer is to serve as a bridge between management and market participants. The investor relations officer is responsible for communicating the company's investment thesis in a compelling way and, in the process, attracting and maintaining investor interest. However, the IRO has a second and equally critical role as the carrier of both positive and negative information from the market back to the management team. This intelligence includes feedback to management on investor perceptions of financial performance, management credibility, company strategy, and other issues that influence an investor's decision to buy, hold, or sell the stock. A frequent and ongoing flow of information between top executives and investors can ensure that leaders truly understand market sentiment. Feedback from a broad range of market participants can keep senior managers from becoming insular in their thinking—from listening only to either company insiders or a static set of top investors. Candid, timely input from the market back to executives is critical, and often it can best be gained and passed through the investor relations function or a third-party consultant. Investor relations officers have a duty to fill the gap between management and the markets by constantly soliciting this type of feedback from their constituency and finding ways to present this intelligence internally in a constructive fashion. Guidelines issued in April 2002 by NIRI suggest that investor relations officers take this process one step further by meeting with a committee of independent board members (preferably the audit committee) to give this market feedback directly to the directors.[2]

On a practical level, the responsibility of the investor relations officer can be broken down into four key areas:

1. **Financial reporting and disclosures.** Always at the core of the investor relations department responsibilities, effectively communicating financial results and disclosures to the investment community has never been more complex and, at the same time, has never been more important.

2. **Marketing the company's investment thesis.** Also central to the duties of corporate investor relations officers is the job of responsibly communicating why their companies are good investment opportunities.

3. **Corporate governance communications.** As one of the top investor concerns in the early twenty-first century, corporate

governance issues are a topic that investor relations officers
must incorporate into their communication programs.

4. **Public presence.** Management of the company's public corporate
presence and reputation is typically conducted in partnership
with a firm's media relations team. Investor relations officers must
now play an integral role in managing and strengthening corporate reputation.

Financial Reporting and Disclosures

Corporate reporting and disclosure practices have come under heightened scrutiny as regulators and others search for ways to help rebuild
investor confidence after a series of high-profile business failures.

Pro forma reporting. Aside from cases of outright fraud, "pro
forma" reporting—or use of nonstandard performance metrics—has
been one of the most widely criticized corporate reporting practices.
Although frequently associated with financial reporting from young,
growing companies, a study by NIRI released in January 2002 found
that companies with market capitalizations above $1.5 billion were
more frequent users of pro forma reporting methods.[3]

If used appropriately, pro forma figures allow companies to help
analysts, investors, and the media understand underlying strengths
that might be obscured by one-time, unusual events. The choice of
pro forma figures provides perspective on the market drivers on which
senior executives focus most. Additionally, pro forma reporting is frequently useful in cases of business combinations or divestitures to give
investors a common basis for comparison of financial results.

Unfortunately, in their zeal to meet analysts' consensus expectations, numerous corporate issuers took the use of pro forma reporting
to the extreme, resulting in communications that confused
investors and misled the market about the underlying strength of the
businesses.

The market itself appears to be forcing a degree of cleanup in this
area, although regulators have already adopted stricter rules on the
use of pro forma reporting. The NIRI study found that of 233
companies examined, only slightly more than half reported pro forma
figures with prominence.[4] Interestingly, 90 percent of the companies
using pro forma numbers voluntarily followed suggested reporting

guidelines published by NIRI and the trade group Financial Executives International (FEI) in April 2001.[5]

In January 2003 the SEC adopted a new rule for issuers that sets guidelines for use of pro forma reporting. The rule mandates that companies using pro forma figures also include the most relevant generally accepted accounting principles (GAAP) measure and explain how the pro forma measures differ from related GAAP figures.[6]

Although the SEC rule puts in place a more defined mandatory framework for using pro forma reporting, blue-chip companies should seize this opportunity to set an example by going beyond the strict legal interpretation of current or future rules. This type of action demonstrates the values of an organization and can help rebuild credibility and trust within the investment community.

In addition to using a principle-based approach, companies that issue earnings reports including pro forma measures should consider the following practices:

❏ Include GAAP figures prominently and provide reconciliation between the two measures, as the SEC now mandates and FEI/NIRI had proposed. The reconciliation might be in the form of an explanation in the text of the release or in tabular form, depending on its complexity.

❏ Provide detailed, clear definitions of pro forma measures and consider how they compare to metrics used by others in the same industry. Even basic metrics such as operating earnings may be defined differently from company to company within one particular sector. Companies should understand how their definitions differ from competitors' disclosures and make a conscious decision about whether to use accepted industry standards or to define metrics in a different way. The company should keep definitions consistent and make them easily accessible to investors through the company website and as a regular addendum to the earnings release.

❏ Include all key information in the release that will be discussed on the related conference call with analysts, investors, and media. As FEI/NIRI notes in its proposed guidelines, it is important to include comments that will be given on the conference call on topics such as context or factors affecting the operating performance, as well as outlook for future performance, using appropriate safe harbor warnings.

Qualitative disclosures. In addition to meeting the concerns about pro forma reporting and quantitative measures, blue-chip investor relations officers must examine their disclosure practices for qualitative information to help ensure that their reporting effectively conveys the company's economic condition.

The qualitative portions of annual and quarterly reports, particularly management's discussion and analysis (MD&A) sections, are tools that can be of great value in an investor communications effort if they are used to paint a picture of the company's performance and the factors driving it. These disclosures present the opportunity for management to describe its perspective and to help investors better understand the softer factors driving strategy and results. Unfortunately, companies frequently do not take advantage of this opportunity, and these documents become little more than a recounting in prose of the numbers presented in the accompanying tables.

Marketing the Company's Investment Thesis

The dynamics of today's market—damaged executive credibility, shifting relationships with sell-side analysts, and volatile operating performances—make proactive marketing to investors more difficult, but more important than ever before. It is a buyer's market, and even the most respected blue-chip companies cannot afford to sit back and let quality investors find them. Many blue-chip investor relations officers are besieged by demands from current and potential investors for management's time. By taking a proactive approach to managing these demands and keeping the pipeline of new investors full, investor relations officers can ensure the interest of the most desirable shareholders and make the best use of management's time.

To succeed in proactively managing the shareholder makeup, the company should take the following actions:

❏ **Demonstrate what is behind the numbers.** Talk beyond the most recent financial metrics. Use a marketing program to ensure that audiences understand the factors and forces driving the results.

❏ **Set multiple benchmarks for success.** The appeal of the single consensus earnings number is decreasing, and investors are looking at other metrics to incorporate into their analyses. By using marketing meetings to reinforce multiple benchmarks, blue-chip companies can proactively guide investors to the metrics that most appropriately demonstrate the value of the company. When investors begin to consistently look beyond one quarterly consensus number, they will have a better understanding of performance that can help build their confidence, which will decrease stock volatility.

❏ **Don't hide when times are bad.** Management accessibility and consistent information flow in the time of a crisis can help stabilize a situation and maintain or rebuild credibility. Companies typically are rewarded or penalized based on the manner in which they handle a crisis, not solely because of the cause of the crisis itself.

❏ **Understand which investors are buying and selling your stock.** Most blue-chip companies arrange for shareholder identification studies at least on an annual basis. The most successful efforts go well beyond an annual or even six-month review. Knowing which investors are coming in and out of a company's shares on at least a monthly basis is one of the few concrete ways that investor relations officers can begin to understand stock movements and gauge the success of marketing programs.

Corporate Governance Communications

In addition to communicating basic financial and strategy information as part of disclosure and marketing activities, blue-chip companies must increasingly address concerns about corporate governance policies. Many blue chips have scrambled recently to publish policies and update old practices, but Pfizer, for one, has long made governance a priority and set an example for others to follow.

Defining the term. In 1992 Pfizer took an unusual step and named Terrance Gallagher vice president for corporate governance. Few people understood the role of this new position. Even five years later, *Business Week* ran a story about him titled "Vice-President for What?"[7] It is hard to imagine the term "corporate governance" stirring much bewilderment today. However, while it has become one of corporate America's hottest topics, few companies know what to do with it.

This confusion arises partly due to the difficulty in defining corporate governance. The term broadly refers to a nonfinancial, intangible asset that undoubtedly affects a company's strength and long-term performance. Essentially, corporate governance describes intangible assets such as the quality and effectiveness of the board of directors and high-level policies put in place to help ensure protection of shareholder interests.

Until now, an afterthought. General counsels and corporate secretaries have typically handled corporate governance issues, but in the past actions have often centered on issues of protocol. Even as large investors became interested in governance in the late 1980s and the California Public Employees' Retirement System (CalPERS) formalized its standards, it was a sleepy topic. It certainly remained so throughout the 1990s boom.

Recent scandals, however, have damaged public trust in companies and raised questions in the minds of investors about the ability of executives to act ethically without a system for monitoring their activities. In a June 2002 survey of 400 opinion leaders in the United States by Edelman's Strategy One research group, only 40 percent of respondents said that they had a favorable opinion of business institutions and 48 percent said trust in business had declined during the past year. Moreover, only 41 percent said they trust business to do what is right.

Decline in trust and accompanying scandals have focused the attention of the internal investment community, governments, and even the general public on corporate governance issues. A Thomson Financial survey found that 89 per cent of institutional investors see corporate governance as either a primary or secondary consideration in their decision to invest in a company.[8] Moreover, shareholder resolutions, often a sign of conflict, are presented more frequently, news articles on corporate governance appear continuously, and analysts increasingly pay closer attention to management practices when covering a company. In short, corporate governance practices affect a company's reputation today more than ever.

To help manage the reputation risk that corporate governance can play in a company, consider the following strategies:

Keeping an open dialogue. One of Gallagher's most successful strategies as vice president of corporate governance for Pfizer was open dialogue. Many investors, even today, complain that companies do not listen to them. As a first step, Gallagher visited Pfizer's twenty largest institutional investors to establish an ongoing discussion of governance issues. According to news reports, this willingness to communicate was one of the factors that helped convince TIAA-CREF to abandon its contest against Pfizer's poison pill (attempt to prevent a hostile takeover).[9] Moreover, shareholder activists are increasingly media-savvy, often fighting their battles in the press. Witness billionaire investor Sam Wyly's very public campaign against Computer Associates, which unnecessarily displayed the company's dirty laundry and ended in a controversial $10 million payout.[10]

Maintaining an open dialogue also keeps a company ahead of the curve. Often best practices germinate from investors' ideas. According to a Dow Jones article written at Gallagher's retirement in 2000, TIAA-CREF backed down on its poison-pill objections because Pfizer worked with it and other institutions to create a shareholder rights review process every three years by the wholly independent governance committee.[11]

Blue chips today should look to Pfizer as a model. Many large companies with active, vocal investors still tend to haphazardly and ineffectively disperse governance responsibilities. One company that has taken a more serious approach of late is Tyco. Beset by investor disillusionment and a crumbling reputation, in 2002 the company appointed Eric Pillmore senior vice president for corporate governance, as part of an effort to restore confidence in the company with its audiences.[12]

Increasing the importance of intangibles. In addition to keeping the dialogue open, every investor relations officer should leverage the company's intangible assets. Investors today ask as many questions about the nonfinancials as they do about the financials. Intangibles, such as corporate governance, director independence, strategy, and management strength, seriously influence their investment decisions.

It's important to remember that having effective governance does not mean merely complying with recent stock exchange listing standards. Those standards represent minimum best practices. It is not enough to prove that the majority of board members are independent; companies must also prove that they can govern effectively. To do this, blue chips can leverage the important intangible factors that are not part of the public record, but which are critical to articulate, such as board members' various expertise, irreproachable character, and commitment to the company, as well as a culture that fosters independence of expression and diversity of thought.

To make sure these points find their way to investors, investor relations officers should add important detail about the board and its activities to the annual report and the company's website. According to an analysis by Toronto-based IR consultant Blunn & Co., of 135 investor relations websites from leading companies, immediately following the New York Stock Exchange board's approval of its new listing requirements proposal, 84 percent did not have a stand-alone corporate governance section.[13] Additionally, the Edelman Strategy One survey found that 74 percent of respondents did not find company websites to be "extremely" or even "very" credible sources of information. Other tactics that demonstrate an engaged and effective board might include raising the profile of the audit committee during earnings conference calls and increasing the visibility of board members at the annual shareholders meetings.

Public Presence

With corporate and management reputation playing an increasingly important role in the investment decision-making process, investor relations officers must consider how to ensure that overall public perception of the company and management supports, complements, and enhances the very specific objectives and messages for the investment community. Investor relations audiences—analysts, shareholders, potential investors—are all influenced by overall perceptions in addition to the direct financial communications put forward at the time of earnings, one-on-one meetings, and investment conferences.

Most often, general corporate and management reputation is shaped by media coverage, although activities such as philanthropy and executive civic involvement also play a role.

In order to help manage the overall company reputation, investor relations officers must work closely with the organization's media relations team, which, at many blue-chip companies, is structured as a separate department reporting to a different senior executive. In addition to the organizational separation, professionals in the two groups often have distinctly different professional backgrounds and experiences, making it sometimes hard to find a common language and platform from which to operate.

Although it can be difficult to overcome the divisions between the two departments, it is worth the effort. By working productively together, media relations and investor relations professionals can team up to ensure that overlapping corporate messages and communications objectives are not only coordinated, but are financially responsible and substantive while being compelling and effectively delivered at the same time.

The cooperation of the investor relations officer and media relations team in dealing with the regional, national, and international business media is critical to successfully managing corporate reputation, especially because the media landscape has changed dramatically during the past five to ten years. Among the changes, note in particular the following:

♦ Reporters have become more sophisticated and critical about financial topics as the public appetite for business and financial news has increased. Many reporters have proactively sought education, cultivating their own sources to serve as instructors. In some cases, news organizations have provided tutors. As a result, many business reporters now have better understandings of formerly arcane accounting rules, disclosure regulations, and the overall business and competitive landscape. This additional level of knowledge among reporters is enabling them more than ever before to ask the tough, challenging questions once received only from analysts and institutional holders.

♦ Intense competitive pressure among news organizations and individuals drives many reporters on an eternal quest for the "next big story." Investigative financial journalism is common today, with reporters poring over details of corporate securities filings to find disclosures that may surprise the markets or be hidden to all but the most careful reader. In fact, the major wire services have dedicated reporters to focus on corporate filings and the stories that result from them.

♦ The media also has more sources for fueling ideas about potential news and investigative stories. Information generated by research reports from short sellers as well as information posted on Internet chat boards may be unsubstantiated and in many cases untrue. Nevertheless, these sources serve as idea generators for inquiring reporters. Even at the numerous respected national news organizations today that maintain strict rules on fact confirmation and balanced reporting, reporters regularly are turned onto story ideas through short reports and chat room postings. Although these leads in their raw form may not be entirely accurate, reporters may frequently use the ideas as a starting point for uncovering a related story.

Given this demanding environment, a true partnership between the investor and the media relations teams can be a powerful combination for today's blue chip in managing its reputation. The most successful programs typically involve efforts from the investor relations team to add their financial knowledge and up-to-date market intelligence to the messaging savvy and knowledge of the media relations group. This combination forms a base of underlying support for the proactive investor relations efforts and serves as a first line of defense against media crises.

In addition to the need for investor and media relations teams to work closely together, the key underlying principles of these successful programs often include the following efforts:

❏ Educate reporters about the company and its industry to provide a background when there is no immediate breaking news. Although these efforts are not designed to generate specific stories, this type of outreach, which can include lunch briefings, meetings with executives, tours of facilities, and other activities, gives reporters the knowledge needed to accurately report on the company and to critically evaluate rumors fed to them by opponents of the company.

❏ Build media relationships in advance with both the communications team and senior executives. Although a friendly relationship does not guarantee a company a positive story, having an advance working relationship with a reporter typically provides that the company's opinions and responses have a fair hearing.

❏ Communicate substance over spin. The investor relations departments' in-depth knowledge of the business and financial issues can add significantly to efforts to communicate with reporters. At the same time, an investor relations officer's market intelligence gathering can help the media professionals plan for potentially difficult issues and reporters' questions that may be on the horizon.

❏ Coach the principal spokespeople in advance on both content and technique. Some executives are natural media spokespersons, but many are not. Training and role playing in advance can help them feel more comfortable when talking to the media, allowing them to focus entirely on their content at the time of an interview. At the same time, this advance training with executives provides a valuable opportunity for the communications team to test and refine messages about the company in general or in response to a particular issue.

Outlook for the Future

The field of investor relations is at a crossroads. Changing securities regulations, new demands from skeptical investors and analysts, and increasing financial sophistication of the media are combining to require a thorough and robust assessment of investor relations practices and the function's role within a corporation.

Investor relations officers at blue-chip companies have a duty to go beyond their traditional roles as chief disclosure officers and investment community marketing advocates. Investor relations officers must embrace their responsibility as bridges for information between investors and senior managers as well as constantly strive to set benchmarks in transparent and fair shareholder communications.

Chapter Notes

1. National Investor Relations Institute, *Who's Who in Investor Relations,* 2002–2003 edition, p. i.
2. National Investor Relations Institute, "NIRI Ten Point Program to Help Restore Investor Confidence," *Executive Alert,* April 9, 2002.
3. National Investor Relations Institute, "NIRI Releases Survey: An Analysis of Corporate Use of Pro Forma Reporting," *Executive Alert,* January 17, 2002.
4. National Investor Relations Institute, "NIRI Releases Survey: An Analysis of Corporate Use of Pro Forma Reporting," *Executive Alert,* January 17, 2002.
5. National Investor Relations Institute, "NIRI Releases Survey: An Analysis of Corporate Use of Pro Forma Reporting," *Executive Alert,* January 17, 2002.

6. U.S. Securities and Exchange Commission, "Proposed Rule: Conditions for Use of Non-GAAP Financial Measures," Release No. 33-8145, 34-46768; U.S. Securities and Exchange Commission, "SEC Adopts Rules on Provisions of Sarbanes-Oxley Act," Release No. 2003-6.

7. John A. Byrne, *Business Week,* "A Vice-President for What? Terrance Gallagher helped Pfizer build a reputation as a governance stalwart," December 8, 1997.

8. Howard Stock, *Investment Management Weekly,* "Institutions Prize Good Governance," October 28, 2002.

9. John A. Byrne, *Business Week,* "A Vice-President for What? Terrance Gallagher helped Pfizer build a reputation as a governance stalwart," December 8, 1997.

10. Marcelo Prince, Dow Jones News Service, "Computer Assoc. To Pay $10M To Wyly To End Proxy Fight," July 24, 2002.

11. Phyllis Plitch, Dow Jones News Service, "Pfizer's Retiring Governance Chief Is No 'Dinosaur,'" April 12, 2000.

12. Tyco press release, "Tyco Appoints Eric M. Pillmore Senior Vice President of Corporate Governance," August 6, 2002.

13. Howard Stock, *Investor Relations Business,* "Most Companies Don't Disclose Governance Policies Online," November 4, 2002.

3 | Litigation IR and the Duties of Corporate Disclosure and Governance

THEODORE J. SAWICKI, ESQ.
SCOTT P. HILSEN, ESQ.
Alston & Bird LLP

INVESTOR RELATIONS OFFICERS are on the front lines of corporate disclosure and governance as never before—including during those unfortunate periods when a public company is under legal assault or restating financials. Adding to the pressure, since the advent of the Internet with its all-news-all-the-time-in-your-face financial media and even after-hours trading, IR professionals are under the gun to disclose not only accurately but also very quickly. In short, like athletes, IR professionals have to be better and faster than they were just a generation ago.

As the 1990s and the secular bull market came to an end, so did the trust and confidence investors placed in American corporate management. Investors read one tale after another of corporate fraud on a scale unparalleled since the Roaring Twenties ended with a crash. Following that period, the Securities Act of 1933 and the Securities Exchange Act of 1934 brought much-needed control over the securities markets and necessary protection to investors. As a result, American public companies in the 1930s shifted from closely guarding their financial conditions to periodically disclosing their current situations. Investors, given timely statements about their investments, naturally placed more faith in Wall Street—and that is a fundamental reality that should always be remembered: Greater transparency and disclosure nearly always result in greater investor confidence in capital markets and in individual companies, with benefits for all.

But by the mid-1990s, some contended that, if anything, Wall Street was being held too accountable, even to those with specious interests, such as plaintiffs' lawyers. Mired with frivolous class action lawsuits filed at the instant a stock price declined, public companies called on Congress to reform securities litigation. The Private Securities Litigation Reform Act of 1995 (the 1995 Reform Act) was designed to protect public companies and, ultimately, their investors from "strike" suits alleging violations of the Securities Act of 1933 and the Securities Exchange Act of 1934 in the hope of compelling a quick settlement that lined the pockets of attorneys. Backers felt the Reform Act evened out the playing field and returned a level of confidence in securities markets.[1]

However, the pendulum has swung again. The avalanche of news stories covering overt corporate malfeasance even at name-brand companies, and the complicity of a then major Big 5 CPA firm in the Enron Corp. meltdown, shocked investors. The key to investor knowledge—public disclosure—has been undermined by suspicion and distrust. From the crippling debt hidden in off-balance sheet entities by Enron, to the improper accounting of staggering expenses reported by WorldCom, Inc., to the lavish pilfering by executives at Tyco International Ltd. and Adelphia Communications, corporate scandals have dominated the headlines. Even sophisticated institutional investors must wonder if they can truly trust any management.

The disclosure systems designed to regulate and protect investors have been skirted by executives who misstated earnings to achieve artificially high stock prices. Weaknesses in corporate governance, stock-based executive compensation, and a lack of integrity in the accounting profession all have contributed to an environment that mirrors the pre-1930s stock market.

The vital upshot of the recent scandals is that public company officers and directors today have increased responsibility and personal accountability for the accurateness of public disclosures. These increased responsibilities and risks to officers and directors concomitantly have affected insurance protections. Even the personal assets of officers and directors are not off-limits from disgruntled shareholders or regulatory and legal agencies. Jail time is a potential reality.

Unfortunate as it may be, even straight-arrow executives will find their public disclosures are no longer blindly accepted as truth, but instead are studied for flaws and deceptions. The cost of compliance with disclosure requirements has increased considerably as companies struggle with new and untested rules and regulations. And, in this litigious environment, a company's exposure based on the quality and accuracy of its communications with investors and the public has raised the stakes for investor relations officers. The IR officers are the shock troops in this new battle for investor confidence and proper compliance. The IR team must not only tell Wall Street that a company has good prospects (if it does), they must also assure investors and the financial media that proper corporate governance and disclosure is a priority at all times.

How We Got Here

Prior to the 1995 Reform Act, public companies often were saddled with frivolous class-action lawsuits. These strike suits, as they are called, primarily were generated by plaintiffs' attorneys seeking a quick settlement. The excessive cost of locating and producing massive amounts of documents and the disruption to business operations caused by depositions of executives outweighed the cost of settling the claims.

As the Chairman of the Senate Committee on Banking, Housing, and Urban Affairs, Alfonse D'Amato, remarked:

> There is broad agreement on the need for reform. Shareholders' groups, corporate America, the SEC, and even lawyers all want to curb abusive practices. Lawyers who bring meritorious suits do not benefit when strike suit artists wreak havoc on the nation's boardrooms and courthouses.[2]

Strike suits also acted to quell the information being disclosed to investors. Companies were fearful that communicating freely with investors and analysts would make them vulnerable to shareholder litigation.[3] As a result, voluntary disclosures, especially forward-looking statements, were chilled. For investors, less information is bad for the market. Investors and markets thrive in a climate of transparency and disclosure.

The 1995 Reform Act brought about measures to rescue business from the stifling costs of frivolous class actions. Among other things, the 1995 Reform Act imposed a stay of all discovery against the company (such as document requests and depositions) until after the court determined the threshold viability of the class action complaint.[4] Plaintiffs' attorneys also are required at the initial complaint stage to set forth facts with particularity that show a strong inference that the defendant intended to make a misrepresentation or omission.[5] The Reform Act specifically protects forward-looking statements by creating a safe harbor generally for projections of financial results and economic performance and statements of management's plans and objectives.[6]

Of importance to lawyers and IR professionals, however, the Reform Act did not dramatically reduce the number of securities class actions. In 1994, approximately 220 securities cases were filed, which represented a 41 percent increase from 1993, and a 30 percent increase from the average of the prior three years.[7] This increase in 1994 can be attributed, in large part, to plaintiffs rushing to file claims before the Reform Act took effect. Nevertheless, securities class action filings have steadily increased since 1995 and have averaged over 200 filings per year between 1995 and 2001. Of course, the stock market meltdown and onslaught of corporate governance scandals since 1999 have brought forth a gusher of suits.

As *Figure 3-1* shows, the practice of filing lawsuits against public companies is a thriving one. If there is a silver lining, it is that although the number of filings is high, the numbers of cases that are being dismissed at an early stage has increased. Before the Reform Act, only 12 percent of cases were dismissed compared with 26 percent after the passage of the Reform Act. Investor relations professionals are well within their prerogatives to quickly inform the media and institutional investors when a suit is dismissed, or that they are reasonably moving for dismissal, if defense lawyers so advise.[8]

On the downside for public companies, however, the lawsuits that survive dismissal have succeeded in satisfying the heightened pleading standard and have a stronger factual basis. More often than not,

FIGURE 3-1   **Lawsuits Filed Against Public Companies**

Year	Number of Filings[9]
1996	122
1997	167
1998	245
1999	207
2000	201
2001	483[10]
2002	180[11]

these cases lead to settlement—and a job for an IR professional explaining to investors and rating agencies the true fallout of the settlement.

Also worth noting is that the stakes are higher than ever before. Public companies that were sued in 2001 lost more than $2 trillion in market capitalization combined during the class period (the period in which shareholders lost value), which was 157 percent greater than the losses of all the companies sued in shareholder class actions in 2000.[12] Cisco Systems, Inc. has the dubious honor of leading the pack with a loss of $331 billion in market capitalization during its class period from August 1999 to February 2001, followed by Intel Corporation with a $231 billion loss.[13] Enron Corp. placed sixth with a $60 billion drop in market capitalization.[14] No wonder investors are peeved.

These vast losses have, not surprisingly, led to a dramatic increase in the size of settlements. Prior to the passage of the Reform Act, the average settlement in a securities class action was just under $8 million.[15] By 2001, the average settlement value increased almost 150 percent to $17.2 million.[16] When allegations of improper accounting practices are added to the mix, lawsuits filed in 2001 cost 280 percent more to settle than nonaccounting cases.[17] It is clear that proper accounting procedures, good corporate governance, and solid IR have a role in minimizing legal costs.

Restatement

The most dreaded word in financial reporting is restatement. In today's litigious environment, a company that restates financial statements, except perhaps as a result of an accounting change, virtually guarantees that it soon will be a defendant in a securities class action. IR professionals would be well-advised to prepare battle plans well before a restatement is issued. Restatements are considered by plaintiffs' lawyers as nothing less than an admission by the company's management and auditors that its accounts were materially misstated.

It therefore should come as no surprise that the most significant settlements have resulted from restatements. For example, Cendant Corp. recently restated earnings and was compelled to settle a class action for $2.83 billion.[18] MiniScribe Corp. settled a restatement case for $550 million, and Waste Management Inc. settled for $220 million.[19]

Restatements have increased every year since the Reform Act, from 116 in 1997 to 270 in 2001.[20] Investor relations professionals may wish to note that no industry sector is immune to restatements. From 1997 to 2001, 25 percent of companies in the manufacturing sector restated financial statements, 16 percent of all software companies announced a restatement, and 10 percent of service companies had a restatement.[21] Thus, it is highly advisable for investor relations professionals to have contingency plans on the shelf, in the event of a restatement. Of course, IR professionals should always counsel clients that conservative accounting procedures, indeed procedures relatively immune to restatement, might be a course well worth considering.

Change in Investor Demands

Whereas the revolution of securities laws in the 1930s focused on periodic disclosures, the paradigm shift in 21st century disclosure philosophy is that of instant transparency. No longer are public companies allowed to reserve disclosures for periodic filings. With the dawn of instantaneous communication through the Internet, webcasting conference calls, real-time market participation, the wire services, and the growing practice of "preannouncements" (making early announcements that the company will not make quarterly earning estimates), companies now must immediately disclose material information. Indeed, with after-hours trading and trading on foreign exchanges, IR professionals are in effect on call 24/7. Furthermore, under SEC Regulation Fair Disclosure (Reg FD), press releases and other disclosures cannot be limited merely to securities analysts and insiders, but also must be made reasonably available to all investors. Investor relations truly has pushed to the forefront of corporate communications.

The Sarbanes-Oxley Act of 2002, passed in the summer of that year, represents another defining moment for investor relations professionals. The far-reaching act establishes a host of new corporate governance, reporting, and disclosure requirements for public companies. The act enhances criminal and civil liability provisions of the securities laws, and also adds a new layer of checks and balances to financial reporting by establishing a new accounting industry oversight board, funded by publicly traded companies, to monitor CPAs who vet financial statements. Although the act responds to many shortcomings in the accounting profession, the primary targets of reform clearly are corporate executives. As the *Wall Street Journal* reported, "The law gives a straight path of liability to the pocketbooks of individual executives."[22]

Some of the notable provisions of the Sarbanes-Oxley Act, especially as they relate to investor relations, are the following:

♦ **Enhanced financial disclosures and accuracy of financial reports.** The act requires that financial statements filed with the SEC reflect all material correcting adjustments under generally accepted accounting procedures (GAAP) and SEC rules that have been identified by the auditor.[23]

♦ **Real-time disclosures.** Of particular challenge to IR professionals, the act requires companies to disclose on a "rapid and current basis" information concerning material changes to their operations and/or financial condition. In practice, of course, each company is unique. But IR professionals should likely be in daily contact with accounting, audit, and legal departments, on the lookout for items that might soon require a "hurry up" release. It would not be dramatic to require that IR professionals have the home and cell phone numbers (and e-mail addresses), and vice versa, of their colleagues within the accounting, audit, and legal departments. Thus, it often falls upon IR to smooth ruffled feathers and restore confidence in the company. Management must disclose material facts immediately, then get on with the business of running the company.[24]

♦ **Off-balance-sheet transactions.** In direct reaction to the Enron debacle, the act mandates that the SEC adopt rules requiring annual and quarterly reports filed with the SEC to disclose all material off-balance-sheet transactions, arrangements, obligations (including contingent obligations), and other relationships of the company with unconsolidated entities or other persons that may have a material current or future effect on the organization's financial condition. Again, although this topic seems arcane, IR professionals must be versed in the full range of a company's financial obligations and capital structure.[25]

♦ **Pro forma financial disclosures.** The act mandates that the SEC adopt rules requiring companies to reconcile any published pro forma data to the financial condition and results of operation calculated according to GAAP.[26]

♦ **Management assessment of internal controls.** The act requires the SEC to adopt rules requiring companies to include in their annual reports an internal control report.[27] This report must contain a statement by the company's management that it is responsible for creating and maintaining adequate internal controls and procedures for financial reporting, and an assessment of the effectiveness of those controls and procedures as of the end of the company's most recent fiscal year.[28]

In addition, the company's auditor must report on and attest to management's assessment of the company's internal controls. IR professionals should be aware of the potential land mine created if the company's outside auditing firm decides to issue a qualified opinion as to a company's internal controls— somewhat akin to when an outside auditing firm does not fully endorse a company's reported figures. IR professionals need to know about any tension between auditing firms and management and be prepared to handle the news of an qualified opinion, should it occur.

♦ **Corporate responsibility for financial reports and officer certification.** The act requires the SEC to adopt rules requiring CEOs and CFOs of public companies to certify in all quarterly and annual reports filed with the SEC that the officer has reviewed the report and that there are no untrue or misleading statements, that the officer is responsible for and has reviewed internal controls, and that there are no deficiencies in any internal controls. Already, many companies are moving to boilerplate statements in this regard, so this does not appear to pose much of a challenge for IR professionals.[29]

♦ **Forfeiture of certain bonuses and profits.** The act requires that any CEO or CFO preparing to make an accounting restatement because of misconduct in compliance with SEC financial reporting requirements must forfeit any bonuses or other incentive-based or equity-based compensation, including profits from the sale of company securities, received during the twelve-month period following the publication of the financials being restated. Again, this rule is fairly straightforward and should not pose a challenge for IR professionals.[30]

♦ **Insider transactions.** The act requires directors, officers, and any entity owning more than 10 percent of the company's outstanding stock to disclose any transaction (as required under Form 4) within two business days following the transaction. It is illegal for any insider to purchase or sell any security of the company during a "blackout" period. Insiders certainly have the right to sell their stock, whenever it is legal. However, IR professionals may wish to be informed as quickly as possible about sales, or pending sales, so as to be ready to field questions from institutional investors. And if anyone consults with IR prior to a sale, the answer should be "don't." Investors never like to see management sell stock, no matter how, where, or when it is reported.[31]

♦ **Securities litigation and statute of limitations.** The act modifies the previous statute of limitations for securities litigation of one year after discovery of the alleged violation or three years after the violation, to the earlier of two years after discovery or five years after the alleged violation.[32]

♦ **No bankruptcy discharge.** The act amends federal bankruptcy laws to immediately prevent the discharge of debts under any claim relating to a violation of state or federal securities laws, or any securities fraud or manipulation.[33]

Suffice it to say that the Sarbanes-Oxley Act, even with its sweeping reforms, will not end the call for accountability. As the horizon is scanned by those calling for reform, individuals and entities outside the company are coming into view as potentially responsible parties. Historically, accountants, attorneys, and bankers who were involved in advising the company with respect to financial reporting and disclosures have avoided liability for securities violations as aiders and abettors. The United States Supreme Court, in *Central Bank of Denver, N.A. v. First Interstate Bank of Denver,* (N.A., 511 U.S. 164, 114 S. Ct. 1439 [1994]), overturned years of precedent in ruling that the securities laws do not provide the basis for a claim against any person or entity that aids another who makes material misstatements.[34] The Supreme Court acknowledged that it could not amend the securities laws, but instead that Congress has the authority to write laws that could make outside lawyers and accountants liable for abetting misdeeds at publicly held companies.[35]

A resounding call has been sent recently to Congress by plaintiffs' lawyers to accept the Supreme Court's implied invitation to revise securities laws to include liability for aiding and abetting securities violations. Several bills even were proposed on the coattails of the Sarbanes-Oxley Act that would have included civil penalties for aiders and abettors.[36] In fact, former SEC Chairman Arthur Levitt opined that a key failure of Sarbanes-Oxley was the absence of an aiding and abetting provision, which would, in effect, hold the feet of complicit accountants and lawyers to the fire as well.[37]

With the outcry for reform, liability for secondary actors such as CPAs and attorneys will likely come into focus. Indeed, the policies behind imposing such liability are difficult to question. Individuals who intentionally assist others in committing torts and crimes have long been held responsible for their involvement.[38] Although aiding and abetting liability for securities law violations has not yet been resurrected in most jurisdictions, the tide may be turning. For investor relations professionals, this may pose new challenges. In particular, if a law or accounting firm is fingered in a bad deal at a public company, should its work be trusted with any public company? (In part, this lack of trust played a role in the demise of Arthur Andersen.) Alert IR professionals must be ready for such bad news, certainly given that most major accounting and law firms today have national practices.

The waves of change also may begin to erode the protection for corporations put in place through the 1995 Reform Act. Consumer groups, plaintiffs' attorneys, and a growing contingency of lawmakers are casting blame on the 1995 Reform Act for creating an environment conducive to fraud by corporate executives.[39] Class action lawsuits are thought by some to be an effective deterrent to corporate fraud, and the 1995 Reform Act's provisions increasing the standards to file such lawsuits are seen as hindering this restraint.[40] The climate was different when the Reform Act was passed in 1995. The economy was in a boom, Congress was Republican-controlled, and corporate fraud was not headlining the news. In fact, Arthur Andersen, the accounting firm decimated by the Enron scandal, was out front leading the charge in favor of the Reform Act.[41] Now, with investors losing billions of dollars as the result of corporate wrongdoing, the 1995 Reform Act's restraints on securities class actions are under fire.

So far, the efforts to "reform" the Reform Act have faced resistance among lawmakers. Most of the legislators who supported the Reform Act remain in Congress and continue to defend the securities litigation reforms.[42] Indeed, the Sarbanes-Oxley Act did not include any substantive changes to the Reform Act. Whether that line can be held remains to be seen. It is an area IR professionals must watch.

Another factor for IR professionals to consider is that personal assets of executives and board members will be at risk as never before. Changes in director and officer insurance protection are being considered to better protect their personal assets: such as regulating entity coverage that has limited coverage for individuals, increased coverage for officers and directors, and excess coverage of officers and directors for claims in which the company is not permitted to provide an indemnity.[43] IR professionals must consider how to convey the reality of these protections to institutional investors, without suggesting that directors and officers are making themselves bullet proof, despite wrongdoing. The reality of increased executive liability, it should be noted, can also be a legitimate angle for an IR professional to pursue. "I don't think the chief executive would do anything to endanger his own finances," is an argument with merit.

Another consequence resulting from changing investor demands has been reforms to executive compensation practices. The primary source of executive compensation over the past decade has been stock options.[44] Options ten years ago accounted for only 27 percent of median compensation to CEOs, compared to 60 percent today.[45] Some critics have contended that one effect has been to push executives into focusing on short-term stock price gains instead of valuing the long-term health of a company.[46] Some have also complained that CEOs and CFOs, worried about their options, approved accounting procedures which inappropriately propped up stock prices. However, stock options remain an appealing way to align executive and shareholder interests, something IR professionals need to emphasize to investors.

Still, when corporate executive salaries and bonuses reach stratospheric levels, IR personnel are the first to hear complaints. Indeed, some famous investors with followings, such as Warren Buffett, have lamented about executive compensation. IR professionals will have to work in a climate in which big compensation carries with it not an aura of great success but a whiff of cronyism, or even corruption. Executives like Kenneth Lay of Enron Corp. and Bernard Ebbers of WorldCom, Inc. made millions, even hundreds of millions, while their companies crumbled, leaving shareholders and employees empty-handed. Jack Welch, the retired chairman of General Electric Corp., was provided with a retirement package—since amended in the harsh light of the bear market—that included a $9 million-a-year pension, use of a company jet, a shining new Mercedes-Benz, and tickets to premiere events.[47]

Moreover, the disparity between executive and corporate earnings has dramatically increased, surely causing even more disgruntled investors. According to a recent study of twenty-three companies under investigation for accounting practices, the top executives pocketed $1.4 billion in compensation during the past three years, while the share values plunged $530 billion, or about 73 percent of their total value from January 1, 2001, through July 31, 2002.[48] That's a tough sell for IR professionals. In response to abuses in executive compensation, the Conference Board Commission on Public Trust and Private Enterprise (a twelve-member commission including a former Federal Reserve chairman, a former SEC chairman, and former U.S. senators) recommended strengthening independent compensation committees, encouraging performance-based compensation, expensing fixed-price stock options, and providing advance notice by executives of an intent to sell stock.[49] Adopting these kind of compensation reforms could go a long way to changing investor perception— and could give IR professionals some much needed ammunition and advance warning for dealing with institutional investors.

There must be symmetry, however, between protecting against manipulation of compensation practices and providing motivation for growth and innovation. Incentives should always exist for talented and qualified individuals who are willing to take a chance or create new products and services, or who deliver consistently better earnings per share through careful cost controls and stock buybacks.[50] Communicating these objectives to investors in a way that restores confidence in the market will be the challenge of investor relations personnel in every industry.

The IR Challenge

The challenge to investor relations personnel in this brave new world is to restore investor confidence in a highly politicized and changing corporate atmosphere. No longer are public companies presumptively on the moral high ground with respect to disclosures, and no longer are investors blindly accepting corporate communications as fact. The presumption that corporate executives deal honestly with the public has been eroded by a few examples of corruption. The burden now lies squarely on public companies to rebuild trust with investors and to restore the integrity of financial reporting. Investor relations personnel will no doubt shoulder much of this responsibility.

One consequence as the pendulum swings toward greater regulation is the flood of new disclosure rules that have not been tested or applied. Many companies are taking a wait-and-see approach before implementing changes; however, any delay could squander vital time.[51] As Lou Thompson, chairman of the National Investor Relations Institute warned, "To put it simply, time is not on our side in the battle to restore investor confidence."[52] Moreover, the speed in which the Sarbanes-Oxley Act was passed likely will give rise to difficult interpretive issues and, consequently, future clarifying amendments and SEC statements.

Investor relations personnel will need to actively communicate with investors about a company's existing corporate governance policies, as well as any changes to those policies.[53] If the company governance policies and disclosure practices do not comply with current standards, then investors should be told what the company is doing and what it intends to do.[54]

A misconception is that waning investor confidence and problems with governance are limited to large companies with huge market capitalization; on the contrary, it is likely that the opposite is true. If even blue-chip companies are not exempt from suspicion, why would any investor trust a smaller shop, perhaps not even audited by a national CPA firm? Thompson said, "Anyone who doesn't recognize that the scandals created by a few greedy executives have painted Corporate America with a broad brush is not seeing the big picture."[55]

As regulations tighten, so does the margin for error. Investors today are less tolerant of public disclosures that are ambiguous or lagging. In the new age of instant transparency, any minor stumble could lead to a serious fall. Disclosures will be dissected and any mistakes are more likely to be blown out of proportion or misinterpreted as intentional. Again, for IR professionals, the stakes are raised quite a bit: You have to speak clearly and quickly, and you have to get the message right the first time you put it in print or open your mouth. IR is no longer a game for the genteel. And IR professionals must tell management that only sterling corporate governance standards are acceptable on Wall Street today. Wall Street wants strong audit committees, good, solid, independent boards of directors, and conservative accounting strategies. These themes are critical to effective communications with investors and will remain so for the foreseeable future.

ALL IS NOT LOST. Despite the increased scrutiny placed on corporate actions and corporate communications, and the recent falter in investor confidence, business in America is resilient. Patience and perseverance are needed to move past the scandals and recriminations that have dominated the recent upheaval. Notwithstanding the present downturn, investors can count on the fact that the vast majority of directors, officers, and IR personnel have the integrity and the intent to restore faith in their companies and in Wall Street.

Chapter Notes

1. In passing the Reform Act, Congress noted that "The hallmark of our securities laws is broad, timely disclosure to investors of information about the financial condition of publicly traded companies." Sen. Report No. 104-98 at 5 (1995), reprinted in 1995 U.S.C.C.A.N. at 684.

2. Sen. Report No. 104-98 at 5 (1995), reprinted in 1995 U.S.C.C.A.N. at 684.

3. Ibid.

4. The stay takes effect if the company files a motion to dismiss. See 15 U.S.C. § 78u-4(b)(3)(B).

5. 15 U.S.C. § 78u-4(b)(2).

6. 15 U.S.C. § 78u-5(i)(1).

7. PricewaterhouseCoopers, 1997 Securities Litigation Study, 1.

8. National Economic Research Associates, Securities Litigation Study, figure 11.

9. PricewaterhouseCoopers data.

10. The 2001 figures include 308 cases relating to the allocation of shares to purchasers of stock in Initial Public Offerings (IPOs). Although these cases are not traditional securities class action alleging violations of the Securities Act of 1933 and the Securities Exchange Act of 1934, it is possible that they replaced temporarily traditional class actions.

11. Through August 2002, according to "Class-Actions Lawsuits Target Bigger Fish," *Investor Relations Business* (September 23, 2002): 1.

12. "Companies Face a Record Number of Shareholder Lawsuits," *Investor Relations Business* (April 22, 2002): 1.

13. Ibid.

14. Ibid.

15. Ibid. See also, National Economic Research Associates, Securities Litigation Study; PricewaterhouseCoopers, 2001 Securities Litigation Study, 7.

16. National Economic Research Associates, Securities Litigation Study; PricewaterhouseCoopers, 2001 Securities Litigation Study, 7.

17. PricewaterhouseCoopers, 2001 Securities Litigation Study, 6–7.

18. William Cotter and Chris Barbee, National Union Fire Ins. Co. of Pittsburgh, Pa. 2002 D&O White Paper, 6.

19. Ibid.

20. William Cotter and Chris Barbee, 7.

21. Ibid.

22. Sullivan & Cromwell, memorandum entitled "Congress Passes Broad Reform Bill in Substantially the Form Passed by the Senate Last Week: President's Signature Expected Shortly," July 26, 2002.

23. H.R. 3763, 107th Cong. § 401(a)(2002)(enacted)("Sarbanes-Oxley").

24. Sarbanes-Oxley, supra note 23, § 409.

25. Sarbanes-Oxley, supra note 23, § 401(a). Pursuant to Title IV, Section 401 of the Act, the SEC must adopt these rules within 180 days of the enactment of the Act.

26. Sarbanes-Oxley, supra note 23, § 401(b). Pursuant to Title IV, Section 401 of the Act, the SEC must adopt these rules within 180 days of the enactment of the Act.

27. Sarbanes-Oxley, supra note 23, § 404(a).

28. Ibid. A similar requirement was enacted in 1991 and has been imposed on depository institutions through Section 36 of the Federal Deposit Insurance Act.

29. Sarbanes-Oxley, supra note 23, § 302(a).

30. Sarbanes-Oxley, supra note 23, § 304(a).

31. Sarbanes-Oxley, supra note 23, § 306(a).

32. Sarbanes-Oxley, supra note 23, § 804(a).

33. Sarbanes-Oxley, supra note 23, § 803.

34. 511 U.S. at 177, 114 S. Ct. at 1448.

35. Ibid.

36. Senators Richard Shelby (R-Ala.) and Richard Durbin (D-Ill) introduced legislation in February 2002 that would have added liability to aiders and abettors. The bill, however, was denied in a vote on the Senate floor. Similarly, the House Financial Services Committee rejected a bill on a party-line vote that would have clarified the Supreme Court's decision. Shawn Zeller, "Holding the Line on Investor Lawsuits," *National Journal* (July 27, 2002).

37. Ibid.

38. Accounting Industry Oversight Board Before The House Committee on Financial Services, 107th Cong. 2d Sess. (April 9, 2002), testimony of Professor Donald C. Langevoort.

39. Dan Carney, "Don't Toss This Stock-Fraud Law. Just Fix It," *Business Week* (August 5, 2002).

40. Lisa Girion, "Battling Over Shareholder's Right To Sue," *Chicago Tribune,* August 6, 2002.

41. Ibid.

42. Ibid.

43. William Cotter and Chris Barbee, National Union Fire Ins. Co. of Pittsburgh, Pa. 2002 D&O White Paper at 15.
44. Tim McElligott and Toby Weber, "Drum Beat of Reform Grows Louder," *Telephony* (September 23, 2002).
45. Ibid.
46. Ibid.
47. "Companies Should Heed Ethics Recommendations," *Austin American-Statesman,* September 23, 2002.
48. Sally Roberts, "CEO Pay Draws D&O Scrutiny, Underwriters Looking Closer At Compensation, Corporate Boards," *Business Insurance* (September 16, 2002).
49. Ibid.
50. Tim McElligott and Toby Weber, "Drum Beat of Reform Grows Louder," *Telephony* (September 23, 2002).
51. "Semantic Hair-Splitting May Stall Current Disclosure's Adoption," *Investor Relations Business* (September 23, 2002).
52. Ibid (comments of National Investor Relations Institute Chairman Lou Thompson).
53. Ibid.
54. Ibid.
55. Ibid.

4 | The IR-PR Nexus

DAVID SILVER, APR

Silver Public Relations

I T HAS BEEN ROUGHLY FORTY YEARS since Marshall McLuhan, the famed communications theorist, popularized and defined the terms "mass media," "global village," and "Age of Information." McLuhan wrote in 1964 in his seminal work, *Understanding Media: The Extensions of Man,* "In a culture like ours, long accustomed to splitting and dividing all things as a means of control, it is sometimes a bit of a shock to be reminded that, in operational and practical fact, the medium is the message."

One could argue his vision becomes truer with each passing year. With the rise of business news cable stations and the Internet, the medium plays a leading role in shaping public opinion on the scandals raking public companies, accountants, and sell-side analysts on Wall Street—and, importantly, how individual companies and managements are perceived in the mix.

Consider the flood tide of financial television shows such as CNN's *Moneyline,* CNBC's *Squawk Box,* and Fox's *Your World with Neil Cavuto,* as well as 24/7 Internet news services such as TheStreet.com and CBSMarketwatch.com. The medium (somtimes as slickly staged as a Broadway production) provides viewers—and investors—oceans of financial information on public companies, their management, and the surrounding regulatory and business environment.

The New Paradigm

In the wake of the Wall Street scandals about ersatz brokerage research and creative accounting—and the resulting tougher regulatory environment—there is a new investor relations and public relations paradigm for public companies to follow, if they wish to use the mass media to get their story to institutional investors and the 100+ million individual investors. The more than 8,000 public companies listed on Wall Street must consider coordinating, if not proactively merging, their IR and PR programs. There is little sense anymore in treating institutional investors as important and serious through a cogent and significant IR program, while having a Wild West—or even unrelated or underfunded—PR campaign underway.

In addition, IR and PR professionals, while working and talking with each other, must become familiar with the phalanx of new and stringent federal regulations governing corporate disclosure. Ideally, corporate managements should be secure in turning to their IR/PR staffs for guidance on proper and timely disclosure (although IR and PR staffers should never presume to walk on a legal counsel's turf).

The convergence of IR and PR has become so important that not combining those functions could have negative consequences for a public company's share price. Today it is a fiduciary responsibility of management and directors to make sure IR and PR work together (at the minimum), and certainly not at odds. Although certainly accelerated by Wall Street ethics issues, the need for blending IR and PR has been building since the 1980s. The market capitalization of public companies is increasingly determined by "intangibles," which include a solid senior management team; employee satisfaction; and ethical, but profitable, business partnership arrangements. But the most important intangible is a company's reputation. In particular, Wall Street must trust management and its accounting procedures.

Some market studies indicate that as much as 40 percent of a company's market capitalization is determined by the intangibles. That percentage probably rose even higher in the late 1990s, although maybe not for the right reasons. By the 1990s a typical company's book value represented less than half its market capitalization, which still holds true in this decade.

The investor perception of intangibles means a stock could trade for, say, $20 a share, or $14 a share, based on the fundamentals but also depending on how Wall Street perceives management, and its "story." Like it or not, management is often perceived through the lens of the financial news media. The resulting obligation of management and directors is to make sure that the IR team and the PR team are in fact on the same team. As a result, we are now entering what could be called the "Golden Era of Investor Relations and Public Relations."

The seemingly endless flaps over brokerage or "sell-side" research, crooked corporate management, bogus accounting practices, and the recurrent Wall Street obsession with quarterly earnings statements have made for an equities market as volatile as any in memory. Managing IR and PR is especially necessary in choppy waters, and the wavy ride in the markets has caused some companies—even such giants as Coca-Cola Inc., AT&T, and PepsiCo.—to forgo providing financial earnings guidance for analysts and investors.

Although it may seem self-serving to say so, the awkward situation corporations find themselves in plays to the benefit of IR and PR professionals, who have key roles to fill in educating investors, employees, and the financial media. This includes communicating that the quarterly-earnings game cycle will not always be of utmost importance, especially for those companies now stepping off the field of the quarter-by-quarter game. IR and PR professionals will have to intelligently argue that strategic positioning and long-term fundamentals will be the value drivers in the future, backed up by the company's reputation. It always behooved a company to be open and aboveboard to gain Wall Street's trust, but with the flood of new regulations from Washington, such behavior is now mandatory. With the new laws and regulations, most notably Regulation FD and the Sarbanes-Oxley Act of 2002, public and investor relations executives or consultants at public companies must help—even lead—in representing their company's financial information to institutional and individual investors.

Certainly, with Reg FD in place, any thought of the IR team confidentially telling institutional investors the "real story," while the PR team keeps up a rosy facade for the financial media is not only outdated but also illegal. Given that reality, there never has been a better opportunity for public relations and investor relations executives to become trusted and important advisers to boards, CEOs, and CFOs to help interpret and communicate important information about a company's financial health and reputation to the financial, legal, and mass media.

This new role has been recognized within certain industry groups, including the Washington, D.C.–based National Investor Relations Institute (NIRI). NIRI recently created the Center for Integrated Communication to deal particularly with issues of IR and PR integration. President Louis Thompson Jr. declared that the center would advocate the importance of integrated corporate communication, conduct or foster research on integration as it relates to corporate value creation, and provide development opportunities for IR and PR professionals.

Reputation

To get a premium price for a stock based upon the fundamentals, there are three things that really count: (to borrow an approach from real estate mavens) reputation, reputation, and reputation.

Every company has a story to tell, be it growth, or share buybacks, or value. Presumably, that story should be self-evident to management and IR and PR professionals, and not hard to repeat to investors. (If you don't know what your story is, you are soon going to need a lot more than just IR and PR help.) The reputation of a company determines how much faith Wall Street investors place in a story. That reputation, by and large, is earned by being able to talk to investors, analysts, and the financial media quickly, cogently, and without an "attitude."

Yet many a public company operates on a daily basis without understanding the crucial importance of managing its number one asset: reputation. Sometimes companies let calls from financial news reporters go unanswered or refuse to comment on rumors, even ones that are patently false. Recently a publicly held real estate investment trust (REIT) listed on the Big Board did not respond to a reporter's question about whether a dividend would be maintained (a very important question, from an investor's perspective, especially for a REIT). The reporter did his job and wrote a story stating the company did not return calls about the dividend. You can imagine the result. This same company almost certainly would not have disregarded a call from a major institutional investor. But the effect on the stock price was just as real.

The IR and PR teams in this example were not working together; in fact, the REIT planned to maintain its dividend. There was even a secondary fallout from the unanswered reporter's call: institutional investors wondered why management didn't alertly respond to the reporter's call—were they asleep at the switch? Did they hire incompetent in-house PR staffers? If they had incompetent PR staffers, who else was running around loose? Did management have a policy so rigid that it could not respond to a basic question about its dividend? Bad PR was in fact bad IR.

The company cited here did not guard its reputation. One blunder did not ultimately harm the REIT (although shareholders who sold shortly after the story might have a different point of view). However, a company cannot endure too many flubs like this one without hurting shareholders on a more permanent level.

Gatekeepers

The example of the Wall Street REIT illustrates the point: As unlikely as it seemed only ten years ago, today's gatekeepers of a company's financial information on Wall Street must be part of an integrated investor relations and public relations team. With the proliferation of financial media, the posting of news stories on Yahoo! company sites and message boards, and day traders pouncing on rumors, it makes little sense to treat the two functions separately. Both functions serve to enhance the perception of a company's fundamental value.

Key Responsibilities

It was only a few years ago that companies viewed public relations officers as news release writers, more tactical than strategic, and investor relations officers as the disclosers of company numbers and handlers of the "dog and pony shows" on Wall Street. But not any-more. Today's IR and PR officers must understand regulatory man-dates and obligations that affect their jobs, while at the same time alertly fielding questions from institutional investors, analysts, and the media.

The IR/PR team must also decide (with management approval) how to package the company "story" so that it is consistent and true. Shading the story for retail or institutional investors or the financial media simply doesn't hack it anymore. In addition, and as impor-tantly, the IR/PR team must actively put management before investors and the media (naturally, it helps if management is charis-matic, but intelligence and earnestness will carry as much weight on most days). With investors retreating from equities, and with more than 8,000 public companies competing for the investor dollar, pub-lic company management must be proactive in meeting with investors and the media. Wallflowers rarely make the party happen.

Naturally, there will be managers who do not feel like being "paraded around" to handle reporter's questions, or being "brought out on the carpet" in front of institutional investors. Their reserva-tions will be greatest during or after any bad quarter. The IR/PR team must try to convince management that running a public com-pany inevitably entails public obligations, much like holding public office. Part of the job, given the enormous power of institutional investors and the pervasiveness of the media, is to be the company's face. Management teams cannot hide from investors and the media and expect to be trusted. Shareholder value will suffer. Anything that hurts market capitalization is a breach of fiduciary responsibilities to shareholders.

At times, getting management on board is a difficult task. Many managers are accustomed to being answered to, not the other way around. However, the appeal of being in the media is also great. In addition, institutional shareholders tend to be a rather genteel lot when discussing matters affecting their stock value.

Meanwhile, it will fall upon the IR/PR team to develop new rigor in regards to the chairman's letter (which accompanies annual reports) and, critically, the management discussion and analysis sec-tion of annual 10-K and quarterly 10-Q filings. In particular, liquidity under different scenarios (such as slower sales) must now be addressed.

A competent IR/PR team should play a role in helping senior management frame messages in 10-K and 10-Q filings, as the perceived accuracy, honesty, and transparency of these messages will create corporate value. The team must also micromanage the company's website so that shareholders and potential investors will have updated, accurate material financial information. The team will have to involve the CEO, CFO, and internal house counsel in working on key messages for investors, the media, and employees.

The financial media and the investing public want to know more about corporate governance and ethics than ever before. The company website should make clear that the company is devoted to transparency and has independent directors, particularly on the audit committee of the board. Investors are still willing to place their bets on Wall Street—but only if they can trust the public companies they are considering.

Now, some specifics on the new rules mandated from Washington, D.C., and their effect on IR and PR practices.

Regulation FD

In 2000, the Securities and Exchange Commission adopted Regulation FD (fair disclosure, or "Reg FD"). This rule was enacted to ensure that all investors, but especially individual investors or out-of-management-favor analysts, concurrently receive the same "material information" regarding a public company that select institutional investors and market makers had been getting first.

Reg FD was and is intended to level the playing field and also to create more information, as even "tough" analysts would not be "locked out" or punished as before. More honest analysis, and thus more accurate market information, was the intended goal. Many public companies immediately abided by the new regulation, and without undue difficulty. After all, it is only right that material information be available simultaneously to all investors and analysts. But other companies decided not to communicate at all unless forced to do so in an earnings announcement or other material information that a public company was required to disclose.

This was, and is, a seriously flawed response to Reg FD. Indeed, some companies have been hammered on Wall Street, as they choose to be mute, while the investing public is being drenched in media stories about corporate fraud and accounting shenanigans.

The markets can be efficient only when company IR/PR officers communicate sufficient and appropriate information to a wary investing public so that investors can understand, value, and feel comfortable with a company's stock. Therefore the IR/PR teams' disclosure of material information on an ongoing basis will be seen as maintaining market efficiencies and fair valuations for those public companies.

On another level, Reg FD is good argument for the coordinating of IR and PR teams. The same message has to be delivered simultaneously to everybody. A company cannot deliver materially different messages to different groups of investors or analysts, or give material information to institutional shareholders, but not to the financial media. If IR and PR are not coordinated, mixed, possibly illegal, messages could result—to nobody's benefit.

Regulation G

In 2003, the Securities and Exchange Commission (SEC) adopted Regulation G regarding earnings release disclosure requirements. This ruling affects both investor relations and public relations professionals at publicly traded companies. In fact, its adoption was considered so important that NIRI issued an executive alert on Regulation G for its thousands of members.

The NIRI clarification is worth mentioning. Briefly, if a public company issues an earnings release, then the SEC requires the company to furnish the earnings release under the new item 12 of an 8-K, whether or not the earnings release contains non-GAAP information. If a company uses non-GAAP information in the earnings release, the information must be reconciled with the relevant GAAP information in the release. GAAP information must be presented with the same prominence as the non-GAAP information. Additionally, the release must state why the non-GAAP information is relevant.

Public companies that present information regarding a completed reporting period during an accessible conference call do not have to provide this information in a Form 8-K after the conference call if:

◆ the accessible conference call is held within forty-eight hours of the earnings release

◆ the earnings release was furnished on Form 8-K prior to the call

◆ the company issued a widely disseminated news release notifying the public of the date and time of the call and how to access it, and then placed that information on the company's website

◆ the conference call is accessible to the public by webcast, dial-in conference call, or similar means

◆ the financial information included in the conference call is provided on the company's website, along with accompanying disclosures required by Regulation G

It is of paramount importance that public relations and investor relations professionals understand and comply with the new government regulations that affect publicly traded companies. Mistakes or misstatements could be costly to a public company's reputation and the credibility of its public relations and investor relations.

The Need for Coordinated IR and PR Teams

Since this chapter advocates the melding of the investor relations and public relations function in public companies, it is appropriate to review how both of these professions evolved—and why they should now be coordinated, or even merged.

The Rise of Public Relations

The rise of public relations as a profession correlated with the rise of mass circulation newspapers and magazines from 1900 through 1917. During this period, known as the "Seedbed Era" in American corporate history, there were fifty well-known national magazines with circulations of more than 100,000—remember, there was no television. *Ladies Home Journal,* which was founded in 1883, had a circulation of close to 1 million. The muckraking journalists of this era—Lincoln Steffens, Upton Sinclair, and Ida Tarbell—used these national forums to rail against abuses of big business and corporations. This was also the time when high school education had become compulsory and literacy in America rose dramatically.

Corporations at this time, in general, had a policy of not commenting to the press, and, of course, there was no SEC to require accurate disclosure. But as the negative stories kept coming out, the public attitude toward large enterprises darkened, in some quarters to near black. President Theodore Roosevelt still figures prominently in history books for his legislation against the "robber barons" and for his trust-busting endeavors. One could argue that Roosevelt followed and answered to the national press. Corporate America learned a lesson— no one is above the court of public opinion in an age of national media.

One of the first serious practitioners of proactive public relations in representing corporations was Ivy Lee, a former journalist. He all but pioneered the field of public relations, attempting to represent corporations in an honest and professional manner. In the early 1900s, Lee issued a "Declaration of Principles" that set the professional standards of modern public relations and mailed his manifesto to all relevant editors of newspapers and magazines. It read in part:

> This is not a secret press bureau. All our work is done in the open. We aim to supply news. This is not an advertising agency. In brief, our plan is, frankly and openly, on behalf of business concerns and public institutions, to supply to the press and the public of the United States prompt and accurate information concerning subjects which is of value and interest to the public to know about.

Lee was among the first public relations professionals to issue "press reports," which today we would classify as news releases, to reporters on a large scale. Among his clients was John D. Rockefeller Jr., who at the turn of the century was a favorite target of Ida Tarbell, a skilled muckraker. She wrote the *History of the Standard Oil Company,* in which she lambasted both Rockefeller and the Standard Oil Company. For a spell, Lee was successful in helping to "balance" Rockefeller's image in the media, by artfully representing Rockefeller's business accomplishments and philanthropy to journalists.

Another early leader in public relations was Edward Bernays (interestingly, a double nephew of Sigmund Freud). Bernays started practicing PR in the early 1900s and continued providing public relations counsel until his death in 1995 at 103 years. In many regards, Bernays laid the theoretical groundwork for the field of public relations in 1923 with his seminal work *Crystallizing Public Opinion*. Much of his work remains cogent today, in that it recommends proactive PR.

Bernays pioneered the technique of using "third party authorities" to plead for his clients' causes. "If you can influence the leaders, either with or without their conscious cooperation, you automatically influence the group which they sway," he wrote. In order to promote sales of bacon, for example, he conducted a survey of physicians and reported their recommendation that people eat hearty breakfasts. He sent the results of the survey to 5,000 physicians, along with publicity touting bacon and eggs as a hearty breakfast.

Bernays's clients included President Calvin Coolidge, Procter & Gamble, CBS, the American Tobacco Company, General Electric, and Dodge Motors. To this day, corporations that commission "independent" studies are following in the footsteps of Bernays (although the public has grown a lot more skeptical of industry-financed studies).

As important as these pioneers are, it is more important to remember that they operated in an era before the huge upsurge of financial media, particularly the electronic media. Giants they may have been, but they didn't have to wrestle with CNN, or Yahoo! company websites and message boards. They navigated a world dominated by general circulation newspapers and magazines, many of which were susceptible to skilled PR campaigns, perhaps backed up by advertising dollars.

As a result, corporate PR emerged first, and separately from IR, and was thought of more in connection with marketing, government relations, and general corporate image campaigns.

The public relations profession is changing rapidly, and for the better. Bernays and Lee would be very impressed with how the reputation of the field is being elevated, most recently by the federal courts.

In a groundbreaking ruling in a federal court in New York in June 2003, the judge ruled that legal advice that is intended to shape public opinion and that is part of discussions between lawyers and public relations executives and individuals under investigation (such as Martha Stewart, among other Wall Street corporate executives) is now protected under attorney-client privilege. In a previous case ruling, this privilege had been recently granted to accountants—a field that is currently under investigation and undergoing scrutiny as well.

The ruling relates only to legal advice that is discussed among lawyers, public relations professionals, and individuals under investigation, but with all of the scandals brewing on Wall Street, public relations is fast becoming a sought-after specialty by law firms and their corporate clients under investigation. Public relations counselors are now strategic corporate players on Wall Street and with large national law firms representing public companies in litigation matters. The boardrooms are now opening for public relations and investor relations professionals, especially if that position is integrated and functioning in a senior management role that provides counseling on a range of issues to the CEOs and CFOs of public companies. The investor relations side of the team is fast becoming an important part of this equation.

The Advent of Investor Relations

Investor relations emerged into its own in the 1960s, often associated, as has been noted, with the so-called dog and pony shows for sell-side analysts and retail investors, usually held at the offices of securities brokerages. At the time, the important clients were stockbrokers with "big books" (lots of rich clients) and individual investors—Wall Street was a much smaller avenue back then. Soon, earnings news releases, annual reports, and other financial disclosures became the province of IR.

However, from the 1970s through the 1990s, the money managed by institutional investors swelled—indeed, exploded. Assets of equity mutual funds (let alone insurance companies and pension funds) jumped to $4.31 trillion in 2000, from a mere $37.5 billion in 1975. Appropriately enough, IR evolved into handling relations with the new, sophisticated, jumbo investors that stalked heavily down Wall Street.

In IR, it became important to know how to "talk the talk." More Wall Street professionals started going into investor relations, often from the broker-dealer and investment banking side of the business. Furthermore, the rise of institutional owners, many armed with trigger fingers on the sell button, led to companies' placing much greater emphasis on "making the numbers" and the quarterly earnings statement.

As with PR, the IR function really evolved before the financial news explosion of the 1990s, or the Internet, and, of course, before Reg FD and the Sarbanes-Oxley Act. It goes without saying, IR emerged before the present-day ability of financial news reporters to access online nearly all news articles ever written about a public company. Today, a "bad" story is archived and permanently retrievable, a part of a company's reputation forever.

Historically, the financial media was not important enough to be a priority client of either IR or PR. This allowed the two trades to evolve separately. But times have changed.

Today's Integrated Function

We are now in many ways living McLuhan's vision, that the "medium is the message." Business news stations market their journalists like rock stars, with labels such as the "Money Honey," and "The Brain." There is an incessant demand to fill the "news-hole" at financial cable stations. Effective, proactive IR/PR teams use the electronic media to help get their story out to investors. Airtime is always likely to be brief, and so it is wise to decide before going on the air what message needs to be told, and then to stay on point throughout the interview. It is fair to make interviews conditional, in that only certain topics are to be addressed (although once on the air, anything can happen).

Bear in mind that McLuhan's observations are more apparent in television than anywhere else. Being technically correct won't help if a company executive appears ill humored or unsure. And if the ground rules are too loose, the whole interview could revolve around a surprise topic, such as sexual harassment. An executive wandering "off point" could easily make an innocent gaffe, but one with repercussions on Wall Street.

But on a more substantive level, financial reporting has never been more sophisticated or trenchant, certainly at premier publications such as *Forbes,* the *Wall Street Journal, Business Week, Investor's*

Business Daily, or the *New York Times.* And, as mentioned, these articles are archived and accessible for other reporters and investors—for good or ill, they become part of a company's record. A significant portion of the financial media, in a very real sense, aspire to the same level of sophistication as these major publications, with access to numbers that IR used to provide solely to institutional investors. In any event, a company's financials are now available online 24/7.

Given these realities, it is imperative that the IR and PR functions be at least coordinated, or even combined, in public companies, so the same "story" is consistently told to investors, shareholders, and the media. And it better be an accurate story. Chief executive officers, chief financial officers, and their investor relations/public relations officers who think they are clever in deceiving shareholders, investors, and analysts are, rather, grotesquely myopic. Once the media perceives the deceit, the company becomes the center of negative stories that will hurt the reputation of the company for quite some time.

To gain a competitive advantage, inspire trust, and have consistent messages, it is recommended public companies using the new hybrid investor relations/public relations model follow these basics:

❏ Update company information on operations and finance issues for analysts and investors on a regular basis, while adhering to Regulation FD and Regulation G.

❏ Determine levels of interest with sell-side and buy-side analysts, brokers, and portfolio managers. Spend as much time as possible with managers and analysts who "like the stock." Keep them comfortable, keep them in the loop, and try not to surprise them.

❏ Have an easy-to-use interactive website for all audiences, especially for viewing financials. Consider using a few examples of real-time reporting on your website—such as daily sales at stores, or units produced. Although much information may be proprietary, investors today like to know that a company is able to track its performance daily. Find a way to show investors you can, and feature it on your website.

❏ Outside IR/PR consultants can be extremely helpful to a public company, especially on the media side. Large-cap and midcap companies can often get positive results in media relations from the regional IR/PR firms that have built relationships with the local media. This can be crucial should a crisis PR situation arise.

❏ In some situations, make the outside consultant an integral part of the company's IR/PR team. The consultant can be an intelligence gatherer for the company and quickly discover the media's perception of the company.

❏ Remember, the media drives what much of Wall Street thinks about public companies. Reputation management is the most important aspect of a company's perception with investors, shareholders, government regulators, and employees. Be alert, respond quickly, and act in a way that demonstrates the conviction that running a public company entails responsibility to the public and capital markets.

❏ Employees are a public company's foot soldiers in the credibility campaign in the marketplace. Be sure to communicate with them on a consistent basis.

When working with the Fourth Estate (historian Thomas Carlyle's description of the press)—whether on a local, statewide, or national basis—make sure you observe the following protocols:

❏ Return phone calls quickly or, better yet, talk with an inquiring reporter immediately. As a rule, reporters are not an imperious lot. But they are working under deadlines. The IR/PR officer who returns a call quickly, engages in friendly banter, and expresses a desire to hear from the reporter anytime, will get called often. Remember names, and call to congratulate reporters on advancements, or for an especially well-written article. And if you think some reporter is too "small time" to deal with, think twice. Some will rise through the ranks. Others may tip bigger reporters off to a story. Nobody likes being snubbed.

❏ As reporters write their stories, be proactive and keep an open line of communication between the reporters and your senior management. Provide the media with analysts who cover your company, and push those analysts to talk. The later you return a call, the less chance you will get to "tell your story" and to make sure that the reporting is balanced. If you return a call past deadline, you may discover just how surly a reporter can be.

❏ Consider developing a list of reporters' e-mail addresses. On a monthly basis, shoot out a message with company news or your latest observations on Sarbanes-Oxley, corporate governance, or ethics, and make sure to include your phone number. If an official at your company is brave enough to become a regular commentator on proper corporate governance—in the process perhaps occasionally alienating others—you will have earned a prized position.

❏ On earnings calls, make sure you comply with the Regulation FD rule and Regulation G. Communicate all material company information to reporters and put out a news release on a news wire such as Bloomberg, AP, Reuters, or Dow Jones.

THIS IS A WATERSHED ERA for Wall Street and Washington, and reputations will be made for those public companies savvy enough to understand how to work with a public company's diverse audience base. Converging the investor relations and public relations functions, and becoming known as a public company that is transparent will win big points with analysts, investors, and the media and will enhance market capitalization.

Even though the opportunities for IR and PR officers with financial and communications skills have never been better, the demands are also greater. Today, IR/PR professionals not only have to be proactive and media-savvy, they also must have a working command of finance, accounting, economics, and the capital markets. The more information that is relayed to investors, shareholders, analysts, and the media in a factual, truthful, timely manner, the more senior management will view the IR/PR function within a public company as a crucial component, important to growth and higher market capitalizations.

PART 2

IR Implications *for* Selected Financing Scenarios

5 | Sustained Stock Buybacks: An IR Tool for Mature Companies

NEIL G. BERKMAN

Neil Berkman Associates

Wall Street and the financial media love the explosive earnings-growth story, the next Microsoft, the next Amgen, the Next Big Thing. They love the story, even though in reality the company they are chasing could be the next Tyco International, Worldcom, Enron, or Global Crossing.

So how do you run an established, solid, profitable company and keep the earnings-growth story alive? It's common knowledge that most merger-and-acquisition campaigns fail. Yet if your firm responsibly sticks to its knitting, there is a strong possibility your stock will be overlooked among the more than eight thousand publicly held enterprises and trade at a lower price/earnings ratio than any number of flimsy but hyped unseasoned stocks.

Investors may be fickle, but they are your shareholders. In days of yore, established companies paid good dividends and produced slick annual reports to foster loyalty. Modern tax planning eschews dividends, which, even after the 2003 tax cuts, on average, are taxed at higher rates than capital gains. And hardly anybody is seriously impressed by well turned-out annual reports in this era of online filing with the Securities and Exchange Commission. Nevertheless, it should be remembered that only a generation ago, paying dividends regularly was seen as a reassuring sign of financial strength.

So what to do now? For many companies, a sustained stock buy-back program, coupled with a reaffirmed commitment to transparency, good corporate governance, and a vow of Spartan leadership and management, is a course well worth considering. Indeed, the regular stock buyback may be poised to become what the regular dividend was thirty years ago: a sign of financial resilience and management commitment to shareholders. Of course, Wall Street must be clued in to such a strategy through regular and sustained investor relations.

The operative words here are *regular* and *sustained*. Too many companies announce buyback programs that are sporadic or simply investor relations hype. Wall Street can be fooled for a while but generally is not impressed with this sort of grandstanding. The key is sustainability, an understanding that management intends to buy back stock this year, next year, and annually into the foreseeable future, just as dividends were paid a generation ago.

The dot-com era may have been fun while it lasted, but it underlined one of life's truisms: Trees do not grow to the sky. It is the rare gem of a company that can sustain double-digit earnings growth for more than a few years. It's even rarer to find companies with organic growth opportunities that can support above-average growth indefinitely. Even the most reliable growth companies with the longest records of success ultimately encounter the limits of their opportunities. Such glory stories as IBM, McDonald's, and Home Depot come to mind. As in life, every company enters a stage when it may be considered "mature." At this stage—which, not incidentally, defines the bulk of public companies—it's up to management to articulate to Wall Street its plans to enhance shareholder value. The old "we're going to grow earnings by 20 percent every year" won't hold water and, in fact, will lead to a vicious backlash when projected earnings fail to materialize. Effectively communicating a sensible strategy—whether it consists of targeted new-product development, more intensive sales and marketing, debt reduction, stock repurchases, or some combination of these—is the essence of investor relations and the key to protecting a company's multiple and shareholder value.

The Mergers Fallacy

There are tempters aplenty for managements who seek overnight facelifts for their mature companies. Wall Street is full of professionals who brandish merger plans as corporate fountains of youth. Investment bankers are expert at identifying likely candidates and arranging financing, and they will aggressively call upon public-company executives unbidden.

Investment bankers know how to package and sell a proposed acquisition to company management and investors. They know how to make even the most mundane transaction look attractive, loaded with a magic "synergy" that will sustain rapid growth for years to come and be "accretive" to earnings. Besides, it's fun to make acquisitions. The road shows, the meetings with professional investors, the travel are exciting, at least for a while. There is the undeniable thrill of being at the helm of a larger company, having more underlings, the perceived muscle to move into new markets and gain access to larger lenders and institutional investors. And if the benefits turn out to be more apparent than real, the remedy is simple: Do another deal, or jump ship to another company, leaving shareholders to hold the bag.

This acquisition strategy always works for the bankers and the brokers, whose fees are paid regardless of the outcome. The strategy even works on rare occasions for the companies involved, although the investment universe is littered with the remains of acquisitions gone sour, synergies that failed to materialize, cost-reduction programs that somehow didn't lower costs, and once-lofty multiples that are now nothing but painful memories. For an excellent account of the perils of M&A mania, see *Profit From the Core*, by Chris Zook and James Allen (Harvard Business School Press: 2001).

The M&A strategy is analogous to the hare in the fabled race between the tortoise and hare. The prosaic alternative to the M&A rush for huge profits is the share buyback plan, executed slowly and relentlessly, just as the tortoise walks. It's easier to increase earnings per share when the share count is falling and you are demonstrating to Wall Street that you have extra cash, and thus the financial strength, to buy back shares every year. You are also demonstrating to Wall Street that you would rather put money in shareholders' pockets than engage in Wild West roundups of like companies or even unlike companies. Moreover, if Wall Street is told, and is shown evidence, that the share count will be falling for a long, long time, a group of patient investors will form who are willing to buy the stock.

Switching analogies from fables to Hollywood, the stock buyback strategy could also be characterized as "build it, and they will come." With more than nine thousand mutual funds, thousands of professional money managers, and millions of individual investors out there, a company that delivers higher earnings per share on a sustained basis, for clear and understandable reasons, will develop "sponsorship," or a following. If the company doesn't, it needs to hire better IR staff or consultants.

Another word on the IR challenges presented by M&A campaigns: These deals fly in the face of the new Wall Street, which demands transparency and clarity from managements and balance sheets. Analyzing a company in one line of business is itself a demanding job. When a company branches into multiple businesses, serious forecasting of revenues and, especially, of profits becomes still more problematic and unreliable. Even acquisitions of like companies lead to dubious pro forma statements and write-downs. Going forward, there will likely be heightened suspicion that profits are being "managed" in any conglomerate or merger campaign and, along with that, heightened suspicion that the company in question may soon take a fall. It is worth noting that Howard Schilit, author of *Financial Shenanigans: How to Detect Accounting Gimmicks and Fraud in Financial Reports* (McGraw-Hill Trade: 2002) and founder of the Rockville, Maryland–based Center for Financial Research and Management, believes that merger campaigns and industry "roll-ups" are "time bombs with a live ticker running." Any company on a buying binge will almost certainly purchase a dud along the way, since sellers know a lot more about what they are selling than buyers know about what they are buying. Not surprisingly, many companies have been spinning off divisions lately, in an attempt to pay down debt and become focused, for themselves and for Wall Street.

Indeed, Wall Street's preference for transparency increases with every fresh accounting scandal and instance of egregious corporate transgression hidden behind an impenetrable veil of complexity. The market value of transparency has also been enhanced recently by the proliferation of increasingly stringent disclosure requirements. By encouraging open conference calls, webcasts, and timely disclosure of material information to all market participants simultaneously, Regulation FD has enhanced the value of a simple story. Similarly, the Sarbanes-Oxley Act of 2002 has increased the value of transparency by mandating, among other things, that senior executives certify their companies' financial statements. A CEO and CFO would surely find affixing their signatures less worrisome in a focused company than in a conglomerate.

All of this is not to say that an acquisition-led growth strategy is always and everywhere a bad choice. Perhaps in certain very depressed markets, buying on the cheap makes sense. But it does suggest that management should consider other ways to sustain earnings growth and perhaps pursue a diversified value-enhancement strategy that limits overall risk. The simple expedient of reducing the number of shares outstanding through stock repurchases can usually become a key component of such a plan.

Why Not Buy Back Stock?

Although acquisitions can be risky as sources of consistent growth, the Street frowns on the accumulation of cash for its own sake, especially when the returns on the cash are far below the returns normally earned in the business. There are times when a company should not to do a stock buyback, or at least not when it is a hastily conceived and temporary fix. When a company's stock price declines suddenly —whether because the company has failed to meet earnings expectations, because of rumors that it won't make its numbers, or for reasons not immediately clear—Wall Street often demands that management "do something!" The common knee-jerk reaction to this demand is to hastily convene a board meeting and announce a stock buyback. Such repurchases rarely achieve any material impact on earnings per share, nor do they work to reverse any decline in the company's market value that may be rooted in the fundamentals. In long bear markets, moreover, when the prices of stocks tend to fall whether a company is meeting expectations or not and the best outcome may be simply not to get clobbered, a onetime buyback will almost certainly fail to stem the tide.

Such on-the-fly repurchase programs, entered into under duress, can have at most a minimal, transitory effect, although they probably will please outsiders who are looking to dump their stock and are glad to have a ready market in the form of the company's treasury. On a recent conference call announcing a disappointing quarter, an irate institutional shareholder of a midcap stock asked if the company would purchase its shares, which that day had declined to just a fraction of tangible book value. The company agreed that this might be a wise idea. To no one's surprise, the block of stock that traded the next day turned out to have been sold by none other than this same irate shareholder. Unfortunately, since the eighty-five thousand shares repurchased represented only about 1 percent of those outstanding, this onetime buyback did little to improve the outlook for earnings per share but did set back the company's treasury.

Unlike the announcement of an acquisition or some other corporate event, a share repurchase program is not dramatic or particularly visible, although IR should put it on investors' radar screens. Rather, such a program is like the tortoise that succeeds through perseverance. In fact, a large, permanent repurchase authorization can have long-lasting impact, compared with the onetime variety.

However, although simply announcing the adoption of a buyback program may once have been sufficient to generate fresh buying in the stock by Wall Street professionals, it has been a long time since such an effect could be depended upon. Today, Wall Street wants to see a company actually repurchase shares if it announces that it has the authority to do so.

Advantages of a Permanent Repurchase Program

Because many shares must be repurchased over an extended period to have a significant impact on earnings per share, stock buybacks are most effective when used as a permanent element of a company's long-term strategy to build shareholder value. Thus, in keeping with this strategy, the implementation of a buyback program should be announced during a regularly scheduled earnings release conference call or at the annual meeting of shareholders, rather than under the duress of a weak share price. Announcements at such regular events send a positive signal that management is bullish about the company's prospects and that it is serious about using all the tools available to enhance returns for its shareholders. Looked at in this way, buyback programs are essentially no different from continuing programs to enhance productivity through employee training and investing in new technology. They serve the same function as efforts to source raw materials from the lowest-cost providers and are every bit as important as advertising programs to increase market share.

One element of stock buybacks has undeniable appeal over and above those other types of programs. A spiffed-up advertising program may or may not work, and efforts to cut costs can be swamped by unexpected events, such as electricity shortages or unforeseen bottlenecks. In contrast, a stock buyback program, adhered to over the years necessarily pushes earnings per share higher than they would be otherwise. In effect, it is something investors can count on.

Additionally, a properly handled, permanent repurchase program gives management the flexibility to quickly purchase blocks of stock that might become available from time to time at attractive prices, such as from the disgruntled institutional shareholder mentioned above. Such negotiated trades are not subject to the strict volume, timing, and tick restrictions of open-market repurchases. Although a hastily arranged buyback initiated in panic mode can also accomplish this task, under these circumstances a company is typically able to repurchase only small amounts of stock, certainly too small to have a meaningful impact on future earnings per share. But with a permanent, sizable authorization always in place, over time a company can repurchase a significant amount of stock and make a meaningful contribution to building value for shareholders.

Consider the example of a midsized manufacturing company that supplies highly engineered parts to the cyclical but enormous automobile industry. This company dominates its niche, steadily increases market share, earns the highest returns on capital in its industry, has a substantial and rising cash position and no debt, and has never made an acquisition despite Wall Street's best efforts to encourage it to do so. The company demonstrates its commitment to building shareholder value in every aspect of its operations. Management takes justified pride in maintaining gross and operating margins that are among the industry's highest in good times and bad. Although still small, the cash dividend has increased every year for more than fifteen years. In addition, the company has consistently repurchased its stock. Its board sees to it that at any given time management is authorized to repurchase up to about 20 percent of shares outstanding. When this authorization has been used up over several years, the board authorizes the repurchase of another 20 percent.

In its regular quarterly earnings releases, the company routinely reports the number of shares repurchased during the past three months and how many shares are left to repurchase under the existing authorization. Repurchases have amounted to several hundred thousand shares in some quarters, when the stock price was low for whatever reason, and have shrunk to zero from time to time when the stock price was high. Over the many years that this buyback program has been in place, neither the analysts who cover the company nor any of its institutional shareholders have ever suggested that the number of shares repurchased in a given quarter is too low or too high.

Over the past five years, the company has repurchased approximately five million of its shares on the open market. As a result, the average number of shares outstanding has fallen from the roughly 30 million there would have been in the absence of the buybacks to only about 25 million. So instead of reporting, say, diluted earnings of $1.00 per share without the repurchase program, the company actually reports something much closer to $1.20. Of course, the exact increment to earnings per share attributable to the buybacks depends on the interest income foregone on the cash used to repurchase the stock (or the increase in interest expense, if the company borrowed to finance the repurchases). Assuming the multiple remains constant, this company's shareholders end up with nearly 20 percent more value with the buyback than they would have received without it.

Interest costs, in the current low-interest rate environment, are favorable for buybacks. The loss in interest income is reduced when Treasury yields hover around 4 percent.

Countering the Counter-Arguments

The suggestion that a company initiate a stock repurchase program often elicits groans from management, which may incorrectly see the adoption of a buyback plan as an admission to Wall Street that the company has exhausted its high-growth investment opportunities. A typical response is "I didn't raise money from the public to use it to buy back my shares. I raised it to grow my company." Managers sometimes fear that the announcement of a buyback plan sends a signal to Wall Street that their company lacks organic growth opportunities and will thus put pressure on the multiple. This is a serious concern and one that calls for good investor relations.

One solution is to tell investors that they should watch the price at which a company is buying back its shares. A plan to buy back stock at or below tangible book value, for example, would probably, and perhaps correctly, be perceived by Wall Street as a negative signal. On the other hand, repurchasing shares at a substantial multiple of earnings, albeit a multiple below some prior peak, signals management's belief that the current multiple does not fully reflect the long-term growth opportunity. Thus stock buybacks offer a subtle way for management to tell Wall Street that the growth expectations built into the current stock price are too conservative. In this context, a buyback is a bullish, and not a bearish, sign.

In one case, a small publicly traded California wine producer leaked to the media that it would buy back its own shares whenever they fell below $4 a share, and in fact it did. This effectively placed a floor on the stock and helped keep some institutional investors on board. When the company later stopped buying back shares at under $4, the stock fell sharply.

If a company stops repurchasing shares when its stock reaches a higher multiple, isn't that a signal that management feels the stock is fully priced? Yes, it is, which suggests the further question: Why should Wall Street be expected to pay more for the shares than the company itself feels they are worth? If, on the other hand, the company continues to buy back shares at the higher multiple, the consistent upward pressure on earnings per share will have a positive and telling effect. This is because, without saying so directly, a management that buys back shares at certain price-earnings ratios is informing Wall Street there is a floor under the stock price—a not insignificant advantage, in bearish markets.

A company goes public to fund growth and provide a vehicle to monetize management's accomplishments, so it's natural for management to worry about defending the stock price. Wall Street, in contrast, must make buy, hold, and sell decisions continuously, based on an outlook for growth that may change every day. A company's past growth is irrelevant to the market, whether the story has improved or deteriorated. What matters to Wall Street is simply whether today's stock price appropriately discounts current growth expectations: If not, then buy; if so, then sell. Properly implemented, a stock repurchase program is an effective way for management to nudge expectations in the right direction.

A common argument against a buyback authorization is that a company won't earn a premium multiple if its earnings per share growth results from a shrinking number of shares, rather from the sexier cause of rapidly increasing earnings. As stated at the beginning of this chapter, Wall Street and the financial media love the next Big Thing or hot stock. If earnings are growing rapidly anyway, buying back shares during temporary downturns in the stock price is not likely to reduce the long-term multiple, and in situations where earnings growth is slowing, the multiple is going to decline anyway. Buybacks are not an either-or proposition. Stock repurchases are but one element of a complete program to build shareholder value.

Certain circumstances make it difficult to buy back shares despite management's best intentions. The most common obstacle is financing. Bank lines of credit often explicitly prohibit the funds from being used to repurchase stock, and cash often is in short supply at precisely those times when the buyback opportunity is most attractive from the company's point of view. A permanent buyback program permits the repurchases to proceed at a deliberate pace, perhaps more rapidly when cash flow is strong and not adequately reflected in the stock price but never so fast as to "break the bank" or dangerously deplete cash reserves in the event of a temporary slump in business or an extended recession.

A large, permanent repurchase plan allows a company to buy shares whenever financial circumstances and the stock price warrant, without having to seek explicit board approval or make an announcement to Wall Street. Again, buyback programs must be thought of in terms of years and even whole decades. While business prospects for even key products or services might wither from season to season (depending on competition or markets), a properly executed stock buyback program is a fundamentally sound idea now and ten years from now.

Float Consideration

A serious issue, especially for smaller companies, is float. Specifically, companies fear that reducing an already small public float through buybacks will harm the stock in the long run by reducing liquidity and making it harder for potential institutional shareholders to establish positions. Moreover, institutional shareholders, as witness such behemoths as Fidelity or Capital Research & Management, have tended to become larger in recent years.

Note, however, that many stocks trade actively and at attractive multiples even with floats of less than a million shares. And although many institutions will be precluded from participating in a particular situation because of a small float (or more typically a small total market capitalization), many other institutional investors running tens to hundreds of millions of dollars specialize in precisely such situations. The relevant issue is growth in earnings per share, not float per se. Besides, the smaller the number of shares outstanding, the fewer the shares that need to be repurchased to make a dramatic difference to earnings per share. Remember, moreover, that stocks can be split.

As noted previously, properly implemented stock repurchases financed with corporate funds can send a bullish signal to Wall Street. An even stronger signal is sent when a company's stock is purchased in the open market by members of senior management using their own money. Small changes can have large effects. Insider purchases make a dramatic statement of management's confidence in the future even when the number of shares involved is small relative to the company's own formal buyback program. Anyone who reads Yahoo!'s and other sites' online message boards about public companies knows that many shareholders—especially bear theorists and short traders—watch management purchases and sales closely.

FAR FROM AN ADMISSION OF DEFEAT, far from representing the last gasp of a company on the slippery downslope of its growth opportunity, a large, permanent stock repurchase program is an excellent way for management to signal its confidence to Wall Street and add value for shareholders. It takes company performance plus effective communication to build a premium multiple. A large, permanent stock repurchase program is among the most effective tools available to bring your story to Wall Street's attention. There is no substitute for action. Repurchasing shares is a savvy investor relations strategy.

6 | Investor Relations in M&A Transactions

JOHN F. HARTIGAN, ESQ.
Morgan, Lewis & Bockius, LLP

G OOD INVESTOR RELATIONS practices during corporate merger-and-acquisition (M&A) transactions are crucial in keeping companies from running afoul of federal securities laws and, ultimately, to the success of the transaction. Recognizing the importance of shareholder communications, the federal securities laws are structured in a way that enhances public disclosure of information. The disclosure requirements are intended to achieve efficient securities markets through the mandatory disclosure of firm-specific information.

In addition to efficiency, the securities laws seek to achieve fairness and investor protection based on the premise that complete information allows market participants to fully evaluate their investment and voting decisions before acting. Investor relations teams and management must not only honor these principles but also adopt them as their own.

The type of investor relations strategies available to companies are dictated largely by rules and regulations promulgated by the Securities and Exchange Commission (SEC). With evolving deal structures and advancements in technology, the regulatory schemes are periodically revised and amended to keep pace with these trends to maintain the correct balance between the interests of the transaction parties and those of the investors and the markets.

In recent years the SEC has adopted two rules that have changed the landscape of information disclosure in M&A transactions. The first, Regulation M-A,[1] seeks to provide greater transparency in business combination transactions by allowing parties to a transaction to have more freedom in communicating with investors and the markets. The second, Regulation FD,[2] seeks to protect investors by prohibiting selective disclosure of material, nonpublic information.

Regulation M-A

In October 1999 the SEC released a comprehensive set of amendments to the rules governing mergers, acquisitions, tender offers, and similar extraordinary transactions entitled Regulation of Takeovers and Security Holder Communications, the so-called M&A Release[3]. The changes were prompted by trends that have emerged in the M&A arena that the SEC believes are likely to continue. These trends include the increased use of securities as consideration in M&A transactions, the increase in hostile transactions involving proxy or consent solicitations, and the increase in the amount and speed of communications with security holders and the markets as a result of advancements in technology. The intended purpose of the revisions promulgated by the M&A Release, as noted previously, is to create a more well-informed and efficient marketplace. To effectuate this purpose, the amendments allow companies to communicate with security holders and the markets more freely and on a more timely basis. In addition, the amendments serve to harmonize the disparate treatment of cash and stock tender offers in the regulations, to simplify and centralize the disclosure requirements, and to eliminate regulatory inconsistencies in mergers and tender offers.

In making its cost-benefit analysis, the SEC concluded that an environment conducive to earlier and less restrictive communications regarding business combination transactions would enhance price discovery and market efficiency and, at the same time, be consistent with the protection of investors. The amendments permit companies to disseminate oral and written information about a planned transaction more freely to security holders prior to and after filing a registration, proxy, or tender offer statement; such activities were previously restricted by the Securities Act of 1933 and the Securities Exchange Act of 1934.

Business Combinations

Before the amendments, a business combination or exchange offer involving the issuance of securities was considered an offer of securities, triggering the registration requirements under the Securities Act. So-called gun-jumping restrictions prohibited most statements regarding such a transaction before a registration statement was filed. Rule 165 of Regulation M-A creates safe harbors under the Securities Act for communications in stock-for-stock mergers and exchange offers. Under the rule, parties to a stock-for-stock merger or exchange offer are not subject to a violation of Section 5(c) or Section 5(b)(1) of the Securities Act for oral or written communications about a transaction made prior to filing of a registration statement, during the waiting period before effectiveness of the registration statement, and in the posteffective period, so long as any written communication from and including the first public announcement until the closing of the transaction is filed upon first use. The rule further clarifies that "an immaterial or unintentional failure to file or delay in filing" will not result in the loss of the exemption as long as "a good faith and reasonable effort was made to comply with the filing requirement" and the filing requirement is satisfied "as soon as practicable after discovery of the failure to file."

The challenge for companies and their IR professionals is to be familiar with current rules and regulations and to interface with counsel to ensure that releases comply with those rules and regulations.

Proxy Solicitations

The M&A Release also removes restrictions on communications during proxy solicitations. Before the amendments, persons intending to initiate a proxy solicitation not involving a contested election or other exempt solicitation were prohibited from making public statements about their intentions until preliminary proxy materials were filed with the SEC. In line with the new rule as applied to securities mergers and exchange offers, there is safe harbor under the proxy rules as well for communications in which target or acquirer stockholder votes are solicited. The revised rule, which applies equally to security holders and companies, allows oral and written communications regardless of when the proxy statement is filed if all solicitation-related written communications include the information required by the rule and are filed on the date of their first use.

The revised rules dealing with proxy solicitations significantly loosen restrictions on management and parties to a transaction in communicating with investors on matters that could potentially require a vote. However, the SEC believes that the necessary safeguards are in place to protect investors, including the antifraud provisions of Rule 14a-9. Furthermore, the M&A Release makes it clear that the amendment does not allow parties to secure a shareholder's vote prior to providing a proxy statement.

There is now more room for developing and implementing IR strategy than before, and to do so effectively, IR professionals would be well advised to consult with experienced legal counsel or proxy solicitation firms when preparing strategies, news releases, and communications with shareholders.

Cash Tender Offers

Rules dealing with communications during cash tender offers have also been amended. The tender offer rules in effect prior to the revisions restricted bidders' and targets' communications regarding proposed tender offers. The so-called five business day rule provided that an offer "commenced" once the identity of the bidder and the target, the tender price, and the amount of securities sought were publicly announced, unless a tender offer statement was filed and disseminated to security holders within five business days or withdrawal of the offer was subsequently announced.

The revised rules thus eliminated the five business day rule and modified the definition of "commencement" to denote the time "when the bidder has first published, sent, or given the means" to security holders to tender securities in the offer.

Bidders are now permitted to communicate freely regarding a planned tender offer, both orally and in writing, prior to commencement of the offer. As in the other contexts, the rules require filing of all written communications related to a tender offer on the date the communication is made, beginning with the first public announcement of the transaction.

Benefits of the Amendments

In adopting the revised rules contained in Regulation M-A, the SEC intended that the increased flow of information would help security holders in making well-informed voting or investment decisions. Another benefit the SEC expected as a result of the amendments was a reduction in the occurrence of selective disclosure. By requiring the filing of all written communications relating to a transaction, the amendments would make the information available to a broader base of investors. The SEC did not ignore the possibility that the amendments may lead companies to use oral rather than written communications to sidestep the filing requirement. It concluded, however, that the market would "likely demand that information be reduced to writing and companies generally [would] want to disseminate information broadly in order to sell their transaction to the market," thus reducing selective disclosure overall.

Note that the SEC adopted Regulation FD to deal specifically with the problem of selective disclosure, as discussed later in this chapter.

Flexibility in Timing

The M&A Release also provides bidders in exchange offers more flexibility with respect to the timing of exchange offers. Prior to the release, bidders were prohibited from commencing an exchange offer until after the filed registration statement became effective. The amendments allow the beginning of an exchange offer without having to wait for its becoming effective, as long as the registration statement has been filed. The SEC provided this added flexibility as an incentive for issuers to file their registration statements sooner, which would lead to increased public disclosure of information and a decreased incentive to selectively disclose the information to a limited number of investors.

The SEC recognized that by allowing an early offer, the amount of time needed to complete an exchange offer would be shortened, thereby shortening the time a security holder had to consider the available information. The SEC believed that the investors would be adequately protected in this instance by various rules. For example, a bidder is only permitted to purchase securities in an exchange offer once the registration statement becomes effective, and exchange offers cannot expire until after twenty business days have elapsed from commencement. Furthermore, bidders offering securities must disseminate supplements to investors disclosing material changes to information previously provided, and investors can withdraw their tendered securities any time prior to a bidder's purchase.

Investor Access in Tender Offers

Another benefit the amendments provide is that bidders are allowed more access to investors in tender offers. If the target company maintains a list of non-objecting beneficial owners, the bidders are permitted to contact and communicate with them directly, similar to the proxy context. The SEC noted that this change would be beneficial to both bidders and investors by making communications regarding tender offers more efficient.

Potential Risks Created by the Amendments

In addition to the benefits, the SEC also considered the potential risks created by the new regulatory scheme. One risk the SEC recognized was that the more permissible communications could lead some individuals to "condition the market with false, misleading, or confusing information." Nevertheless, it concluded that the new and existing regulatory safeguards, as discussed below, would sufficiently deter such behavior. Furthermore, the SEC believed that investors would benefit from the more timely receipt of information and the fact that before they made an investment decision with respect to a particular transaction, they would receive a registration, tender offer, or proxy statement. Therefore, investors would have adequate opportunity to review the full information made available to them in the mandated disclosure document along with any prior information that had been disseminated, before making a voting or investment decision.

Because issuers are permitted to disseminate certain information prior to filing certain disclosure documents, another risk is that investors may make investment decisions prior to having complete information. However, the SEC concluded that although some investors might act prematurely, the risk was no different from what it had been under the prior rules. As discussed above, for instance, five business days were allowed between the announcement of a tender offer and the filing of the required disclosure statement. Even upon filing, the security holders might not have received the information until several days after the filing, given possible delays and vagaries in the delivery of that information, whether by mail or other means. The amended rules permit the dissemination of transaction-related information prior to the filing of a mandated disclosure statement, as long as all written communications are filed. The SEC stated in the M&A Release that these rules would provide investors with more information and more time to come to a better informed investment decision rather than lead to premature decisions. It is important for the IR community to recognize that guidance from legal counsel should be sought whenever communications relating to an M&A transaction are involved. Careful planning and choreography are required to comply with the rules. Written communications themselves, for example, must include a prominent legend that advises investors to read the applicable registration, proxy, or tender offer, filed or to be filed with the SEC, because they contain important information. The legend must also advise that copies of the filed document can be obtained for free at the SEC's website and explain which documents are available free from the filing person or issuer, as applicable.

These written communications must be filed on EDGAR, the SEC's electronic filing system, on or before the date of first use, which may require coordination with financial printers. Because the process of filing requires some time, dissemination of the information should be planned in advance, and to the extent possible, written communications should be EDGARized ahead of time. Legal counsel should always be contacted before the written communications have been released and never after the fact.

Since certain communications may not appear to trigger the filing rules at first glance, IR professionals should also be aware of the scope of the rules' coverage. Letters and e-mails to a company's employees discussing the effects of a potential merger on them, for instance, may require filing. IR professionals should also be mindful when it comes to all publicity and communications during a transaction, including road shows and slide shows. In addition, the M&A Release states that "written communications include all information disseminated otherwise than orally, including electronic communications and other future applications of changing technology." Videos and CD-ROMs, for example, should be transcribed and filed on EDGAR.

Antifraud Provisions

Numerous antifraud provisions are in place to protect investors from false or misleading information, and all IR professionals should understand these provisions thoroughly. All communications remain subject to Rule 10b-5 under the Exchange Act, which may impose liability for materially false or misleading information. Section 12(a)(2) of the Securities Act also continues to impose civil liabilities in transactions involving the Securities Act. Furthermore, registration statements that are ultimately declared effective must include all material facts and must not be false or misleading in order to avoid liability under Section 11 of the Securities Act.

Proxies are subject to the antifraud provisions of Rule 14a-9, and tender offers are subject to Section 14(e). The SEC adopted an additional safeguard to protect security holders from possible misleading information in the tender offer context. To encourage only bona fide tender offers in the absence of the five business day rule, the SEC adopted Rule 14e-8, which makes it fraudulent to announce a potential tender offer if the bidder

1. has no intention of commencing the offer within a reasonable time and completing the offer,
2. intends to manipulate the bidder or target's stock price, or
3. does not reasonably believe that it will be able to purchase the securities sought in the offer.

The SEC concluded that, in aggregate, these safeguards would adequately discourage parties to a transaction from disseminating false or misleading information, while the amendments of the M&A Release would enable investors to have access to an increased flow of information on a more timely basis.

"Plain English" Requirement

In addition to these safeguards, the M&A Release puts into effect another investor protection mechanism. The rule requires "plain English" disclosures for all issuer and third-party cash tender offers, cash mergers, and going-private transactions.

Disclosure documents for these transactions often include detailed information that is difficult for investors, even sophisticated investors, to understand. The required plain English summary term sheet is intended to facilitate their understanding by providing a concise summary of the important and relevant information regarding the transaction, allowing investors to better inform themselves prior to making a voting or investment decision. Again, IR professionals need to review the "plain English" summary sheet carefully to affirm that it is sufficiently clear and accurate.

Regulation FD

On August 10, 2000, a controversial set of rules was adopted by the SEC called Regulation FD (for "fair disclosure").[4]

The SEC provided three reasons for adopting the regulation: First, the SEC wished to cure what it perceived to be an unfair advantage given to market professionals and institutional investors at the expense of the general investing public. The SEC believed that public companies were selectively disclosing material, nonpublic information to a small group of Wall Street professionals before making the information public. Those in possession of this information, in the view of the SEC, could potentially make profits or avoid losses to the detriment of investors not privy to the information, ultimately resulting in an erosion of investor confidence in the integrity of the securities markets.

The second impetus that led to the adoption of Regulation FD was the SEC's concern that material nonpublic information was being used as a tool by corporate management to influence analysts and institutional investors to report favorably about a company or else risk losing continued access to the selective information. A prohibition on selective disclosure would relieve this pressure on analysts, resulting in unbiased reports.

The final reason the SEC adopted Regulation FD was because technological advancements have made the broad dissemination of information economically and logistically feasible. Previously, limitations in communications technologies necessitated the use of market analysts to act as intermediaries in disseminating information. Since various cost-effective, broadscale methods of communicating directly with investors have become available (for example, through the use of Internet webcasting and teleconferencing), the use of such intermediaries is no longer necessary or desirable.

The proposed adoption of Regulation FD ignited a flurry of public comment. Although most comments were from individual investors favoring the adoption of the regulation, many Wall Street professionals voiced their concerns that Regulation FD could have a chilling effect on information flow to the marketplace. Company officials would become too restricted in the manner they released information, it was argued. These commentators believed that due to the uncertainty in determining whether information would be deemed "material" under the rules, issuers would refrain from disclosing information altogether rather than risk potential liability.

Scope of the Rule

Regulation FD prohibits the selective disclosure of material, nonpublic information by an issuer, or persons acting on its behalf, to certain enumerated persons, including market professionals or holders of the issuer's securities, under circumstances in which it is reasonably foreseeable that such persons will trade based on the information. If such disclosure is made to the enumerated persons, then the issuer must at the same time publicly disclose the information, if the disclosure was intentional, or do so promptly thereafter, if the disclosure was unintentional.

Although Regulation FD does not exclusively apply to business combination transactions, the SEC lists mergers, tender offers, changes in assets, and changes in control or in management, as "types of information or events that should be reviewed carefully to determine whether they are material." For IR professionals, the central point is that information about mergers should be tightly controlled, and safeguards should be put in place to protect against inadvertent or selective disclosure.

It should be noted that the SEC limited the application of the rule to "enumerated persons" in an attempt to narrow the rule's scope of coverage. Communications to those persons who owe a duty of trust or confidence to the issuers and would therefore be expected to maintain confidentiality, including lawyers, accountants, and investment bankers, are excluded. Similarly, disclosures made to credit rating agencies, those made to persons who expressly agree to keep disclosed information confidential, and those made in connection with most securities offerings registered under the Securities Act are also excluded. It should be noted that communications continue to be subject to prohibitions against insider trading under Rule 10b-5. Regardless of whether the person is an "enumerated person," selective disclosure of material nonpublic information could result in, for example, tipper liability. IR professionals should educate themselves and keep abreast of developments in this area.

Materiality

The major difficulty companies are having in following Regulation FD is in determining what is material, especially in the preliminary stages of initiating a business combination transaction, tender offer, or proxy or consent solicitation. Unfortunately for IR professionals and others, the SEC does not define "materiality" for purposes of Regulation FD, rather leaving its interpretation to existing case law. The FD Release cites the 1976 case, *TSC Industries, Inc. v. Northway, Inc.*, a seminal Supreme Court case holding that information is material if "there is a substantial likelihood that a reasonable shareholder would consider it important" in making an investment decision, and a reasonable shareholder would have viewed the information as having "significantly altered the 'total mix' of information made available."

This definition does not afford a bright-line or formulaic test for companies seeking to initiate a transaction to apply. Instead, companies and their IR professionals would be well advised to consult with experienced legal counsel in making a good faith determination of what is "material" under facts and circumstances of a particular situation. Some commentators have suggested that the fact that a particular transaction is being considered by a corporation may, under

Regulation FD, be considered material, since it could move the market for the company's stock if that fact became public.

In the preliminary stages and throughout a transaction, companies should, therefore, enter into confidentiality agreements with third parties to protect themselves.

Reg FD in Practice

With the adoption of Regulation FD, company and consultant IR professionals must be more mindful when communicating with analysts, the public, and other investment professionals about their firm's M&A-type transactions, whether planned or actual. Numerous commentators have suggested tips on how companies should proceed in dealing with Regulation FD.[5] Indeed, it should be highlighted that Regulation FD specifically applies to IR professionals, and all others "acting on behalf of the issuer."

On the side of caution, the National Investor Relations Institute (NIRI) has suggested that companies adopt a written disclosure policy authorizing only a limited number of spokespersons to speak on behalf of the company. Further, they suggest that those employees not covered by the rule should be advised to refrain from communicating with analysts and other market professionals, since analysts might particularly target such employees as a source of information (this is an example of how FD might indeed inhibit the flow of information to the markets, even while making for a more flattened playing field).

Regulation FD does not specifically require policies be in place, but the SEC noted in the FD Release that "the existence of an appropriate policy, and the issuer's general adherence to it, may often be relevant to determining the issuer's intent with regard to selective disclosure."

Once the company knows that it must make a public disclosure of its material nonpublic information, it must decide how to disseminate the information. The FD Release provides considerable flexibility in the acceptable means of public disclosure. The rule states that an issuer can make a disclosure by submitting the information on a Form 8-K or "through another method (or combination of methods) of disclosure that is reasonably designed to provide broad, nonexclusionary distribution of the information to the public." Generally, companies use the business news wire services to issue a news release.

If disclosing through a Form 8-K, the issuer has the option of either "filing" the information under Item 5 of the form or "furnishing" it under Item 9. This distinction is important in that a filing is subject to liability under Section 18 of the Exchange Act and Section 11 of the Securities Act, whereas furnishing information on Form 8-K in the manner designated is not. All Form 8-K disclosures, regardless of whether filed or furnished, remain subject to the antifraud fraud provisions of the securities laws.

To alleviate the concern of some commentators, the SEC noted in the FD Release that submitting the information on a Form 8-K solely for the purpose of satisfying Regulation FD would not be construed as an admission that the information is material. Alternative methods of public disclosure suggested by the SEC that would satisfy the statute include "press releases distributed through a widely circulated news or wire service, or announcements made through press conferences or conference calls that interested members of the public may attend or listen to either in person, by telephonic transmission, or by other electronic transmission (including use of the Internet)."

In its December 2001 report on Regulation FD, the SEC noted various ways issuers had been complying with that section of the new rule since its effective date.[6] Press releases were still the most frequently used means of dissemination, mainly because Self-Regulatory Organization (SRO) rules mandate them. Another method gaining popularity among issuers was the use of webcasts. Wire services noted significant increases in the number of corporate webcasts during the months after Regulation FD took effect. In practice, webcasts tend to be used in conjunction with press releases.

The report recommends that the SEC work together with SROs to remove obstacles that impede issuers from taking full advantage of new communications technologies. At the present time, the SEC does not consider a posting on a website as sufficient public disclosure. As technology improves and the Internet becomes more accessible to investors, however, the SEC envisions this medium becoming an acceptable method of public disclosure. (This prospect may be a bit surprising to some, in that most people, even investment professionals and the financial media, are not online at all times and rely heavily on wire services to bring them pertinent information.) Whatever standard may develop in the future as to sufficient public disclosure, in the interim, companies should be careful not to post material, nonpublic information on their websites without making other arrangements to satisfy the disclosure requirement.

Interplay Between Regulation FD and Regulation M-A

During an M&A transaction, companies must consider the implications of both Regulations M-A and FD. As discussed above, Regulation FD excludes from its coverage communications made in connection with most securities offerings registered under the Securities Act. The policy rationale behind the exclusion is that the registration requirements of the Securities Act provide sufficient protection against selective disclosure.

Although Regulation FD may not require public disclosure in these instances, written statements would have to be disclosed if they fall within Regulation M-A. Unregistered offerings such as cash tender offers, cash mergers, stock-for-stock mergers done through private placements, and certain proxy or consent solicitations remain subject to Regulation FD and are also subject to Regulation M-A.

Generally, Regulation M-A only requires the filing of written communications. However, when oral communications of potentially material information are made during one of these transactions to an enumerated person as defined under Regulation FD, and that information was never previously filed or made public, the company may be required to publicly disclose the oral communications in satisfaction of Regulation FD. Thus, while Regulation M-A was intended to allow parties to a business combination transaction to communicate more freely, Regulation FD may limit this ability. The SEC has yet to comment on this potential inconsistency in the rules. IR professionals (and, indeed, securities lawyers) will have to watch this corner of the legal world closely and converse with company legal counsel when their company is in, or about to enter, merger talks.

THE ROLE OF THE SEC is to ensure that investors and the securities markets are fully informed in order to preserve the integrity of markets and thereby allow capital to move to its most efficient uses. More information, however, is not useful if that information is misleading or if that information is not received by the investors in a timely fashion. To obtain the right balance and protect investors, SEC rules and regulations serve to determine how and when the information must be disseminated. Regulation M-A attempts to provide investors with an increased flow of information during business combination transactions by providing companies with more freedom to communicate. Regulation FD, on the other hand, restricts selective communications, which could potentially chill the flow of information. Companies are still adjusting to these new sets of rules. Only time will tell whether the SEC will need to step in to recalibrate its scale.

Chapter Notes

1. Regulation M-A, 17 CFR 229.1000-229.1016, 1999.
2. Regulation FD, 17 CFR 243.100-243.103, 2000.
3. 64 Fed. Reg. 61408; SEC Release No. 33-7760; 34-42055; IC-24107; File No. S7-28-98; Oct. 22, 1999, which is available at http://www.sec.gov/rules/final/33-7760.htm.
4. For the complete text of the FD Release, see http://www.sec.gov/rules/final/33-7881.htm.
5. See, for example, Louis M. Thompson, Jr., "Guidance for Compliance with Regulation FD," at http://www.niri.org/publications/alerts/RegFDTips.cfm; Steven E. Bochner and Jason S. Frankl, "Suggestions for Best Practices Under Regulation FD," at http://www.stratosforum.com/images/Regulation.pdf; and IR Guide: Regulation FD, at http://www.ironthenet.com/static/disclosure/guidtofd.html.
6. See U.S. Securities and Exchange Commission, Special Study: Regulation Fair Disclosure Revisited, Dec. 2001, at http://www.sec.gov/news/studies/regfd-study.htm.

7 | Investor Relations for Private Placements

ALEXANDER L. CAPPELLO

Cappello Capital Corp.

THE PIPE, AN ACRONYM that stands for "private investment in public equity," has become a major source of funding for public companies in the last several years, far exceeding the role of initial public offerings. With a PIPE, a relatively large slug of capital is raised from one or just a few equity investors; the equity can be straight common stock or a mix of common stock, preferred stock, convertible bonds, and warrants. Generally speaking, the common stock will be sold to the investors at some discount to its market price.

From an investor relations viewpoint, PIPEs and IPOs are about as different as could be imagined. For an IPO, publicity is sought, road shows are conducted, and hundreds of brokers and perhaps even thousands of investors are educated about a new investment opportunity. For PIPEs, a few large investors must be discreetly approached, at first without even revealing the name of the company seeking to raise capital. Only after serious interest is determined are confidentiality agreements signed, binding all parties to silence until the deal is announced.

Role of the IR Team

The job of the IR team is to maintain silence, review all corporate communications, and ensure that the pending PIPE deal is not inadvertently revealed in corporate releases, statements, or other outlets.

If the IR team is skilled at PIPEs, it might help management prepare materials and presentations for the few select large buyers of stock. Corporate executives may also practice verbal presentations with the IR team.

Investors in PIPEs are generally institutions and, before investing a large amount of capital, will conduct extensive due diligence. This includes meeting at least once and perhaps several times with management. Investors will also ask for access to information generally not publicly available, such as lists of customers, vendors, and financial projections. At this point, in conjunction with lawyers and investment bankers, a good IR team should have all the necessary materials in order to make meetings go as smoothly as possible. The IR team should notify those in charge of "trade secrets" in advance that they will be called upon to reveal this information to a key investor. In general, company employees and management should be schooled to be courteous and efficient. The goal is to solicit a major investment, under a veil of secrecy.

After a PIPE deal closes, the IR team's job is to explain to Wall Street why the deal is a good one for the public company. Of course, filing Form 8-K—the current report—with the Securities and Exchange Commission (SEC) is immediate and mandatory.

As noted, PIPE investors usually buy common stock in large volume but at a discount to market. In addition, they may take positions in convertible bonds or warrants. All of this is technically dilutive, and there is no dancing around that fact. The IR team should not be surprised to receive calls from investors who will want to know why the company sold a large block of shares for $9.50 when they just bought the same equity for $10, the market price. More sophisticated investors will want assurances that when the convertible bonds in fact convert, more dilution will not be a problem. These inquiries will present challenges for the IR team.

Most important, the IR team should explain to investors how the raised capital will be put to use. (The company's PR team should be making the same effort with the financial media.) The team should clarify if the equity funding makes possible business expansion, for example, or a very well-conceived acquisition, or the paying down of debt. The IR team should also point out that an investment bank has just vetted the company and that a large institutional investor has just placed a vote of confidence in the stock.

As for the rationale behind PIPE investors' receiving a discount to market, there are several explanatory responses. First and foremost, the investor is being compensated for illiquidity. Often, the shares sold in a PIPE are restricted and cannot be sold immediately. This can apply even if the stock is unrestricted. After all, a large position in a stock cannot be sold on a whim, and even slow sales of a large position can drag down share prices. In short, a PIPE investor is a long-term investor in a world in which everyone wants profits now and the ability to sell in a minute.

The better the name and reputation of the investment banker and the institutional investor, the more convincing these arguments will be. The IR team should counsel management early to seek out blue-chip names, when possible, for participation in PIPE transactions.

The Importance of Being Discreet

Despite the best efforts of investor relations experts and skilled investment bankers, PIPEs have a way of getting clogged or bursting, usually because of aggressive management, arrogant bankers, or some combination of the two. The following real-world stories are good illustrations of how PIPEs fail or succeed.

Don't Oversell and Don't Leak

Restaurant Corp. (a fictional name) is a publicly traded company and a popular place to eat healthy food in a better-than-usual fast-food environment. At some restaurants, customers wait in lines stretching around the block for a chance to eat. Obviously, this was an idea that could be franchised or duplicated coast-to-coast. Many of the customers also purchased the company's stock, following Warren Buffet's suggestion to invest in businesses you understand. Eventually, the number of shareholders reached several thousand, increasing the stock's liquidity and profile.

At about the same time, the phenomenon of the Internet chat room blossomed, and Restaurant Corp.'s chat rooms were very active. At one memorable annual shareholders meeting, a large ballroom was rented and filled with a standing-room-only crowd of hundreds of shareholders eagerly anticipating announcements. The company had funded an effective IR and public relations campaign, and the results showed.

While Restaurant Corp. was in the midst of completing the first of three private placements, staff of its financial adviser on the deals quietly tracked many of the Internet chat room discussions about the company. Much to the financial adviser's amazement, chagrin, and frustration, items that had been discussed in confidence with management would show up minutes later, virtually verbatim, in the chat rooms. Was it a secretary? A director? An officer? The financial adviser never knew for sure and never found out. In spite of this lack of discretion and violation of legal and ethical protocols by someone inside the company, a private placement was completed for $30 million in convertible preferred stock and $3.5 million in common, necessary growth capital.

At the time of the first financing engagement, the stock was trading for a few dollars per share, with modest volume. Several months following this initial private placement, the stock reached a zenith of $10 per share on heavier volume. The company had "buzz," the result of a great product and excellent (if short-term-oriented) IR and PR efforts.

The problem was that the great product cost a lot to put out, maybe more than could be charged. Approximately a year later, after the company burned through what was supposed to be three years' worth of capital, the financial advisory firm was asked to do another private placement for Restaurant Corp. This was successfully completed for an additional $30 million.

Upon the public announcement of the second financing, which calmed concerns of a shortage of capital, the company's stock again traded up on strong volume for some time. The company was eating money but told investors that growth was expensive. It was true that new shops were being opened, but existing stores weren't exactly gold mines. Operating a high-end fast-food joint was marginal at best. Better IR might have conditioned investors to be more patient and understand that building a national chain is not done overnight. Management also decided to enter a new line of business, blurring the picture and creating new problems for the IR experts who had been selling the story of a successful restaurant chain.

The problem of material information showing up in chat rooms seemed never to go away. Too many people who were close to insiders always seemed to know significantly more than they should before public announcements. Stock traded suspiciously at times.

Investor confidence in the company soon sagged, battered by repeated reported losses and changes in business plans. Institutional investors no doubt noticed the breaches in confidentiality. Eventually the company had to merge with a much larger food service company that brought in all new management.

The IR lesson: Don't oversell a PIPE, don't oversell a stock, and have strict controls on the flow of information.

Be Prepared for the Unexpected

Global Electronics (a fictional name) was the third-largest computer and electronics distributor in the world, when it undertook a $350 million PIPE transaction, this one for convertible preferred stock. A major New York–based securities brokerage evidently took umbrage at a small West Coast shop winning the assignment, and conducted a smear campaign against the chosen firm. It contacted the ten largest institutional shareholders in Global Electronics and repeated stories raising questions about the underwriting firm's competency and ethics. The New York house went so far as to spread "research" that the other company's clients usually tanked.

The large shareholders started calling Global Electronics and asking the CEO why he selected the firm in question to do the job. The West Coast firm had to work carefully with Global Electronics's management for several weeks, to give them the true track record of its clients. When provided with the facts, the company reprimanded the sour bankers at the bulge-bracket firm and told the story to their largest shareholders.

The IR lesson: Sometimes, IR is neither proactive nor defensive. It's just plain old warfare and hard work, and making phone calls, talking to people, and battling misinformation. IR professionals need to be aware that there can be disgruntled investment bankers, snubbed analysts, or short traders who have agendas of their own.

Do What You Say You Will Do

International Pharmaceuticals Corp. (IPC, a fictional name) had been brought public by the investment banking department of a major Wall Street firm. It was followed by several analysts, but regrettably had been dealt a severe blow by the Food and Drug Administration. The FDA was taking about two years longer than expected to approve two separate drug compounds. The cash flow from existing drugs was being consumed rapidly by ongoing clinical development; IPC had invested heavily in marketing and sales infrastructure in anticipation of prompt FDA approvals for its two compounds.

The cost of carrying the additional overhead had severely impacted the company's liquidity, and it had some debt coming due just months ahead. After intense due diligence, the adviser conducting the PIPE managed to place $115 million of convertible preferred and $11 million of common stock with a few institutional investors. Investors were running more than phantom risks—the unpredictable FDA, for example—so their anticipated returns were hefty and thus costly for the company. But the capital IPC earned allowed it to survive and move forward.

The role of the IR team was to be up front with investors about the risk, while at the same time educating them about the drug compounds and pointing out the meaty returns if the company performed as slated. If the stock went up, the convertible preferred stock would return plenty.

During the course of due diligence, the management of IPC disclosed to the PIPE advisers that a certain amount of assets would be written down. These would be non-cash write-offs of an immaterial amount. The company stressed that there would be no need for further write-offs, much to the satisfaction of the investors.

As the PIPE team was gearing up for the placement to save this company from running out of cash, *Forbes,* the national financial magazine, ran a cover story on great short opportunities, with IPC near the top of the list. About the time the PIPE advisers finished reading the article, management called to explain that they had decided to take a major write-off on a substantial percentage of its assets, exactly what it had promised it wouldn't do just a few weeks earlier.

The stock temporarily tanked. No amount of IR, PR, or invest-ment banking could save it at the time. The following year, however, the company experienced improved financial performance and got the FDA approval for its products. The stock then doubled and shortly thereafter sold out to a larger company at an even higher price.

The IR lesson: There were several IR lessons in this experience. The first was the oldest and the same one noted earlier: Never mis-lead your investors, especially on the upside. They will not forgive that. Anticipate major write-offs. Think about what can go wrong, as well as what can go right. Good IR starts with honest management, but IR professionals have to be persistent in asking about possible bad-case scenarios.

The second lesson was that the public relations people have to talk to the IR people. (See Chapter 4, "The IR-PR Nexus.") Did anybody know that *Forbes* was working on a negative article on the company? A shrewd PR professional would have at least gleaned a hint that the magazine had its hatchet out and passed along a warning. True, not all reporters tip their hand, but usually when questions follow a cer-tain tack, one can guess at the tone of an article. Additionally, skilled PR professionals know how to contact reporters and find out what is up. If a reporter is evasive about the tone of an article, that's a clue. Properly warned, the IR team could have told institutional investors that a potentially negative article was being prepared by *Forbes,* although of course, no one knew when or if it would run. A good PR shop might even have been able to steer *Forbes* away from publishing such an article.

Don't Be Arrogant

Some companies seeking PIPE financing seem to think that arro-gance is a selling point. One such firm turned in to the SEC a docu-ment so obscure that the regulatory agency took the relatively rare step of kicking it back as unsuitable for filing. The company was out-raged and blamed the rejection on nitwit regulators, failing to ask the more important question: If even SEC attorneys had trouble deci-phering the document, how would ordinary investors, or even most institutional investors, understand the filing?

This biotech company had burned through $100 million in

investment capital and wanted to raise more. The FDA had yet to approve any of its drugs, however. In a meeting with potential investors, the firm's management appeared to take offense at simple questions, while tossing about obscure acronyms as if all in the audience had been deeply involved in life science research their whole lives. The PIPE adviser doggedly lined up more and more investors to look over the PIPE, which was not a bad deal on paper. There was some promising research, to be sure, possibly of benefit to investors and even to the practice of medicine. But the deal couldn't get funded. Potential PIPE investors noticed that company management wasn't overly concerned at having already spent more than $100 million of investor money. Perhaps the management thought confidence bordering on braggadocio would convince investors that the product was a sure winner. The company didn't raise any more money until after it replaced its CEO. Under new management the company became one of the best-performing biotechs globally in 2003.

The IR lesson: If you are burning through capital and need to raise more, show that you recognize the seriousness of your situation to investors. Be prepared to give away a lot of the company to get survival capital, be happy if you get it, and relate that attitude in your IR. Professional investors in PIPEs are not impressed by arrogance; they have seen plenty of it. On the other hand, it never hurts to look earnest, even with professional investors. Sure, the business plan has to be solid, but management counts, too. In a PIPE, management has to be very accommodating to investors.

You May Get Away With It, But Not for Long

Despite recent press reports, most people who run publicly traded companies are ethical and forthright in all of their dealings. They know the penalties for dishonesty, and they also know that shareholders deserve good corporate governance and transparency. There are, however, management teams that think they can get away with deceitful behavior. Such a team managed a company listed on the New York Stock Exchange, which had a prestigious board of directors, and numbered among its largest shareholders a longtime member of the Forbes 400 Richest Americans who enjoyed an excellent reputation. The placement agent secured a $70 million convertible preferred PIPE rather easily, given its stellar connections. Institutional shareholders trusted the company and the agent. The IR was based not only on the company's prospects but also on the solid group that made up the company's board of directors.

A few months after the PIPE, management informed the advisers that it soon expected to be in technical default on some terms of the placement. One of those terms was to get a registration statement from the SEC covering the common stock underlying the PIPE. That meant the stock was unregistered with the SEC and much less liquid.

The management said that the company was on track to report $50 million in earnings before interest, taxes, depreciation, and amortization (EBITDA) for the latest quarter. On the eve of reporting the quarterly numbers, management reiterated the $50 million EBITDA and confirmed that this was the figure to be reported publicly the next day. That evening the advisers were asked and agreed to waive the penalty provision for a late registration, to allow the company to make a clean report the following day. Just six hours later, the company reported a major operating loss and restatement of its numbers— downward, of course—for prior periods. Needless to say, lawsuits erupted overnight. The capital markets cut this company off immediately. One can only speculate why management chose such an odd course of action. Investigations followed with the bankruptcy filing, and years later, the company is tangled in litigation.

The IR lesson: Just like investment bankers, IR professionals should never allow credentials to outweigh skepticism. It is easy to be impressed with somebody of stature, to be assured by the friendly greeting, the easy handshake, the camaraderie, and the confidence. But IR professionals should keep their eyes focused on fundamentals and try to keep management in the same zone. **Another IR lesson:** Fool with professional investors who put money into PIPEs, and you will lose access to capital forever and end up in court. With recent securities-law reforms, you may end up in prison, too.

Reap Dividends From Being Forthcoming and Honest

As a contrast to the preceding example, consider a Fortune 500 company. This one was consistently honest, open, and candid in its communications throughout the private placement process. Bad news was always delivered promptly, and management was responsive and articulate. Even though a major billion-dollar subsidiary had lost nearly $100 million from operations the prior year, the placement agent was able to procure a substantial line of credit for the company. Because of the quality of the management's communications, its presentations to investors and lenders, and the confidence and trust it instilled, the company was able to privately place an institutional capital commitment in a tough market.

Although the company was largely operating in out-of-favor industries, carried a large debt load, used off-balance-sheet partnerships, and faced another rating downgrade on its debt, it still succeeded. It did so because the management team never did anything to call its integrity into question. Members were open and honest and provided hours of detail in their reports, filings, and conference calls. Whether the disclosures or communications were prepared for the public or for a restricted insider doing a private placement, they were always credible and easy to understand.

The IR lesson: Credible investor relations should be a permanent feature of any public company's operations and should focus on the long term.

Don't Let an Investment Banker Be Your IR Department

Super Tech (a fictional name) was confident but not arrogant. With its business fundamentals and very presentable management team, the company was able to place a $20 million PIPE, in the form of common and convertible preferred stock.

Unfortunately, Super Tech was caught in the "tech wreck" of 2000–2001. Projected sales and profits did not materialize, and it began to run out of money. The convertible preferred had a feature that allowed the company to use its future stock price to settle redemptions or conversions. This would have been a great feature had the stock price gone up, since the company would have had to give away less equity (a smaller ownership stake) when the convertible preferred was converted into common. But the stock instead fell to a lower price, and conversion would mean giving the PIPE investors a substantial chunk of the company, far more than originally anticipated. As a result, management wanted to exchange the convertible preferred for a more traditional fixed-price convertible that would be redeemable for cash at maturity instead.

Asking PIPE investors for a change of rules midgame is never a pleasant task, and such a course requires very deft IR. In a PIPE, you are dealing with professional investors who expect returns on their investment at above-market rates. In addition, PIPE investors, unlike scattered retail investors or even the numerous mutual funds, are few in number and can organize easily if they feel they are being taken for a ride.

Still, Super Tech was determined to change the terms of the convertible preferred portion of the PIPE. To do so, the company chose to hire an investment banker from a major brokerage. The banker proceeded to tell the PIPE investors what the new deal would be, as if being from a large brokerage meant he could dictate to the institutional investors that had invested in this particular PIPE. In the process, he made the company look as if it took its investors for granted because it treated them cavalierly. Any goodwill that remained for the management was eliminated during that first meeting with the new banker. When the investors arrived, they had intended to cooperate and restructure the paper, but a day or two after the banker's presentation they all hired litigators. Fortunately, the original PIPE advisers came back on the scene to help smooth things over and somehow managed to broker a modified deal between the PIPE investors and the company.

The IR lesson: Even if management does a superior job communicating through its investor relations program, in the PIPEs context, a single arrogant adviser or agent can spoil the goodwill earned over an extended period. Public companies should be careful about whom they hire and always emphasize to advisers that it is the shareholders who own the company, not the management. There is a tremendous temptation for management to succumb to obsequious or brash advisers who promise an easy way out of a mess. Shareholders are not stupid and should not be treated as such; they are the real owners of the company. For PIPE investors, that concept is paramount.

Generate Goodwill With Investors

The management at a troubled but promising software company was refreshingly candid. It bluntly stated that the company needed more capital to launch a new range of products—and even that would be no guarantee of success—or else it would need to merge with another company. By carefully explaining to institutional investors the need for the new product line, the financial adviser convinced PIPE buyers of the company's fundamental prospects. As usual in a PIPE, the company had to offer an incentive: Investors would get not only a yield but also a big upside if the company rallied. The management successfully completed a very complicated transaction, placing $29.5 million in convertible preferreds.

A little more than a year later, virtually all of the convertible bonds were still outstanding. But the software company's new product line had produced only marginal results. The firm would run out of cash within a quarter or two, barring a tremendous surge in demand. However, because the management had credibility with all the investors, had always explained that this was a risky situation, and had let them know each step of the way the progress the company was making (or lack thereof), it still had some capital-raising options. The solid IR with PIPE investors all down the line was now going to pay off.

The management sought advice on how to get the group of institutions who held the investment to agree to a short-term standstill/lock-up in order to complete a merger with another industry player that had an interest in acquiring the company. The six institutions were asked to agree to the lock-up but, because the company was publicly traded, were not told why.

The existing goodwill and trust were sufficient to allow the lock-up to be accomplished in a few hours. The management was then able to engineer a deal with its eventual acquirer. The deal saved everyone's investment and allowed the parties to cash out at a profit. All this was only possible because of the superb investor relationships that had been developed.

The IR lesson: When captaining a company, you never know what storms you might encounter or in what directions you may sail. If your investors like and trust you, your options for maneuvering will be that much greater. In this case, because of good IR with PIPE investors, the software company was able to arrange a merger. Without good relations, suspicious investors might have scotched the deal before it could unfold.

THE LESSONS FROM THESE EXAMPLES ARE SIMPLE. What works are the old-fashioned virtues of humility, courtesy, respect, candor, underpromising and overdelivering, communicating often and clearly in plain English, and not surprising people with bad news. Investor relations in PIPEs is unique in that discretion and a certain level of secrecy during the solicitation process are vital. A PIPE is a material event, and the curtains must be kept shut until players give the go-ahead to make information public. In this zone of silence, IR professionals must work effectively to show institutions the rewards of investing.

Investor relations in PIPE transactions is just as critical as in any other type of transaction, and in some respects perhaps more so, because of the close relationship with investors, their sophistication, and the size of their holdings. This is an investor class one can ill afford to alienate. After all is said and done, institutional Wall Street is a small place, where professionals migrate from firm to firm and names are remembered. No manager or IR professional should consider misleading any investor but especially not institutional investors such as those who participate in PIPEs.

8 Investor Relations for the IPO

DOUGLAS M. SHERK

EVC Group

T HE FOLLOWING TRUE STORY is relevant to every chief executive, chief financial officer, and board director of any private company thinking about going public. The names of the people involved and the name of the company have been changed to—well, read on, and you'll understand why.

Max, the chief financial officer of Flying High Technology Corporation, calls in his outside investor relations firm for a meeting barely a year after Flying High completed one of the most successful initial public offerings (IPOs) ever. The meeting is taking place before Christmas, around the time the calendar officially declares the beginning of winter.

"Well, guys," Max says with a sigh as he sits down at the table in the windowless conference room. He pauses to look at Flying High's general counsel, Bart, and the three consultants. "We aren't going to make the quarter. We've got to come up with a strategy for breaking the news."

"If the miss is less than 5 percent, we could just wait until we release actual results in January," says David, the senior counselor from Flying High's IR firm.

CFO Max nods knowingly. "Right now, the best we can do on the revenue side is 12 percent less than we projected on the last call. And," he adds as the consultants pull out their pads to take notes, "we could be as much as 20 percent light."

The consultants all nod their heads and steal glances at one another. "Where are you coming up short?" asks David, his consultant hat on.

"We don't know," responds Max.

The consultant cocks his head to the right as if his hearing has momentarily failed him. "Well, which product lines are off plan?" he asks.

"It looks like the widgets are softer than the other two, but we don't have the details," responds Max.

"What about markets? Are you okay in Europe?" David asks, trying to hide his consternation but perhaps betrayed by the tone of his voice.

Max leans forward, his thick-fingered hands clasped. "Look, I know what you are looking for, but we just don't have the answers. All I know is that we are short, and the best information I can get from the field is that we'll be about $9 million to $11 million below our original estimates. Until we get the new system up and running, we just have to wait for the end of the quarter to get the details. Now, what should we do?"

Three days later, Flying High issues a news release updating its outlook for the quarter ending on New Year's Eve and hosts a conference call. Max and Harry, the company's CEO, aren't able to get much more information on the factors behind the quarter's revision. During the call, their comments reflect this lack of knowledge. Not surprisingly, investors suspect that management has little real-time command of Flying High's "operating metrics"—the ability to track revenues, profits, operating margins, and other important operating trends. The stock flounders badly the next trading day, losing 60 percent of its value.

Unfortunately, Flying High's story isn't unique. Most management teams of IPOs underestimate the need to stay apprised of their companies' operating metrics while a quarter is in progress. They follow the traditional approach to investor relations and start thinking about their IR needs once they are public and the quiet period passes, just after the pricing, or, at best, shortly after Form S-1 (signaling a company's intent to go public) has been filed with the Securities and

Exchange Commission (SEC). By then, it is too late to do the detail work required to be optimally prepared for the operational surprises and ensuing communications issues that invariably develop. By then, it is also too late to create and implement the systems needed to properly monitor operating performance as a quarter progresses and be a "best practices" publicly traded company.

Be Optimistic, But Be Realistic, Too

As of early 2003, the 976 companies that had completed IPOs since the beginning of 1998 (and for which information was available) were trading at only 54 percent of their offering prices. That constitutes a large sample—nearly 1,000 companies—and it highlights a fact: Most IPOs are not going to the moon, either on Wall Street or operationally.

Many such companies trade at half-off IPO pricing because, at some point in their relatively young lives as publicly traded stocks, they have either negatively surprised Wall Street or proved to have an undistinguished product, service, business model, or some combination thereof.

This chapter discusses the steps you should take to avoid matching the average performance of those 976 IPOs. It supplements the comprehensive list of investor relations dos provided by SEC legal counsel and the large accounting firms. A few of those basics are covered here, but the focus is on a step-by-step process to maximize the potential of a company's IPO and minimize the risks on the pricing date and into the future. At the same time, the process recommended here may lead the board and management to determine that going public is not the best way to maximize the value of the company.

Getting Started

A variety of factors cause boards and management teams to think about going public. In many cases, the motive is to bring wealth to the early backers and members of management. In other instances, being public provides increased visibility that enhances marketing opportunities; competitors have a harder time telling your prospective customers that the company is about to go under when financial statements are being filed with the SEC that prove otherwise. Finally, companies sometimes go public to diversify their sources of capital.

Whatever their reasons, after deciding to go public, most company managements become swamped during hectic days that run into the weeks and then months. The board and the other interested parties keep the heat on to get the deal done while the market is receptive. Management typically loses control of various aspects of the process when warnings about the consequences of delay become the cry of the day. En route to the IPO, it finds itself not only trying to run a company and outwit competitors but also sitting through endless meetings with lawyers, accountants, investment bankers, and other experts.

Additionally, as would be expected, many managements haven't yet been through an IPO, or their experience has become outdated by new corporate governance requirements. As a result, they defer to experts, and experts try to get the deal done as quickly as possible, motivated by the lucrative fees they stand to earn. Routines are followed, but to management they are new routines. Reliance on the routine process means that the typical management team isn't as prepared to be publicly traded as it could or should be.

Rather than wait until you're caught up in the IPO whirlwind, start preparing as soon as you receive the first inkling that your company could be an IPO candidate. Among the signals to watch for are the following:

- A competitor just filed an S-1 with the SEC to offer shares.
- Investment bankers are calling on your company and talking up an IPO.
- The venture backers or board members have brought up the subject.
- Companies with similar investment characteristics are being well received in the market.
- Your company is the only private company among your competitors.
- Your company is growing rapidly and will need additional capital to fund additional growth.
- Your debt has become more expensive than diluted equity.

♦ Your company has achieved certain internal milestones and is progressing toward a long-planned entry into the public markets.

Peer Group

From an investor relations perspective, the first step in preparing to go public is to identify a peer group. Which companies will your company be gauged against by the investing public? Which companies have similar operating characteristics or compete for the same customer base? Although every management team believes its company is one-of-a-kind, the market prefers comparisons and analogies. Analysts, investment bankers, and fund managers seek to compare your company with other publicly traded companies as a way to determine valuation. Many one-of-a-kind businesses are less diligently followed by analysts and less desirable to institutional investors once they become publicly traded. This is especially true for smaller-capitalization companies. The IR goal should be to align your enterprise with a peer group and then be one of the stars of that group.

Look at the potential peer group from a 360-degree perspective. Aside from your competitors, what other publicly traded companies are in industries related to yours or have financial fundamentals similar to yours? In late 2002, a hospice care company went public. At that time, only one other publicly traded company focused solely on hospice care. In creating a peer group, the newly public company determined that many of the analysts following its sole pure peer also followed "bricks and mortar" health care companies such as hospitals and skilled nursing facilities. Understanding the operating metrics of that broader peer group became important to understanding how those analysts might view the company.

Operating Metrics

Once the peer group is created, identify the specific operating metrics used by investors to evaluate the companies. These can be gleaned from reviewing information published by the companies, conference call transcripts, analyst reports, discussions with professional investors, and the investor relations representatives of the peer group companies. Revenue, gross margins, operating margins, and net margins are a few of the operating metrics used to evaluate companies in general. Other metrics are specific to particular industry segments.

EVC Group has identified as few as twenty-four operating metrics for a company and as many as thirty-seven. For example, with the hospice client, employee turnover became an important operating metric to follow because the industry's level was quite high. Our client's level of employee turnover was comparatively low and became a distinguishing investment characteristic—a selling point to investors.

Another example occurs more commonly with companies using distributors to access their customers. Monitoring sales and inventory levels within the distribution channel during a quarterly period has become critical to understanding the progress of a business. Yet many companies still get reports from their distributors quarterly or, at best, monthly. In this age of real-time information, finding out that sales from an important distributor were less than expected for the last month of a quarter creates the impression that management doesn't have control over the business. Better to set up real-time, or close to real-time, reporting systems for sales well in advance of an IPO, or even talk of an IPO.

Analysis

Apply some analysis to the list of operating metrics. Determine if there are any other operating metrics that could help to distinguish your company within its peer group. Consider the example of a company in the recycling industry. This company was rare in that it had facilities along waterways that made shipping to customers both easier and less expensive. Because of onerous regulations and land costs, potential competitors had little chance of getting permits to build facilities with similarly advantageous shipping locations. Obviously, this distinction is not going to be readily apparent to Wall Street investors, who usually spend their days far from industrial waterfronts and dumps. Until effective IR positioning was brought to bear, investors didn't appreciate this operating metric, which was a value enhancer.

The analysis of operating-metric distinction must include an evaluation of how long the distinction might last. In the case of the hospice company, the employee-turnover advantage could disappear as the peer group implements programs to retain nurses. In the case of the recycling company, significant public policy changes would have to occur. And even if that were to happen, they aren't making more waterfront land. For public company management, the point is that once awareness is created for a metric, monitoring has to be thorough and consistent to minimize the surprise factor, should there be one.

Drawing Comparisons

How do your company's operating metrics compare with the peer group's? If its performance is distinctly better, you may wish to consider some strategies to maximize awareness before the IPO process starts. The quiet period, the SEC-mandated hiatus during which a company must do nothing that could be interpreted as conditioning the market to purchase the shares, usually begins when management has selected investment bankers and the organizational meeting—including underwriters, attorneys, and accountants—is held. But it is totally legal to implement awareness programs before the quiet period.

One opportunity is offered by investor conferences held by brokerages. Some brokerages invite a select number of private companies to present to institutions attending their conferences. Giving two to three of these types of presentations can generate awareness and understanding of your company among the institutions that may later be buyers of your IPO. It is also good practice for your senior management team. However, there are some risks that must be considered. The presentation needs to be professional and public-company caliber, or investors will not consider the company ready for prime time, nor their investment dollars. And if your company isn't planning to go public within the next twelve months, any awareness created is likely to recede as time passes.

Another strategy to consider is to establish financial media relations efforts. Coverage of your company in regional or national business media can generate increased awareness among professional investors and have positive implications for business development. However, this awareness strategy needs to begin well before the organizational meeting. Even the most successful efforts can take several months to bear results. In pursuing both the awareness strategies discussed, it is best to use outside professionals with successful track records.

Back to Those Operating Metrics

While building market awareness on stage, companies should be working backstage to ensure their ability to monitor the operating metrics that were identified. In the beginning, the goal should be to produce weekly reports on each metric. For those readers who haven't fainted or slammed this book shut after reading the previous sentence, here's why it is important to aim for weekly reports: A quarter is only thirteen weeks long, and Wall Street is notoriously impatient in the 21st century. Taking the pulse of the business fewer than thirteen times during the quarter reduces your opportunities to create and execute strategies that address emerging operating and financial performance issues.

Monitoring the operating metrics of the business on a weekly basis provides you with a better understanding of the developing financial performance. You'll also have more operating knowledge from which to make decisions, including what to communicate if a situation arises similar to the one faced by Flying High at the beginning of this chapter. There may be nothing management can do in the short term to correct a downdraft in the business. However, there is a lot that management can do to protect credibility and long-term shareholder value if a clear command of the issues facing the business can be communicated.

Some operating metrics are not very volatile, and weekly monitoring will prove to be unnecessary. However, it can be argued that the best time to make that judgment is after your company has been public for at least two quarters. The key motive behind assessing the operating metrics of your company on a weekly basis is to understand how your business is doing relative to the plan you've presented to your investment bankers and to Wall Street in general. Putting systems into place for monitoring your operating metrics before starting the S-1 drafting process will allow management to gain a better appreciation of how the company's financial performance compares with that of its peer group. Such an appraisal can help both the board and management determine the market's appetite for the company's shares and target areas that need particular management focus.

Revenue Forecast Reality Check

There's one more process that should be completed before conducting the contest to choose your underwriting investment bankers: the Revenue Forecast Reality Check ("the Check"). The first step in this procedure is to review the revenue forecasts of your peer group for the past four consecutive quarters. This information can be found in the analyst reports of the peer group companies. In addition, many companies provide quarterly forecasts in SEC filings and during quarterly conference calls. Services such as ccbn.com—the website run by the Corporate Communications Broadcast Network—also sell transcripts of these calls.

The next step is to determine the peer companies' actual revenue results for the same past four consecutive quarters and compare these with their forecasts, creating a ratio of forecast-to-actual revenue results. Now, perform the same analysis on your own company's performance. Have your forecasts been higher or lower than actual results? How does your ratio compare with the peer group average? The answers to these questions can have implications for how your IPO is received by the market.

No Rose-Colored Glasses

One of the greatest mistakes the management of an IPO company can make is to provide potential investment bankers with optimistic revenue forecasts. Once the underwriting process begins, going to the underwriting team and letting it know that the 25 percent growth rate you had expected is now looking more like 21 or 22 percent may result in a bit less underwriter enthusiasm and passion for your company. Management has effectively planted a smidgen of doubt about its control over operations and its ability to monitor and forecast the performance of those operations. There is also the practical matter of what type of valuation the market will give a 21 percent grower versus a 25 percent grower.

There are other issues to consider. A peer group that has consistently exceeded company guidance or analyst revenue forecasts has an investor base accustomed to results that exceed expectations. Consequently, Wall Street may very well expect your company's actual results during the first few quarters of its public life to be better than analysts had predicted. Such expectations can create tremendous pressures on management, especially if its own forecasts were optimistic to begin with. Implementing the Check before sharing forecasts with potential underwriters can reduce these pressures and forestall investor disappointment, enhancing the market's regard for both the company and its management team.

Here's a real-life example to consider. EVC Group conducted the Check for a company whose peer group, on average, posted about 95 percent of their forecasted revenues. In other words, the peer group often undershot expectations by 5 percent. This company forecast a 35 percent revenue growth rate for the next year. However, after the Check results for the company's peer group were presented to management, they decided to cut back revenue forecasts by 5 percentage points, to a 30 percent growth rate. (This rate turned out to be the company's norm in recent years.) Six months later, the company was having a very good year, growing at that 30 percent rate, not the originally expected higher one. As a result, management gained a reputation in the marketplace for having a solid command of the business and fostering the fastest growth in its peer group, without the added pressures or opportunity for disappointment the original, higher forecast would have created. Good IR dictates sensible revenue and profit forecasts, with an eye for potential shortfalls. This is true in particular for IPO companies.

Disclosure Policies and Procedures

Disclosure Policies and Procedures (DPPs) provide the written framework for all disclosure decisions. Most companies have some form of DPPs, but they are typically informal. As a company prepares to go public, underwriters of directors-and-officers (D&O) liability coverage will require that the DPPs be put into writing. And since no director in his or her right mind will serve on the board of a publicly traded company without proper D&O coverage, your company is going to need to create a formal DPP document.

Just like many other aspects of the IPO process, the creation of corporate DPPs tends to follow a template and not be very effective.

Customized DPPs make the disclosure process less complicated, help reduce risk, and can boost credibility. So use the DPP template document provided by attorneys or investor relations counsel as a start, but only a start.

Refer back to the list of operating metrics. To the template document, add a discussion of the specific operating metrics your company will periodically release to investors. Including these operating metrics in your DPP document will help focus your entire organization on the company's performance with respect to those metrics and facilitate rigorous monitoring throughout the quarter.

Not every metric belongs in the DPP document. Some items may be highly sensitive from a competitive perspective. Although monitored, these items are not disclosed. The DPP document should note which, if any, metrics won't be disclosed for competitive reasons. The identification of which metrics will not be included should be done early in the underwriting process, so that management maintains tight control over the flow of information from the company.

Guidance

Including specific operating metric disclosure information in the DPP document will also enable the company to avoid a hazard that is sometimes referred to as the guidance trap. Many companies have responded to the passage of Regulation Fair Disclosure (Reg FD) by providing in their quarterly results new releases and during the quarterly results conference calls specific revenue and earnings per share guidance. In less predictable businesses, this approach has increased the risk of shareholder lawsuits and damaged management credibility. Many companies, including Coca-Cola and Gillette Company, have discontinued the practice but still provide enhanced operating metric data. In the case of an IPO, Wall Street may demand some sort of guidance in the first few years, a challenge for management.

Once a company starts providing top- and bottom-line guidance, curtailing the practice can necessitate some difficult explanations to investors. It is possible that IPOs can avoid this dilemma by clearly stating in the DPP document that they will not provide specific top-

and bottom-line guidance. There have not been enough IPOs in recent years to know if this newer approach will stick in future markets. However, if an IPO decides on a "no guidance" strategy, all parties, from investment bankers to senior management, need to be informed of this decision.

There is a middle ground for IR professionals to consider. In place of specific top- and bottom-line forecasts, companies can provide general goals for revenue growth—for example, 10 to 15 percent. These revenue goals are supported by an operating model that outlines how management intends to manage the business from a cost perspective. Operating metrics that are essential to understanding the status of the business should be provided within the operating model. For many companies, these metrics will include gross margin; selling, general, and administrative expenses (SG&A); operating margin; research and development; tax rate; and net income. For these and other operating metrics included in the operating model, the approach should be to provide a very tight range expressed as a percentage of revenue. A sample operating model for a manufacturing company is shown in *Table 8-1*.

This approach allows brokerage analysts and others to develop their own forecasts for the company's financial performance. At the same time, it enables management to focus on running the business, as opposed to just monitoring it, and not to worry solely about short-term results.

One word of caution: Not all investors are content with the operating model approach to guidance. Institutions—the bulk of the market nowadays—tend to want forecasts for the top and bottom lines. They may put pressure on the management of a new public company to provide such forecasts. However, it is our belief that the operating model approach will be accepted by institutions.

Disclosure and Crisis IR

Beyond identifying how the company will provide guidance and the specific operating metrics to be used in doing so, the DPP document includes other information, such as the executives authorized to serve as spokespersons to the media and investment community. The company should identify what types of information, in addition to the dis-

TABLE 8-1 **Sample Operating Model (Manufacturing Company)**

Revenue	100%
Gross margin	52–53%*
SG&A	22–23%*
R&D	9%*
Operating income	15–17%*
Tax rate	30%
Net income	10–12%*

*Percentage of revenue

closed operating metrics, it considers material. The approval process for the disclosure of all information, material or not, should also appear in the DPP document. The company should form a disclosure committee to ensure that the DPPs are regularly reviewed and amended as appropriate.

General guidelines for handling a crisis situation should be included in the DPP document as well. Some companies consider it prudent to attach a crisis communications program. It is also wise to identify the timeframe that will constitute the quarterly quiet period once the company is public. For many companies, this blackout on comment about financial or business performance or prospects begins two weeks before the end of the quarter and ends after the release of results and the conference call.

These are just a few examples of what goes into a thorough DPP document. The general rule should be to create as explicit a document as practicable and recognize that changes to the business will most likely mean changes to the DPPs. Once they are created, the policies and procedures need to be clearly communicated throughout your company. Distributing the DPP document is the traditional mode of communications. However, generating broad understanding of the policies within your company requires a wider effort. Some companies post the DPP document on their intranet and corporate websites. Others conduct meetings to review the key points, and still others require employees to sign a statement acknowledging that they've read the document.

The Presentation

Whole books have been written on the presentation and the "road show" (the presentation made in meetings with investors across the country to pitch an offering) that companies should develop before an IPO. This section discusses some general guidelines for these presentations.

Follow the sequence of activities outlined in this chapter. Developing the pitch to investors before determining the operating metrics, performing the Revenue Forecast Reality Check, or creating the disclosure policies and procedures, presents two potential risks: one, that information later determined to be best kept confidential may be disclosed, and two, that forecasts may be made that later look amateurishly optimistic. Worse, if aggressive outlooks are scaled back, investors may conclude that the company's prospects are souring and that the IPO is being staged merely to give private-equity investors an "exit strategy." Once information is released or forecasts made, it is very awkward to tell investors that a topic is off-limits.

You may use a laptop or printed version of the presentation during a road show, but, keep in mind that it is the company, the fundamentals, and the management team that generate maximum valuation for an IPO, not the most beautiful presentation. Be aware as well that most investment bankers, especially when few IPOs are coming to market, want to control the presentation. It is easier for you to position your company the way you want if you develop a presentation that is used to interview investment bankers. Although this presentation will have other components, it should focus on the following six, essential topics:

1. a brief definition of the company
2. its unique operating characteristics and why they create value for the customer and for shareholders
3. the barriers to other companies replicating those characteristics

4. how long the barriers can be maintained and what is being done to extend them
5. the company's financial performance
6. the operating model to be used in managing the business going forward.

Once the presentation is created, it is necessary to practice the delivery, which should be no more than twenty-five minutes long. It is advisable to invest in a professional presentation trainer who knows how Wall Street works. Even the most polished presenter learns from such training, given the unique characteristics and needs of the professional investor audience.

IR Infrastructure

As its S-1 is being finalized for filing with the SEC, a well-prepared company will put in place an investor relations infrastructure. The first step in building an infrastructure for investor relations is to determine who is going to be responsible for the strategic direction of the program once the company is public. Given the youth of most IPO companies, this responsibility is typically given to executives at the C-level: the CEO or CFO.

The demands of the activities described in this chapter, and the communications demands of being a successful publicly traded company, are onerous. We recognize that they represent a new set of responsibilities for management teams already running flat out. But the reality remains that you have to win not only in your industry but also on Wall Street. There are eight thousand-odd publicly traded companies. Most live in obscurity and many trade for far less per share than they would if they had solid IR.

As a result, it is a good idea for most companies considering an IPO to hire early assistance in developing and executing the program. This assistance can be in the form of either an investor relations professional or an IR consulting firm.

Once the responsibility decision is made and implemented, the plan for the IR infrastructure can be created and acted upon. It goes without saying in this era of Internet communications that IR Web content needs to be created and managed. Because of the limitations of the pre- and postoffering quiet periods, it is advisable to leave an investor relations component off the website until twenty-five days after the period ends. However, the website should be used during the quiet period to collect the names and e-mail addresses of interested parties for post–quiet-period follow-up. One way to accomplish this is to place a notice on the home page that allows people to send their names and e-mail addresses for future postoffering announcements. Once people send their information, they receive automatic responses thanking them for their interest and referring them to the digital address to review the S-1.

During the quiet period, the IR Web content can be built. Various services provide good templates for this content, and some will even host the content. Outsourcing this aspect of the IR program can be quite effective for those companies not willing or able to dedicate the internal resources or whose managements are already stretched. An outsourcer can provide seamless links from other site content, match the corporate branding with regard to look and graphics, and ensure prompt posting of news releases and links to SEC filings. The National Investor Relations Institute (www.niri.org) and many outsourcers provide excellent input on what makes for good IR Web content.

Another decision to be made regarding the infrastructure is how to manage the inquiries that will come in beginning on the day the S-1 is filed. These include inquiries from the media, from individual investors, brokers, analysts, and institutions, and possibly even from credit-rating agencies. Although each group needs to be managed differently, they all need to be managed promptly if the company is going to be successfully received in the public markets. The general rule of thumb here is that the media need to be asked what their deadlines are. Institutions and analysts should have their calls returned within the same day. Brokers and individual investors should have their calls returned within twenty-four hours.

An investor relations voicemail box should be set up so that there is a convenient place for the operator to direct calls from the main number. That voicemail box needs to be checked daily and should have a greeting that indicates what the company's general response policy is, to help manage the caller's expectations.

Vendors should be selected during the quiet period. These include any outside providers of IR Web hosting, conference call providers, and news release distribution services. Years ago, using one of the major news release distribution services became a commonly accepted means to satisfy SEC disclosure requirements. The key is to select one of the internationally known services and not a small upstart. It is too chancy to rely on a service of unknown quality and quantity to meet SEC disclosure needs.

Another component of the infrastructure is the information that will be distributed in response to inquiries. During the first twenty-five days after the IPO is priced, the only document that should be distributed is the final prospectus. But after those twenty-five days, the restrictions loosen up. Then kits can be created that include recent news releases and a fact sheet and other digestible information that helps investors understand the company. Do not include analyst research reports in these kits, regardless of any disclaimer that might be imprinted on their covers.

EXECUTING THE IR FUNCTIONS presented in this chapter requires an investment of time and money. Many companies may well wonder why they should go public" if it entails developing weekly monitoring systems for much of the their operating and financial data (the metrics) and then enduring a skeptical Wall Street that wants hard forecasts to be met to the penny, if not exceeded.

The benefits of being a public company are well known, however, including access to capital and profits for pre-IPO equity investors. Once the decision is made to go public, a company might as well do it in a way that allows shareholders to benefit to the greatest degree. Good IR for IPOs will significantly reduce the risk that your company will end up like Flying High Technology. This preparation will benefit management, early investors, and public shareholders.

PART 3

IR Tactics in Proxy Wars *and* Other Crisis Scenarios

9 | Crisis Investor Relations

MICHAEL S. SITRICK

Sitrick and Company, Inc.

T HE CALL CAME IN EARLY on a Wednesday afternoon. It was the chief executive officer of a large pharmaceutical company, and he sounded frantic.

"The short sellers are at it again," he told me. "We just got a call from a reporter at the *Wall Street Journal* who wants to speak to one of our executives about some accounting issues. Our IR firm has advised us to refuse comment. They say this reporter is in the shorts' pocket." The CEO paused, then asked plaintively, "What do you guys think?"

It was a classic dilemma. A publicly traded company receives what it takes to be a hostile inquiry. Fearing that no matter how it responds, its position will be misrepresented, the company is inclined to stonewall. The temptation to batten down the hatches in such circumstances is both understandable and hard to resist. But it is almost invariably the wrong thing to do. Which is exactly what I explained to the CEO.

"Just because the reporter got his information from short sellers doesn't mean it's not true," I advised him. "I'd recommend calling the reporter to find out exactly what he knows and exactly what he wants. After that, we can decide whether or not to comment."

The CEO agreed, and I called the reporter. It turned out he had information indicating that the company hadn't disclosed a significant purchasing arrangement between it and an entity controlled by the CEO. Not surprisingly, he wanted to ask the CEO about it. I said I'd see what I could do.

When I informed the CEO, he told me flatly that the reporter's information was wrong.

"In that case," I said, "if we go through it allegation by allegation, providing as much documentation as we can, we can probably kill the story."

Within thirty minutes, we had assembled not only the answers to the reporter's questions but also documentation for the assertions we were making. In the end, our efforts prevailed.

"Well, I guess I won't be writing that story," the reporter told me. "Thanks for your help. I know you know that I want to get it right."

Needless to say, the CEO was pleased.

To Win the Game, You Have to Get In the Game

As I am fond of telling our clients, if you want your side of the story to be represented in the media—or on Wall Street, for that matter—you have to tell it. While not responding to a media inquiry doesn't excuse the reporter from ensuring his or her story is accurate, your company can certainly be guilty of, at a minimum, contributory negligence if you don't, at least, (1) find out what the reporter is writing, and (2) even if, for whatever reason, you can't comment, tell the reporter that he's got it wrong.

Not too long ago, most public companies expected their investor relations departments to focus solely on the Street. Reflecting this, the post of IR director was usually held by a former treasurer or financial executive whose job it was to "give the analysts guidance" and handle institutional shareholder relations. Not anymore.

Over the past decade, investment news has moved from the third section of the *Wall Street Journal* to the home page on most Americans' computers. We now live in a world where accounting scandals have become major media events. What's more, analysts, fund managers, and even business executives have become media personalities themselves. To put it another way, media relations and investor relations have become intertwined.

The interplay between the Street and the media became readily apparent at the height of the dot-com boom, when an executive's appearance on CNBC's *Power Lunch* would often result in his or her company's share price getting a boost in the afternoon trading session.

Just as Wall Street has bonded with the media, so too must the IR executive. Where traditional IR was based mainly on Street work and contact, crisis IR also incorporates media, CEO positioning, messaging, process control, and extensive consulting at a much higher level than ever before. In short, investor relations is really morphing into financial communications.

Ironically, the reaction of many companies' executives to this increasing flow of information has been to bury their heads even deeper in the sand. That's especially true since the implementation of full-disclosure rules and, more recently, with the sight of chief financial officers of major companies being led away in handcuffs. The result is a greater reluctance at many companies to talk. Increasingly, executives are hiding behind quiet periods and speaking at only a handful of well-choreographed press and analyst conferences.

One problem with this type of response is that it can be counterproductive. Analysts who no longer get the level of detail to which they've been accustomed start to feel left out. As a result, some may resort to attacking companies via the media. Lack of corporate communicativeness tends to push the investment and analyst community—to say nothing of the "shorts"—even further into the arms of the media.

As information from companies becomes more difficult to obtain, news organizations find themselves forced to rely more and more on outside sources. This trend poses grave risks for public companies. Not only does it allow a company's image to be determined by third parties, it also, and all too often, results in the publication of incorrect information, whether because an analyst was misquoted or simply misinformed. An important point to remember: Reporters are not obligated to get your side of the story in their articles. They are only obligated to provide you with the opportunity to respond.

Traditional IR Versus Crisis IR

People often ask me to define the difference between crisis investor relations and traditional investor relations. More often than not, I say, it's nothing more than a phone call. I am reminded of the call a retailing executive got from one of the country's leading newspapers asking him to comment on reports that vendors had stopped shipping goods to his company because of concerns about its financial viability.

"That is hogwash," the executive said and slammed down the phone.

The next day, the newspaper published a major article in which three vendors were quoted, with attribution, as saying they had stopped shipping goods to the retailer because of concerns over its financial stability. The thirty-column-inch story also contained the executive's three-word response.

The company was immediately flooded with calls from other vendors worried that they were going to become creditors to a company that might be headed for bankruptcy. Although the company assured the callers that the three vendors named in the article had actually been cut off because of late delivery and quality problems, the story so panicked the company's other vendors that it became a self-fulfilling prophecy. Vendors began demanding cash on delivery, and before long, the company was forced into bankruptcy.

How could the problem have been avoided? For one thing, instead of snarling an angry response and hanging up the phone, the executive should have asked the reporter to name the vendors who had supposedly stopped shipping goods. Had he done so, he would have been able to explain why they were bad-mouthing his company. The executive should also have offered to provide the reporter with the phone numbers of fifty or one hundred other vendors who were continuing to provide the company with credit on an ongoing basis. Had he done this, chances are that the story would have either been killed or taken a very different tack.

Another distinction between traditional and crisis investor relations is that while the former is about maintaining relationships with Wall Street and keeping the Street apprised of the company's progress, the latter is about solving problems—ideally, before anyone outside the company is aware of them.

In this sense, crisis IR is not just about short sellers or properly handling a media call. It is about having the wherewithal to handle situations that could have a major impact on the company and its market value. This includes situations such as proxy battles, earnings restatements, announcements of significant losses, aborted acquisitions, delayed bond payments, unexpected management changes, product recalls, and shareholder or other significant lawsuits. At the very least, such crises can severely dent both a company's credibility and its share price. In extreme cases, they can mark the beginning of a death spiral that ends in bankruptcy court or worse. Crisis IR specialists can explain the facts to investors and the media and ensure, whenever possible, that perceptions reflect reality.

A classic example of how crisis IR can correct misperceptions occurred late in 2002, when a merger was announced between two publicly traded companies in the health care industry. The deal was applauded on both Main Street and Wall Street, and everything appeared to be going fine. Then, just before the closing was scheduled to take place, the acquiring company uncovered what it believed to be accounting irregularities in the overseas operations of the target company. All of a sudden, it looked as if the deal might fall apart.

The news broke on a Friday evening. Sitrick and Company was called in on Sunday by the target company to help "deal with" Wall Street and the press. As is almost always the case, the facts were not quite as they appeared.

After receiving a complete briefing from the company, working with the company's management and attorneys, we drafted a news release putting the matter into perspective and explaining that, while it might affect the price somewhat, this discovery was not expected to derail the merger. At the same time, the release explained that no deal is done until the ink is dry and that if for some reason the transaction did not go through, the fact was that the company was in terrific shape and would continue to prosper on its own. The release included facts and figures to support this contention.

We also put together a fact sheet for investors and the media outlining the company's strengths, including the potential of the market in which it operated. Concurrent with these activities, we initiated and responded to investor, analyst, and media calls.

The strategy, which obviously our client supported, was full disclosure, no denials, and a proactive explanation of what the company was doing to make sure this sort of irregularity never happened again. We issued a news release announcing that the company had terminated the executives responsible for the problem, hired independent counsel to ensure that similar or other problems were not occurring anywhere else in the company, and informed the Justice Department and Securities and Exchange Commission of what was going on.

The results were evident: Both Wall Street and the media reacted favorably, as did the company's employees, customers, and vendors. The merger concluded roughly a month after the initial crisis emerged, with only a minor decrease in transaction value for the client's shareholders.

The Basics of Crisis IR

Although every IR crisis is different, in most cases the tactics used to calm the market, reassure creditors, placate the press, and fend off raiders are relatively straightforward. They can be summed up in the following basic rules:

1. **Understand the facts.** Knowledge is power, especially when facing a crisis. Understand the facts of the situation—not only the proverbial, who, what, when, why, and where that journalists are taught to determine but also how and, most important, "So what?" What happened and why, and what is the significance? Do perceptions reflect the facts? If not, why not? It's hard to explain the facts if you don't know them. The worst thing you can do is provide an explanation that turns out to be wrong. Even if your mistake was an honest one, your credibility will suffer, and a bad situation will be made worse.

2. **Understand your audiences.** To tailor your message properly— or, putting it another way, to address the relevant points of a situation—you must understand the concerns of the company's various audiences. Analysts do not always have the same concerns as investors. Reporters might have a totally different focus, as, probably, will employees, customers, and vendors.

Understanding the mind-sets of your various audiences will help you craft and communicate your message better.

3. **Communicate with all key audiences.** This rule pretty much speaks for itself. If the audience is important and has a concern, speak to it. Nothing feeds fear (or fortifies a short-seller's rumors) like uncertainty, and nothing reinforces the concern that something is worse than it seems than silence.

4. **Be proactive.** You are almost always better off acting at the onset of a problem than waiting until it reaches terminal proportions. Bad news tends to feed on itself. It's like a snowball rolling down the mountainside that turns into an avalanche. Identify the problem, develop a solution, and communicate both to your various constituents. If you don't have a solution, at least let the world know that you have identified the problem and are working on solving it. In this world of 24-hour media coverage and online investor chat rooms, silence is interpreted as secrecy, and secrecy means you have something to hide.

5. **Prepare for every contingency.** In planning to deal with a situation that has caused you to break out the Rolaids, ask yourself what effect news of this event is likely to have on the company's various constituencies. What are the worst-case scenarios? Identify them, and prepare for them.

6. **React appropriately.** Although you should never ignore an incipient problem, overreacting to a situation can be just as bad or worse than underreacting. It can often cause a crisis where none existed before. In assessing the issue, look at the various "what ifs" and react accordingly. Do a risk-benefit analysis of each step in your reaction to the matter. Sometimes, less is more. Sometimes, it is not enough.

7. **Speak with one voice.** Nothing is more important in a crisis, or in business in general, than credibility. Credibility depends on honesty and accuracy, which in turn depends on consistency. It is difficult, if not impossible, to maintain credibility if different people at your company are saying different things. If you have separate IR and PR functions, make sure the two teams are on the same page—both with each other and with your legal and management teams.

8. **Focus on the solution as well as the problem.** Companies often issue news releases that announce the large loss they incurred in the last quarter without addressing what they are doing to turn that loss into a profit. Many times companies talk about a product recall, but not what they are doing to fix the problem behind it. Identifying the solution is just as important to investors as identifying the problem. In fact, it may be more important.

9. **Focus on the future as well as the past.** Wall Street is interested in the past only to the extent that it believes it will affect the future. I am not suggesting that you make earnings projections. Your communications, however, should always focus on the future. This is essential in a crisis.

10. **Be forthright, with others and with yourself.** Three words sum up this rule: "Tell the truth!"

11. **Use experienced professionals.** You wouldn't go to a podiatrist for heart surgery. Neither should you allow a lawyer or IR professional who lacks experience in sensitive, "bet your company" situations to handle your legal, investor relations, or communications activities in a high-stakes crisis. You owe it to your shareholders to get someone who is experienced and has a high level of expertise and an outstanding track record.

Turning Lemons Into Lemonade

Sitrick and Company was recently involved in a case where a large publicly traded utility faced possible bankruptcy because one bank in its syndicate had refused to agree on a renewal of its credit facility.

Our flight from Los Angeles landed at 6 P.M. in the city where the company was headquartered. That evening we met with senior executives, were briefed on the situation, and discussed the various potential outcomes of the bank negotiations. We then went back to our hotel rooms where we worked through the night drafting various contingency documents.

While the company's executive team was focused on getting the bank deal completed, we were preparing for the various eventualities. We drafted a press release explaining that the bank had refused to renew the credit facility, what this meant for the company, and what the management team was doing to deal with the situation. We drafted a second release saying the negotiation had been extended and a third announcing that a deal had been struck with the banks.

We also prepared a variety of other documents, each aimed at one of the company's particular audiences: its investors, employees, customers, creditors, vendors, and regulators. Why so many? Because if any of these groups were sufficiently angry or panicky, they could upset the apple cart, and nothing is more likely to anger or panic a constituency in a crisis situation than feeling they have been left out of the loop.

As it turned out, the recalcitrant bank finally came to its senses. But because we were prepared, the company used this "good news event" as an opportunity to communicate to shareholders—as well as to all the other key audiences—the steps management was taking to implement a long-term plan to restructure and strengthen the company and its balance sheet.

The stock rallied, despite a tough market. Often, when properly executed, crisis IR is about taking lemons and making lemonade.

10 | The Art of Winning Proxy Wars

Based on interviews with

JOHN C. WILCOX

Georgeson Shareholder Communications Inc.

W ITH THE RISE in the number of institutional investors and the increasing willingness of professional investors to pursue corporate agendas of their own, today's investor relations (IR) professionals must have a fundamental understanding of proxy contests. In addition to explaining strategies for winning proxy contests, this chapter is designed to help corporate executives and IR professionals assess their own vulnerability to dissidents, activists, and takeovers, and the role IR can play in addressing those vulnerabilities.

Good, long-term IR is an important ongoing defense against proxy fights. After reading this chapter, you'll gain a "behind the scenes" perspective of the factors driving prominent proxy fights in the media—and how you can prepare for similar actions involving your own company.

Readiness for a Proxy Fight

Is your company ready for a proxy fight? It may all depend on how well your ongoing investor relations efforts defend your company's image as seen by shareholders and the financial media.

If your company is perceived by the public and by shareholders as being open, honest, and reliable, its reputation is less likely to be vulnerable to negative events or rumors. As a result, shareholders may be more likely to back management positions on a wide variety of corporate issues—making your company less vulnerable to a proxy contest. Good corporate governance and accountability to shareholders are essential to effective IR and will serve well in proxy wars.

Being targeted with a proxy challenge can have a broad destabilizing impact on a company. After all, the objective of any publicly traded company is to post earnings that reflect growth and demonstrate success to its shareholders. Any disturbance in a company is a catalyst for investor uncertainty—prompting volatility in stock prices and raising questions about a company's worth. This situation can result in short-selling activities.

Proxy fights are usually "last resort" options that are pursued only when all other avenues have been exhausted by unhappy shareholders. Proxy fights are expensive—in large tussles costs can run into the millions of dollars—time-consuming and draining on corporate resources and public image. In particular, valuable executive time is spent unproductively, while issues such as management compensation and "using the shareholders' money to fight shareholders" are raised.

That's why the best response to the threat of a proxy fight may not always be to fight back. It may make better business sense to take countermeasures and offer compromises to avoid a potentially long and costly legal fight—in both the courts and the media. Proxy fights have a high level of unpredictability: even if you do strategizing and legwork to court the votes needed to win, shareholders can change their minds and switch allegiances right up until the annual or special meeting when the vote takes place.

You want to enter a proxy fight only when you can accurately predict a good chance of success, but you should always consider the very real possibility you may not win—even if you have a strong position. You may do your best to persuade shareholders to vote for your position, but there's always the risk of losing—sometimes due to factors beyond your control.

Proxy fights are rare occurrences within the universe of publicly held companies. In the 2002 proxy season, there were only 38 proxy fights out of nearly 10,000 annual meetings of U.S. publicly traded companies, two fewer than in 2001. Since Georgeson Shareholder started keeping records more than twenty years ago, the record number of contests was 41 (1989), and the lowest was just three (1993). The spike in the late 1980s was a reflection of the junk bond era when ample financing was available for takeovers. Today, proxy fights seem more ad hoc in nature, reflecting specific problems of governance or performance at the companies where they occur.

The challenges of initiating a proxy fight are daunting. Dissatisfied investors often express reluctance to take their case to shareholders because they believe proxy fights are impossible to win, expensive, time consuming, risky, unpredictable, or that "the cards are stacked in favor of management." Indeed, even the simplest proxy war against management, staffed by volunteer labor, costs at least $250,000 to mount.

In today's environment, most of these concerns can be overcome, and proxy fights are expected to increase in the future, reflecting greater focus on good corporate governance and increased activism by frustrated investors.

What Is a Proxy Contest?

How do you define a proxy fight? In keeping with the standards of the New York Stock Exchange (NYSE), a proxy fight is usually defined as a contested solicitation campaign where a dissident mails separate proxy materials and proxy cards. The most common type of proxy fight is an election contest between two competing slates of directors. Votes are solicited by two independent groups: management and dissidents. However, as discussed below, hybrid proxy fights can occur in many situations other than director elections.

Companies may have to deal with what are termed *Trojan horse* proxy fights. For example, shareholders or dissident groups may solicit votes against management initiatives. Or dissidents may solicit support for a shareholder resolution under the shareholder proposal rule—such as a proposal to rescind a company's "poison pill." In response, the company would need to seek the support of shareholders with an aggressive countersolicitation. These are examples of "hybrid" contests that do not involve a change of control and that may not trigger special SEC and stock exchange rules governing proxy fights.

Dissident activity is really not officially a proxy fight until something gets mailed directly to shareholders. However, even if a corporate action undertaken by a dissident group is not considered a proxy fight per se, there can still be a negative impact on the company if the opponent action is not dealt with correctly.

What Triggers a Proxy Contest?

There are many reasons why proxy contests are likely to increase in the future. Shareholder activism tops the list. Investor frustration with management and performance failures, combined with growth in institutional voting power and in shareholder dissatisfaction during a bear market, are important trends that have stimulated interest in proxy contests.

The classic reason for a proxy fight is to change control. Dissidents compete with management for a slate of directors to control or influence a company's board of directors. Or dissident factions may support a hostile takeover bid or election contest, or oppose a merger or acquisition.

Proxy fights are waged for many other reasons as well—and each reason encompasses its own set of scenarios. Among common triggering situations are the following:

Performance problems. A company could experience declining stock prices and lower earnings due to market conditions, management miscues, poor sales relative to the competition, and other factors. A dissident shareholder group may challenge management to remedy the situation with a corporate action. For example, shareholders may pressure management to break up the company's business to improve performance.

Asset distribution disputes. A company may be operating profitably but still be perceived as "sitting on" undervalued assets that could be liquidated or distributed to shareholders. This value may be locked up due to a disagreement over business strategy. Dissidents may seek to unlock these hidden or underutilized assets through a variety of initiatives that can form the basis of a proxy solicitation.

Personnel issues. Every day there seem to be more news headlines revealing company scandals, nepotism, or excessive management compensation. Negative news events are a catalyst for change in a company's board and management.

Corporate governance. A company may have major governance failures, or shareholders may want to impose better governance practices. For example, shareholders can object to the way that a company's board of directors is configured, the independence of board members, committee structure and policies, compensation practices, and antitakeover provisions. Shareholders may want to aggressively overturn a "poison pill" defense against hostile takeovers, for example, or change a board's committee structure, or influence executive compensation practices such as "golden parachutes."

As noted previously, the most common type of proxy contest involves an election contest, governed by SEC Rule 14a-11. In a typical scenario, a dissident slate of directors seeks to unseat either the entire incumbent board of directors or some portion of it. This type of proxy contest most resembles a political election. Both management and dissidents compete to persuade shareholders that their nominees will do the most to maximize the value of the company—while attacking the credibility of the opposing faction. This form of "popularity contest" may be won or lost largely based on the credentials of the board nominees, as well as the business strategy they endorse.

Contests in support of takeover bids constitute another common type of proxy fight. The removal of various obstacles to a cash tender offer may lead to a proxy contest (or a series of contests). This process may involve the solicitation of proxies to rescind a poison pill, for example, or the solicitation of consents to call a special meeting to elect new directors or to eliminate charter provisions that block the completion of a tender offer.

Hybrid contests in support of shareholder proposals are becoming increasingly common due to the willingness of institutional investors to take their case to other shareholders and to be public. The liberalization of SEC rules governing shareholder communications in 1992 opened the door to more aggressive solicitation by shareholders. Hybrid proxy contests in opposition to management initiatives may develop spontaneously and are on the rise for all the same reasons.

Another class of hybrid proxy fights involves competing plans of reorganization for companies in bankruptcy. Such companies may present opportunities for investors who seek control by acquiring debt to block management's reorganization plan and present a competing plan of reorganization. Additionally, some investor groups seek control of public companies by buying convertible bonds (which convert into equity). Indeed, there are convertible bonds known as "toxic convertibles" that allow bondholders to convert their holdings into an increasing number of shares as share prices fall (and thus into a greater fraction of voting shares). Some buyers of so-called toxics are not beyond staging campaigns of short selling to drive down share prices prior to converting their bonds into stock. In such battles, IR is critical to counter efforts by short sellers.

How Vulnerable Are You to a Proxy Fight?

Understanding the causes of proxy contests can help your company analyze its own vulnerabilities. If you can answer yes to one or more of the following questions, you may have to worry about the prospect of a proxy fight:

❑ Does your company have hidden or undervalued assets?

❑ Does your company have unhappy shareholders who are really dissatisfied with your performance or governance?

❑ Has your company's stock underperformed peers and the market?

❑ Has recent bad publicity attracted negative attention to your company?

Your company is especially vulnerable any time a scandal occurs. This could involve fraud, lack of internal controls, executive compensation (such as exorbitant options or bonuses or generous severance agreements when performance has been poor).

Here's another issue to consider: Is your company planning a controversial strategic change that could face opposition from vested interests? For instance, if your company is planning a major acquisition or merger, dissident shareholders may contest this action because they feel the risks for the company outweigh the potential benefits. These shareholders can be very adamant, especially if they have emotional ties to the acquiring company, or have strong beliefs about or connection to that company's "core" business; their position is strengthened by the argument that, in general, mergers rarely produce the promised return.

Preparing a Battle Plan

Before responding to the threat of a proxy fight, it's critical to begin early-stage activities. You should prepare a "battle plan" based on a situation analysis—whether you represent management or dissident interests.

First, you need to do an overall objective assessment of the situation—from both communication and tactical analysis standpoints. You should know exactly:

♦ Who are your shareholders? How is ownership shifting during the period leading up to the "record date" (the date the company closes its books to determine which shareholders have voting rights)?

♦ What vote outcome is likely? Based on an analysis of the ownership and the issues being contested, you and your advisers can accurately forecast the vote outcome. A combination of surveys and interviews can develop information on shareholder attitudes toward the issues that will control the outcome of the contest.

♦ What kind of campaign is required to achieve victory? This strategic analysis will help determine whether you can muster the resources to win.

The strategic analysis needed to formulate a battle plan is best prepared by professional advisers in conjunction with on-staff IR professionals. It will entail gaining a thorough understanding of the following factors:

Shareholder profile. Who are you trying to reach and influence? This is a critical starting point in any proxy contest. Since the outcome of a proxy fight is often extremely close, this initial analysis is crucial.

To prepare a shareholder profile, you should consult such information sources as the most recent 13F and 13D filings, the depository listings, the list of registered holders; the proxy statement, records of management and insider holdings, and employee plans. In addition, a detailed shareholder identification report can be prepared by a professional proxy solicitor to cover accounts not normally accessible through public records and filings. These accounts include shares held in "street" name, that is, shares actually owned by individuals but held in the name of a brokerage; beneficial owners whose holdings are not publicly disclosed (along with their custodial relationships and their voting and investment contacts); foreign accounts; arbitrage positions; and hedge funds.

Some of this work can be done using readily available, "fast and dirty" sources, at least in early stages of the analysis. For example, if one looks at a company profile through the Yahoo! Web service, the largest institutional shareholders and mutual fund holders are listed, based on quarterly updates. Proxy statements, 13D, and 13F filings are also available online, at www.sec.gov. Of course, a company's IR department should always know its largest shareholders. Should questions arise, usually a few hours of work will be enough to get a solid picture of who owns a public company. Of course, if a lot of stock is trading hands, public sources will not capture the needed updates on a timely enough basis.

Vote projection. To project the vote outcome, you need to know the voting policies and practices of your institutional investors and the other groups of shareholders that make up your ownership profile. Institutional investors typically base their votes on economics, but their decision may be influenced by other factors as well. Individual registered holders are usually loyal to incumbent management. But there is a long list of exceptions, such as instances in which a company's dividend has been cut, its stock price has plunged, scandal has discredited management, compensation has been excessive, or a takeover premium has been "lost." Rockville, Maryland–based Institutional Shareholder Services (ISS) reviews corporate proxy statements and advises institutional investors on proxy voting decisions. ISS's voting recommendations should be carefully analyzed in the vote projection. A proxy solicitation firm can provide insight into ISS's likely vote recommendations.

Stock watch/ownership tracking. Many companies monitor their stock's market activity continuously to track and determine the causes of unusual trading. They also analyze ownership changes by carefully reviewing depository listings and transfer sheets. Proxy solicitors and professional stock watch firms have additional resources and "tricks of the trade," for tracking ownership changes. These activities can provide an early warning to a company whose stock is being accumulated by a potential raider or dissident. During the course of a proxy solicitation, stock watch can help determine how shares bought and sold after the record date will affect the quorum and vote results.

Access to the shareholder list. State laws control access by a dissident to a company's shareholder list. Communication with shareholders on proxy matters is generally deemed a "proper purpose" under state law, enabling a dissident to obtain the records needed to conduct a proxy fight. Companies are usually not successful in blocking a bona fide dissident's access to share records (including depository listings and the NOBO [non-objecting beneficial owner] list), although the process may delay the dissident's campaign.

Employee stock ownership plans (ESOPs). ESOPs can be an important factor in contests for control. Shares in these plans are subject to a variety of voting arrangements. Employees have pass-through voting rights, but response is often low. Instructed shares may be voted by trustees at their discretion or through mirror voting. These arrangements can make a big difference in a close contest— enough so that ESOPs should usually be considered as the focus of good shareholder relations in their own right. Analysis of ESOP voting is an important factor in vote projections.

Other regulatory agencies. The Securities and Exchange Commission and individual states are the primary regulators of proxy contests. However, companies in regulated industries may turn to administrative agencies for assistance in defending against threatened changes of control. Analysis of the relevant regulatory players must be done before the contest begins. The results often will determine whether the contest should take place at all—or whether the company has to look for other ways out of a potentially losing scenario.

Proxy Alternatives: What to Do If the Odds Are Strongly Against You

Once you have prepared a comprehensive situation analysis and battle plan, you should be in a position to predict your chances of victory in a proxy fight. As has been noted, it's critical to take an objective approach to determining whether or not to fight. Your decision should be based on a neutral analysis of the factors affecting your position rather than on emotional or personal issues. If your analysis reveals your chances for victory are slim, it is usually not worth engaging in a costly proxy contest if other options are available. Alternate strategies include the following:

Agreeing to a settlement with the dissident. You could change the structure of your board of directors, add outside directors, restructure the business, or take other actions designed to accommodate dissident concerns. Governance adjustments are far less disruptive than a disruptive contest or a change of control.

Finding a "white knight." You could sell the company to a company or group that offers greater potential to maximize shareholder value. If the board and management are persuaded that a change of control should occur, then they have a fiduciary responsibility to hire investment bankers to solicit a bid that will maximize shareholder value.

Involving a strategic investor. You could place additional shares with a third-party investor, in this way introducing additional capital and a strategic voting block. Issuance of additional shares may require shareholder approval, but this can sometimes be avoided through a financing structure known as a public investment in private equity (PIPE). Indeed, a PIPE can be used as a preemptive strike, placing a large block of stock with an ally, quickly, and before the makings of a proxy fight jell. News of pending PIPEs is confidential, but IR is necessary afterwards to effectively "sell" the story of a PIPE to Wall Street and your institutional ownership base.

Adopting additional defenses. You could introduce poison-pill shareholder rights plans or certain other antitakeover charter amendments without shareholder approval. However, introducing defensive provisions in the face of a proxy fight creates the risk of a shareholder backlash—and raises a new issue for dissidents to leverage. The availability of antitakeover protection involves questions of state law that should be thoroughly reviewed with legal counsel. State law may provide takeover defenses that remove the need for additional protection. In general, takeover defenses increase investor relations problems.

Making recapitalization moves. You could recapitalize your company by putting authorized shares in the hands of new investors by issuing new debt or by issuing preferred instruments—some of which can include voting rights. However, there may not be time for such moves if a proxy fight is imminent and shareholder approval would be required. Furthermore, it's important to note that clever corporate maneuvers may work in the short run but fail in the long run. Institutional investors will remember managements who appear to put themselves before shareholders, therefore it is important to convince shareholders that takeover defenses protect their interests.

Initiating aggressive litigation. With the advice and support of legal counsel, companies often bring court actions to prevent or delay proxy fights. This, of course, is often regarded as an extreme measure and if it fails, a company's vulnerability may be substantially increased. Again, the reasoning behind such actions must be bullet proof and not be perceived as harming shareholder economic interests.

A Strategy for Success

Putting Together a Winning Team

An important early step in the proxy campaign is determining which outside players need to get involved. Regardless of your in-house resources and capabilities, it's important to remember that you can't do it all on your own. It's critical to enlist the assistance of proven professionals who can help you ensure that the proxy fight is conducted correctly.

Consider the following members for your proxy team—and the roles they will play in the process:

Lawyers. Legal counsel is essential because everything in a proxy fight must be done in compliance with SEC regulations and state law. Filing, disclosure, and procedural requirements are detailed and burdensome, and they can't be neglected. Lawyers also play a key strategic role.

Financial advisers. You'll need professional help to address valuation issues, to critique the dissident's economic platform, to locate a "white knight" or outside investors, to provide entrée to institutional shareholders, and to make other network connections. Depending on the circumstances, management very likely may be approached by several teams of investment bankers vying for business. There is no harm in meeting with bankers and garnering valuable information and ideas or even holding a "beauty contest," by requiring bankers to submit plans as part of their bid for your business.

Proxy solicitor. The professional proxy solicitor takes responsibility for planning, organizing, and implementing the solicitation campaign. The solicitor's job encompasses tactics, timing, analysis, communications, street name contacts, telephone campaigns, and back-office mechanics. The solicitor also advises on the conduct of the meetings, tabulation questions, and the final review of voting results.

Public relations counsel. Positive public perception sways votes in a contentious proxy fight. A public relations professional deals with the media to ensure a favorable spin for your position, arranges interviews with the media, and helps you craft the content of fight letters. Experienced PR shops with specialized talent in these areas can be rare, so select carefully.

Once your team is assembled, leadership is the critical factor. The leadership of the company's chief executive officer is essential for success. The CEO is commander-in-chief in a proxy fight, coordinating all participants and handling relations with key outside constituencies such as customers, employees, and suppliers. Personifying the company in a proxy fight, the CEO should be both the source and symbol of the company's strength.

Identifying and Targeting Shareholders

The prime audience in a proxy fight is shareholders, especially the largest shareholders. Securing their votes—and keeping those votes in your camp until after the shareholders meeting—is the point of the entire process. That's why all proxy materials need to be geared to the needs and concerns of shareholders.

However, shareholders are not a homogeneous group. A common mistake is to think about shareholders collectively, as though they all have the same goals and act the same way. In fact, shareholders are diverse both in their investment strategies and their decision-making characteristics. You need to identify the specific investment objectives of different shareholder groups and address them in your strategy. That's the point of conducting a thorough audience analysis, as discussed earlier. It's important to know who your audience is because it affects the arguments you want to make and the issues you want to develop during the contest. Some IR firms, well before a proxy fight looms, conduct routine surveys of the largest shareholders and their views of the stock. This is certainly a prudent way to avoid being blindsided by a sudden groundswell of support for a dissident shareholder group.

Once a proxy battle is on or is brewing, consider the following:

♦ What does the proxy fight mean to your primary audience from a tactical and strategic viewpoint? Explain to shareholders how the outcome of the proxy fight will affect their investments, rather than just trying to score points in the debate. What's really at stake for them? Why should they care about your position? How will you maximize value for them? How will you address the problems that concern them?

♦ How are your shareholders divided into groups? Typically, the ownership profile will present a combination of individual retail shareholders, institutional shareholders, insiders, employee shareholders, foreign owners, and arbitrageurs. Each group of shareholders has different priorities that influence the way they vote. Which key messages will appeal to and resonate with each shareholder group?

You may find that individual retail shareholders are driven primarily by their desire for stability and continuity and by their long-term focus. Institutional shareholders are usually more interested in the financial bottom line. They are also often strongly influenced by the recommendation of Institutional Shareholder Services (ISS). Geography also matters; local investors and pension funds may, though not publicly stating as much, be more likely to back managements located in their home state. Employee shareholders are usually more concerned about keeping their jobs than with financial issues, and thus usually are management's best allies in any proxy tussle. Professional investors, including hedge funds and arbitrageurs, are more short term in their focus.

Leveraging Your Investor Relations

Often IR executives are more familiar with investment analysts at institutions than with the analysts' counterparts who make voting decisions. IR during a proxy contest is different from the traditional crisis communications. It must be addressed to the audience of voting decision makers and deal with the specific contest issues. At the same time, proxy IR involves many of the same considerations as those coming into play during any other corporate crisis, including the following:

◆ maintaining ongoing business disclosure
◆ maintaining ongoing IR activities
◆ coordinating contest communications and advertising with ongoing business PR activities and the media
◆ dealing with the concerns of suppliers, customers, and employees whose confidence in the company may be shaken

Consider the following five questions. The degree to which you can answer each in the affirmative may spell the difference between success and failure in mounting an effective proxy fight.

1. **Can you attract media coverage?** A well-positioned, favorable news story or feature can have a significant impact on public opinion and the views of analysts and shareholders, especially if carried in one of the major national financial papers. However, favorable media coverage is a double-edged sword—it can also lead to overconfidence. Don't expect your positive press clippings to do the work of an effective proxy solicitation. Indeed, many professional investors regard financial journalists as amateurs.

2. **Can you write effective "fight letters"?** These are the primary "documents of persuasion" in a proxy contest. Writing fight letters is a delicate balancing act that requires sensitivity to shareholder views. On the one hand, you want to give dramatic gravity to your position. On the other hand, you need to be wary of using scare tactics to rebut opposing arguments. You don't want to win the contest and end up with a mortally wounded company. The most important aspect of the letters is to sum-

marize your position and the key issues in a clear, succinct, and meaningful way. Offer shareholders tangible benefits for your position—and gain their confidence in your ability to execute your strategy and deliver results. Imagine you are selling a product or service, and "brand" your viewpoint with catchy slogans or memorable headlines.

3. **Can you tap into the power of advertising?** You can leverage the messages of your fight letters in ads in national and local publications to reach both your shareholder audience and the broader investment community. Proxy ads help you demonstrate your commitment and determination to shareholders, which is important in maintaining momentum in a solicitation campaign. Look at some examples of clutter-breaking, effective advertisements from well-known proxy contests. Bold headlines grab shareholder attention. "DROP DEAD!" (RJR Nabisco); "Show Us the Money" (ITT); "Don't Be Conned By Kahn" (ICN Pharmaceuticals), and perhaps the most famous of all, "The Directors of Sears, Roebuck & Co.—NON-PERFORMING ASSETS" (Sears/Robert Monks)—all are examples of effective, high-impact headlines used in proxy fights.

4. **Can you conduct effective face-to-face meetings with key shareholders?** There's no substitute for meeting one on one with voting decision makers at institutions that hold large blocks of stock. Your proxy solicitor will prepare institutional contact lists and arrange "road show" tours to reach key decision makers. This approach can also be effective with groups of retail shareholders. For example, in the proxy contest for the merger of Wachovia Corporation and First Union Corporation in 2001, face-to-face meetings helped win the approval of Wachovia's regional shareholders. Reluctant shareholders needed to be personally convinced that the merger was in their best interests and that the hostile takeover attempt of Wachovia by SunTrust was not. In that instance, Georgeson Shareholder Communications set up a series of local town meetings in strategic locations during which company officials presented the merger proposal in person to shareholders and answered their questions.

5. **Can you "keep up appearances" during proxy contests?** It's important to maintain your underlying business without interruption during the contest. This demonstrates your ability to execute your business strategy and maximize value for shareholders.

Remember that proxy fights affect everyone involved with your company—both directly and indirectly:

♦ Employees worry about their job security
♦ Customers worry about the stability of your company in supporting your products and services over the long term
♦ Suppliers and vendors worry about your ability to pay their bills and your long-term viability
♦ Investors worry about the short- and long-term value of their shares

Maintaining the health of your company is paramount—no matter how bloody the proxy fight may become between warring factions.

Clearly Defining the Issues

Management Versus Dissident Positioning

Whether you represent management or dissidents, you must address both sides of the key issues that are in contention in a proxy contest. In a nutshell, these boil down to the following components:

1. How you will strengthen the business and build value for shareholders
2. How the opposition will be unable to do so

When a proxy contest degenerates into a personal struggle with smash-mouth tactics, backbiting, and dirty tricks, it undermines shareholder confidence. Even if you manage to win support for your position with a "scorched-earth" strategy, your company's public image can suffer irreparable damage. Each side in a proxy contest has strengths and weaknesses. Management is typically more familiar with shareholders and has developed relationships with them, especially if good ongoing IR has been in place over the years. But management's position is essentially defensive. This can make it difficult to persuade shareholders that the status quo will improve if, for example, the company is mired in a long downward slide of poor performance and sinking stock prices. The bear market that began in 2000 could result in many managements facing proxy challenges, especially as institutional investors become more assertive.

When a company has been performing poorly, dissidents have the advantage of offering new ideas and a new team. In addition, proxy rules have been liberalized in the past ten years to give shareholders flexibility, whereas corporations still face strict disclosure and filing requirements. This means dissidents can, in effect, wage "guerrilla warfare," while management has to maintain "redcoat formation." In particular, shareholder groups can meet and discuss strategy, and talk to financial media without many of the regulatory constraints faced by management. Management has to honor SEC rules, and must, of course, file and disclose any material information through established channels.

However, dissidents bear the burden of proof that they have a plan to make things better—rather than just different. They also have the disadvantage of being "outsiders." They're typically unfamiliar with the company's inner workings and are often deprived of specific information about budgets, strategic plans and projections, and other matters essential for constructing a persuasive business plan. If the dissidents' credentials are weak and their past business accomplishments unimpressive, they may also be put on the defensive.

Going on the Offensive (Without Being Offensive)

Each side in a proxy fight will try to be the first to publicly state an issue and frame it advantageously for their position. If you can force your opponent to defensively answer difficult or embarrassing questions, it can have a powerful effect on the course of the campaign.

Sometimes each side tries to avoid becoming defensive by ignoring the other side's arguments and issues. This can lead to "apples versus oranges" fights and rebuttals where one fight letter makes a statement and the other side responds with a countercharge—rather than addressing the issues that were raised. The dissident will argue that the most important issue is management's poor past performance, while management will argue that the most important issue is the dissidents' lack of qualifications. In such a situation, shareholders are frustrated because neither side demonstrates how they will improve performance. In the end, if neither management nor dissidents convince shareholders why their position is better—only that it is different from the opposition—the contest can become an exercise in futility that undermines investor confidence and damages the company's long-term prospects.

Ideally, instead of engaging in a war of words, both sides should stake out the high ground and emphasize business over personal issues. Unfortunately, in the heat of battle it is difficult to resist the temptation to get personal and avoid responding to innuendo and personal assaults. In this respect, a proxy war is no different from politics—people with good intentions end up slinging mud and thereby alienating those whose votes they are trying to attract.

Every Shareholder Vote Is Critical

Even with millions of shares voting at an annual meeting or special meeting, the difference between winning and losing may come down to less than a single percentage point. The lesson: Every vote counts; no investor should be overlooked in the search for votes.

One good strategy to avoid losing votes through revocations is to make sure you throw the last punch. Send out a "fight letter" to shareholders shortly before the shareholder meeting, depriving your opposition of time for a rebuttal.

In close votes, don't overlook chat rooms on the Internet. If rumors are rife online, try to dispel them by making official news releases. If serious issues are raised, address the issues seriously and quickly in the same manner.

The Cost of Proxies

The out-of-pocket costs, regulatory requirements, and potential liabilities of a large proxy solicitation deter all but the richest, best-organized, and most committed dissidents. Investors relations professionals generally do not need to concern themselves with gadflies and special interest groups who show up regularly at annual meetings or haunt chat rooms.

There are basic inequities in the financing of solicitation campaigns. Company managers can use corporate (that is, shareholder) money and insurance, while dissidents are denied access to corporate resources. Regardless of whether or not the company spends excessively during a proxy battle, the charge of "using the shareholders' money to fight shareholders" will undoubtedly be lodged by the dissidents. This charge should not be discussed as mere "sour grapes." Governance reformers are looking seriously at the inequities of proxy financing. An ongoing IR effort that stresses efficient and low-cost management practices serves well should an actual proxy war break out. It bears repeating that in recent years dissident groups have become more powerful and institutional shareholders have become less timorous about taking on management. The recent rash of stories about executive mismanagement and malfeasance tends to undermine the credibility of all management to some extent, increasing the defensiveness of all managers in the face of shareholder criticism.

The Winning Combination: Value, Power, and Ideas

To properly develop and execute a winning strategy, remember the importance of proxy mechanics and don't lose sight of what you are trying to accomplish—maximizing a favorable vote response from your shareholders. Consider the viability of alternatives to proxy fights, particularly when an analysis of the odds indicates that you may not win. Nothing is a sure thing in a proxy contest until the final votes are cast and tabulated. For management, your burden is to explain and defend your position, while questioning the credentials and strategy of the dissidents, and demonstrate convincingly how you will maximize shareholder value.

Keep in mind that a proxy fight is not a popularity contest; it's about economic value, power, and ideas. You must be able to prove that you're going to do a better job managing the assets and delivering value.

11 | The Hewlett-Packard Merger: A Case Study

KENNETH R. CONE
DANIEL R. FISCHEL
GREGORY J. PELNAR
DAVID J. ROSS
Lexecon Inc.

THE NEXT FEW YEARS may witness a surge in proxy fights, given the bear market of the recent past. Mutual fund managers and money managers know they must perform or risk losing assets. They in turn will be less deferential to managements who do not deliver for shareholders. In addition, certain Securities and Exchange Commission (SEC) rule changes make it easier for large shareholders to talk to one another without violating securities laws.

Given this likelihood of increased shareholder activism, it is worthwhile for investor relations professionals to review some of the specifics of the contested merger between Hewlett-Packard and Compaq. When the deal was first announced by the two companies' management teams, on the evening of September 3, 2001, it triggered a legal, investor, and public relations firefight between proponents of the merger, led by Carly Fiorina, HP's chairman and chief executive officer, and its opponents, led by Walter Hewlett, son of HP's cofounder and member of the board. In what was generally regarded as the hardest-fought, best-financed, and most closely contested proxy war in years, perhaps ever, both sides presented their positions vigorously to HP shareholders, the broader investment community, and the public. It thus makes for an excellent case study, despite the hard feelings the deal left behind for many of those involved.

The Opposing Positions

Fiorina and other proponents of the merger contended that the deal was beneficial because it provided HP with a more balanced product and revenue mix and would not pose insuperable integration problems, although the track record of comparable mergers in American industry is very mixed. Hewlett, by contrast, strenuously argued that the deal would worsen HP's product mix, making it less profitable, and posed substantial integration risk. It is fair to say that investors' initial reaction to the deal was consistently negative. On September 4, the first trading day after it was announced, HP's stock price plunged nearly 19 percent, from $23.21 to $18.87. A day later, Moody's Investors Service lowered HP's credit rating two notches, to A2. By November 5, HP's stock price had fallen to $16.89, more than 27 percent below its level before the merger announcement. This decline represented a pretty clear thumbs-down by Wall Street.

On November 6, the Hewlett family announced that it would vote its stake against the merger, thus making the deal less likely to be completed. HP's stock price soared in response, rising more than 17 percent to close at $19.81. This was the pattern throughout: Events that made the merger more likely to be completed were generally associated with stock price decreases while the opposite was true for events that increased the probability that it wouldn't go forward. For Compaq shareholders, the reverse pattern was observed, because the market perceived Compaq and its shareholders as the big winners in the deal.

For the merger to be consummated, both HP and Compaq shareholders had to vote in favor. Based on the market's assessment of the transaction, there was never any issue whether Compaq shareholders would approve the deal. They did, and did so enthusiastically. But HP shareholders were a different matter, particularly since Hewlett and his associates owned approximately 18 percent of the stock, which he pledged to vote against the merger. Thus, nearly one-fifth of the shareholder vote was dead-set against the deal from day one. To nix it, Hewlett had to convince just a little less than one-third of other shareholders to vote with him. Nevertheless, HP shareholders did eventually approve the merger by a vote of 837.9 million (51.4 percent) in favor to 792.6 million (48.6 percent) against.

In sharp contrast, Compaq shareholders subsequently approved the merger by a nine-to-one margin. The votes came after Institutional Shareholder Services—a consulting firm whose clients, institutional money managers, owned 23 percent of HP's shares—endorsed the transaction as in the best interest of HP and its shareholders, an item of key importance to IR professionals. The Rockville, Maryland–based ISS often weighs in on corporate governance matters and proxy fights and is regarded by many financial market participants as independent and authoritative.

In any proxy tussle involving large public companies, the IR team must make sure to open up a line of communication to ISS and use it to make compelling arguments. In this case, ISS sided with Fiorina, a stand that, along with other factors, possibly tilted the vote on the deal in her favor. In any event, a subsequent court challenge to the shareholder vote by Hewlett failed, and the merger was consummated.

But Why?

Despite the ISS position, the outcome of the HP proxy fight creates a paradox. Why would shareholders approve a transaction that decreased their wealth? We explore several possible non-mutually exclusive explanations for this paradox below.

Rational Ignorance and the Free Rider Problem

Shareholders rarely have the incentive to expend significant resources when deciding how to vote, or whether to vote at all. Why should they? No single shareholder in the overwhelming majority of cases can expect to affect the outcome of a vote. And even if the outcome could be affected, rewards from superior voting decisions accrue to shareholders based on the size of their holdings, not on their efforts in influencing the outcome. Shareholders, therefore, have strong incentives to take a free ride on the efforts of other voters or simply to follow management recommendations, rather than to make independent efforts to study the issues and vote accordingly.

Additionally, it should be remembered that institutional share-holders usually own portfolios of stocks whose holdings range from dozens to hundreds of issues. Money managers can ill afford the time to get enmeshed in every proxy battle involving one of their holdings or even to study up on them. The roughly seven thousand stocks listed on the NYSE, Nasdaq, and AMEX generate more than eight thousand proxy issues per year.

Corporate democracy exacerbates this problem. Unlike the interests of voters in political contests, the interests of corporate shareholders are closely aligned–everyone wants the company to make profits. This general agreement on goals, and the ease with which shareholders may sell at low cost if dissatisfied, reduces their incentive to safeguard their interests against other voters by investing in independent research.

Furthermore, these stocks are held by at least eight thousand mutual funds, thousands of pension funds, and millions of individual shareholders. It would be costly and duplicative for all these investors to spend time and money analyzing each proxy fight involving each security they own. As a practical matter, few individual or institutional shareholders have an incentive to make that investment.

The marketplace has provided a partial solution for this problem. Institutional investors can reduce their research costs by hiring advisory services that specialize in researching proxy contests and providing vote recommendations. Such services arguably allow institutional shareholders to vote their shares responsibly without studying every proxy issue.

As noted above, one consulting firm, ISS, has achieved exceptional importance in the U.S. market for proxy advice, and its endorsement of the merger may have played an important role in the HP contest. The ISS's 750 clients were estimated to hold about a quarter of HP's outstanding shares. The margin of victory for the merger was only 3 percent, so it can be argued that ISS made a difference in the outcome, particularly since several large institutions announced they were supporting the deal because of ISS's recommendation.

So why did ISS endorse the deal? We considered the explanation that the firm suffered from conflicts of interest, a possibility since it offers some services to corporations as well as institutions. However, a closer review showed that ISS has consistently opposed management-sponsored propositions to increase takeover defenses, a position unlikely to endear it to corporate management. Furthermore, ISS expressed concern in its proxy analysis about claims by Hewlett that HP's board had promised Fiorina a large incentive package for completing the deal. ISS predicated its endorsement of the merger on the fact that HP's board had "thoroughly repudiated" the proposed compensation deal.

Although the review of ISS and its possible conflicts of interest proved fruitless in most regards, it remains a lesson for IR professionals engaged in proxy wars: When fighting for shareholder votes, something more than cogent reasoning and well-drafted arguments are warranted. It is appropriate to research the opposition and look for self-interest in its arguments. Shareholders should definitely be made aware of parties with conflicts of interest in proxy battles, and that is part of what an IR team should do.

In any event, ISS's historical conduct suggests a strategy that generally focuses on keeping management incentives aligned with shareholder interests and opposing propositions where management appears excessively self-interested, rather than on second-guessing the pure business judgment of the insiders. Such a strategy makes sense for ISS, because the firm does not claim that any of its staff members have ever run a major corporation or have particular expertise in either of HP's major businesses: computers and printers. Furthermore, ISS attributed no significance to the stock market evaluation of the merger and was not deterred by the fact that the ISS endorsement itself caused a further decline in the stock price.

There remains the hard question—indeed, the mystery—of why ISS's clients, or anyone else for that matter, paid any attention to its recommendations. Neither ISS nor the institutional investors who were influenced by it provided any explanation of why the judgment of a firm that admittedly lacked expertise on the business merits or drawbacks of the HP-Compaq merger should have mattered more than the consensus judgment of the most sophisticated investors in the world, who in fact had such expertise. Observers might conclude that, for better or worse, ISS's opinion has achieved something of the status of a Good Housekeeping Seal of Approval. IR professionals need to be mindful of that possibility when wading into proxy battles.

Optimistic and Pessimistic Shareholders

The existence of a market price for a stock does not necessarily mean that all shareholders agree on the stock's value. In theory, the stock price could reflect the assessment of only the most pessimistic shareholder and not the beliefs of the more optimistic voting majority. Under this view, a majority of HP shareholders voted in favor of the merger because they believed the deal would increase HP's value, while those who did not favor the deal determined the company's stock price by being active sellers.

The difficulty with this hypothesis is that it cannot fully explain why the assumed optimistic majority who supported the merger didn't buy HP shares from the pessimistic shareholders, causing HP's stock price to rise. For those optimistic shareholders, HP's $4.34 stock price decline when the deal was announced, and the further declines when other events increased the probability that the deal would be completed, created major profit opportunities. No reason exists to assume that the institutional investors who supported the deal were constrained by lack of capital or otherwise prevented from betting on their beliefs. Apparently, there was no "silent majority" of investors who strongly supported the deal because they believed HP's value would increase as a result.

For investor relations professionals, the lesson is that some shareholders will need to be convinced to take a greater interest in the unfolding events of a proxy tussle, and this may require strenuous rounds of phone calls, faxes, e-mails, newspaper ads, and other solicitations. In addition, expert analysis probably should be presented to shareholders. In the case of the HP-Compaq deal, it can be argued that the silent majority sat on its hands or let management lead the way. Moreover, as has already been stated, many institutional shareholders have limited attention spans, because of their pressing commitments to keeping abreast of entire portfolios of stocks, not just particular issues within them.

Long-Run Versus Short-Run Investors

A related explanation for the favorable shareholder vote is that sophisticated investors dismissed the negative stock price reaction to the deal as the product of short-term speculation and not reflective of the merger's long-term impact on the company. But this explanation, although frequently expressed, fails, like the one offered above, to explain the refusal of bullish investors to buy sufficient quantities of the stock to cause its price to rise. Belief in the long-term prospects of the merger necessarily implies a belief that the stock price will increase in the future. This creates an incentive to buy today, an incentive all the greater because of the market's negative reaction to the merger. The fact that bullish investors didn't nullify the stock price decrease suggests that the investors' short-term consensus judgment that the merger was value-busting for HP represented investors' long-term beliefs as well.

Conflicts of Interest

Institutional investors held approximately 60 percent of HP shares, and many of them also did business with HP. If these institutions cared more about keeping Fiorina and HP management happy and protecting these business relationships than about the interests of the outside investors whose shares they controlled, they might have voted in favor of the merger, even if it was wealth-reducing.

This argument, which can explain otherwise illogical behavior by institutional shareholders, is precisely the claim that Walter Hewlett made in his court challenge to the shareholder vote. He alleged that Deutsche Bank, which had initially announced an intention to vote against the merger, changed its vote after Fiorina threatened to terminate HP's business relationships with the bank. It was revealed that Fiorina had indeed had conversations with Deutsche Bank officials, and not just those officials charged with determining how the bank would vote its shares. Although the Delaware court rejected Hewlett's claim, we decided to analyze the conflict-of-interest explanation more generally.

To do so, we compared the announced voting behavior of banks and investment advisers (institutional investors that might have had conflicts of interest because of their potential business relationships with HP) with the votes of pension funds (institutional investors that were unlikely to have such conflicts of interest). The results, shown in *Figure 11-1,* provide some slight support for the conflict-

of-interest hypothesis. Of the 34 institutions that publicly announced their positions, 43 percent, or 9 of 21, of the banks and investment advisers voted in favor of the merger, while about 31 percent,
or 4 of 13, of the pension funds voted yes. If all institutional
investors had voted against the merger to the same extent as did the
unconflicted pension funds had, there may have been no HP-
Compaq merger.

Moreover, *Figure 11-1* may be less significant for what it includes
than for what it leaves out: at least 750 institutions that held a total
of 38 percent of HP stock were excluded because they did not
announce how they were voting the shares they controlled. A cynic
might argue, "Yes, of course, conflicted parties would not draw attention to themselves and announce their vote plans."

These missing data highlight a peculiar fact about corporate proxy
contests: Institutional ballots are secret from the investors who actually own the shares. (The SEC is currently attempting to change this
rule.) This odd definition of a secret ballot can only increase the likelihood of conflicts of interest.

Analyst coverage of the merger also provides some evidence about
the likelihood that conflicts of interest influenced institutional behavior. *Figure 11-2* summarizes the (largely negative) views expressed by
stock analysts concerning the merger. Since most of these analysts
worked for investment banking firms that were potential vendors to
HP, the negative analyst commentary runs contrary to the conflicts-
of-interest hypothesis. On the other hand, and perhaps more
tellingly, it is worth noting that three of the five analysts who supported the merger worked for investment banks that were paid to
assist in the merger or the proxy fight.

The lesson for IR professionals is that one must enter a proxy
fight knowing who has business relationships that will be affected by
the results and thus who may be vulnerable to threats to withhold
financial carrots in exchange for votes. Be on the lookout for such
tactics, and if they are found, bring them to the attention of the public, shareholders, and regulatory agencies in as quick and loud a way
as possible.

FIGURE 11-1 Institutional Votes in the HP/Compaq Merger

For Merger	Against Merger
Money Managers / Banks	
1 Alliance Capital (AXA Financial)	1 Bank of America Capital Management
2 Banc One Investment Advisors	2 Brandes Investment Partners
3 Barclays Global Investors	3 Chicago Asset Management
4 Capital Research & Management	4 Davis Selected Advisers
5 Federated Investors	5 Dreman Value Management
6 General Motors Asset Management	6 Fifth Third Investment Advisors
7 L. Roy Papp & Associates	7 Matrix Asset Advisors
8 Putnam Investment Management	8 Parnassus Investments
9 State Street Corporation	9 Torray Companies
	10 Victory Capital Management
	11 Wachovia's Evergreen Investment
	12 Wells Fargo (Norwest Corporation)
Pension Funds	
1 Florida State Board of Administration	1 CalPERS
2 PA Public School Employees Retirement System	2 CA State Teachers' Retirement System
3 State of WI Investment Board	3 CO Public Employees' Retirement Association
4 State Teachers Retirement System of Ohio	4 New York Common Retirement Fund
	5 NY State Teachers' Retirement System
	6 Ontario Teachers' Pension Plan Board
	7 Public Employees Retirement System of Ohio
	8 State of Michigan Retirement System
	9 Teacher Retirement System of Texas

FIGURE 11-2 **Analyst Recommendations in the HP-Compaq Merger**

Analyst	Support Merger?
Banc of America	Yes
Deutsche Bank Alex. Brown	Yes
Goldman Sachs	Yes
Merrill Lynch	Yes
Salomon Smith Barney	Yes
A.G. Edwards	No
ABN AMRO	No
Bear Stearns	No
Bernstein Research	No
C.E. Unterberg, Towbin	No
Credit Suisse First Boston	No
Lehman Brothers	N/A
Morgan Stanley Dean Witter	No
Robertson Stephens	No
UBS Warburg	No

Notes: Goldman Sachs acted as a financial adviser to HP in connection with the merger, and Deutsche Bank received a fee from HP. Salomon acted as a financial adviser to Compaq in connection with the merger.

Source: Analyst Reports

THE FAILURE OF HP'S SHAREHOLDERS to vote for what we contend was their common interest in HP's proxy fight is especially discouraging because they had several unique advantages in this contest. First, unlike in most proxy votes, where management represents the only organized faction, the HP opposition was led by a highly motivated shareholder whose name was on the company logo, who was a member of the board, and who controlled or strongly influenced 20 percent of the vote, counting both family foundations. Walter Hewlett waged a determined and expensive campaign in which he hired top investment banking, legal, and public relations experts and made extensive presentations to shareholders and investment advisers. His defeat does not augur well for any shareholders standing up to management in proxy wars. Indeed, one might argue, that it does not augur well for good corporate governance.

Second, the stock market evidence concerning the value of the merger was very clear: HP's stock lost $8.4 billion when the merger plan was announced and regained $5.7 billion when Hewlett announced his opposition. Finally, the intense glare of media attention should have reduced the temptations created by conflicts of interest and also reduced the costs to shareholders of becoming informed about the issues. The outcome of this contest paints a bleak prospect for normal corporate votes, where the issues are subtle, the media uninterested, and the opposition far less informed and vocal.

IR professionals engaged in lower-profile proxy wars, if not working for management, should recognize that they will be swimming upstream, maybe even upriver. They must prepare valid arguments and be willing to fight hard to get their views before a skeptical institutional investing community. They should search keenly for conflicts of interest in management and among institutional shareholders and make those conflicts public. They should develop relationships with the financial media, prefacing their comments with concerns about proper corporate governance.

PART 4

Special Case
Perspectives

12 | IR for Non-U.S. Issuers Accessing the U.S. Capital Markets

SIDLEY AUSTIN BROWN & WOOD LLP

As edited by

THOMAS E. McLAIN, ESQ.

YOSHIKI SHIMADA, ESQ.

ALTHOUGH THE RUSH TO U.S. exchanges has slowed in the past few years along with the cooling stock market, many foreign companies still wish to list their shares stateside to achieve the greatest liquidity possible for their shareholders. It is possible that tightened U.S. securities regulations, and the protections and transparency they offer to shareholders, may ultimately result in a second wave of companies listing on U.S. exchanges in pursuit of perceived legitimacy.

An issuer that has decided to offer securities in the U.S. capital markets must prepare its team for the legal, regulatory, and market-practice issues that lie ahead, some of which may require the non-U.S. issuer to take corporate actions in anticipation of its securities offering. Described in this chapter are some preliminary matters that should be addressed by a non-U.S. issuer to ensure that it is prepared for its first U.S. securities offering.

Of course, not only legal and regulatory challenges must be met. The vast U.S. investment community must be made aware of a new investment vehicle, which itself must meet the most current and exacting U.S. standards for disclosure. That is a job requiring intensive investor relations.

Preparing to Offer Securities in the United States

The market-driven pricing and disclosure-based liabilities that are, to varying degrees, part of every international securities offering may be a surprise to a novice issuer. Non-U.S. issuers seeking to access the U.S. capital markets for the first time may have borrowed money previously only from banks, governments, and supranational organizations or, in the case of businesses, may have raised equity capital only from private investors.

The Team

First-time issuers likely are accustomed to negotiated transactions and not to the investor protections afforded by U.S. securities laws and regulations. To succeed in such an offering, which may entail new and unfamiliar business practices and requirements, all parties need to be flexible. The relationships among them must be largely cooperative, not adversarial.

Officers of a non-U.S. issuer who are accustomed to establishing the terms of a financing in a privately negotiated transaction or with the benefit of an exemption from domestic securities laws will need professional assistance to understand the regulatory requirements and market practices designed to protect investors. IR professionals must stress that shareholders sit at the apex of the U.S. public company pyramid, and insist that the IR team have access to all material information, and play a role in when and how to disclose that information in consultation with their advisers.

Foreign companies entering U.S. public capital markets also need to be prepared for the amount of work required for their first U.S. securities offering and the importance of adhering to the agreed timetable. IR professionals may wish to point out that proper compliance and the experience they gain from their first U.S. securities offering will make succeeding U.S. securities offerings much easier.

The Business Profile

A non-U.S. issuer may be advised by securities firms and IR professionals to refine its business profile and clarify its business strategy to facilitate its U.S. securities offering. The IR team needs a succinct "story" or definite image it can project to potential U.S. investors.

Like some U.S. companies, foreign enterprises may decide that restructuring, even serious restructuring, is necessary to meet the desires of U.S. investors. Recent examples of businesses that have had to be thoroughly restructured to meet U.S. standards include some in the People's Republic of China (PRC). Many PRC businesses have traditionally operated like old-fashioned U.S. company towns, providing their employees not only with work but also with housing, education, medical facilities, and other social services and infrastructure. Although it is a sensitive cultural issue, investment bankers have advised these PRC companies that the social services and infrastructure aspects of their businesses detract from their profitability and will result in a reduced valuation by investors.

As a result, before these PRC companies go public on the U.S. markets, they generally separate their social services and infrastructure from their core businesses. This allows a simple and more compelling story to be told to investors who rightfully expect (for U.S.-listed stocks) that management's first fiduciary responsibility will be to shareholders.

Prospective issuers also may be advised to consider disposing of certain business segments, to provide a more focused investment for investors or to eliminate perceived risks that are not integral to the core business. An example of this sort of perceived-risk reduction is the reorganization of certain non-U.S. cement companies to exclude asbestos-related business segments, since asbestos carries the perception of large legal and financial liabilities. IR professionals must be careful to apprise foreign companies who wish to list on U.S. exchanges of these risks.

In general, American institutional investors, and even retail investors, want to see a company with a strong core business and not a collection of companies operating under an umbrella with parental financing. Although some conglomerates have done well, there is a growing sense on Wall Street that predicting their earnings is nearly impossible; predicting earnings for a simple company is treacherous enough. Foreign companies will need advice from IR professionals on how to restructure with U.S. investors in mind.

The Jurisdiction of Incorporation

In some cases, non-U.S. businesses establish a holding company or a subsidiary to issue securities in the U.S. capital markets. Sometimes this is because of legal, tax, or other issues in the home jurisdiction that make it more desirable to obtain financing through an offshore vehicle. In other cases, the requirements of the investors' jurisdiction drive the decision. IR professionals will need to understand these reasons. Examples of the use of such vehicles follow.

- ◆ Several non-U.S. issuers have raised equity through holding companies established in the British Virgin Islands, Bermuda, the Channel Islands, or the Cayman Islands. Some have done so to obtain a corporate form in a jurisdiction with defined shareholder rights that is better known to international securities investors than that of their home country. Others are seeking to avoid having to comply with the requirements that their own country's legal system imposes on securities issued by a domestic company. Still others have substantial international business and set up holding companies in low-tax offshore jurisdictions to minimize their corporate tax liability through deconsolidation or other restructuring. In the case of an initial public offering by a closely held non-U.S. issuer, the move offshore may be made to minimize the tax liability of the group of shareholders that will control the issuer after the offering. Of course, it is the job of IR professionals to clarify to the U.S. investing public these legitimate reasons for seeking certain jurisdictions.

- ◆ For certain types of financing in the U.S. capital markets, such as commercial paper programs and other investment-grade debt offerings, debt issued by a Delaware finance subsidiary and guaranteed by the non-U.S. parent company increases the market of eligible investors, even if the parent company is based offshore. The reason is that many large U.S. institutional investors are limited by asset allocation models, corporate policy, or investment charters in the amount of non-U.S. securities they may hold.

- ◆ An offshore finance subsidiary may provide a convenient way to enhance the credit rating of securities through overcollateralization, guarantees, insurance, or bank letters of credit. The securities issued by these vehicles have generally been limited to debt securities and preferred stock. This approach has been used by non-U.S. businesses for many reasons, such as to minimize the disclosure about the non-U.S. business, to obtain a lower cost of funds through the credit enhancement, to securitize financial assets, to deconsolidate substantial assets, and to implement other types of tax-planning. Finance subsidiaries used for these purposes have been incorporated in Delaware, if the offering is primarily in the U.S. capital markets, or in tax havens such as the Cayman Islands or the Netherlands Antilles, if the primary markets are elsewhere. An offshore finance subsidiary also can be used to circumvent or minimize withholding, transfer, or similar taxes or restrictions on the ability of a non-U.S. business to issue securities.

Corporate Governance and Disclosure

Non-U.S. issuers, particularly those complying with U.S. securities laws for the first time, may need to modify their legal documentation and accounting procedures to meet the standards required in the U.S. capital markets. Indeed, the job of IR professionals will be to advise issuers how best to comply not only with the letter of the law but also with the spirit of the laws—especially since the passage of the Sarbanes-Oxley Act of 2002. To trade for the best price on U.S. markets, a company must earn a reputation for being accessible and transparent. If company management is so inclined, it should meet with key investors to explain the importance it places on compliance with the federal securities laws and its respect for the integrity of the international capital markets. Certainly, such sentiments must be expressed in corporate literature and websites.

Additional contracts or other documentation of business or government arrangements may be required to protect the issuer or to provide more comfort to investors. Examples of circumstances when such documentation is necessary follow.

♦ Existing informal agreements and understandings material to an issuer's business may need to be documented in situations such as corporatizations and privatizations. In these situations, documentation has commonly been required to cover such things as property rights, water rights, energy rights, and purchase and sale arrangements that had previously been represented by unwritten understandings between the issuer and other businesses or government officials. IR professionals, working in conjunction with legal professionals, must first ascertain whether such documents exist and advise the issuer accordingly.

♦ Existing documentation may need to be revised or supplemented to provide the degree of specificity and certainty required by the U.S. capital markets. For example, if a key purchase or supply contract contains material uncertainties, the issuer may be asked by the securities firms or advised by its lawyers to restate or supplement the contract and thereby avoid the marketing or legal risks associated with those uncertainties. With the assistance of IR professionals, issuers should be prepared to answer questions from U.S. investors about these types of agreements and related matters. Indeed, recent scandals have put the onus on issuers to show that they are serious about full and fair disclosure and about adhering strictly to conservative accounting and auditing standards.

♦ Existing financing covenants may need to be revised to accommodate the securities offering, or the issuer may wish to use its ability to access the U.S. capital markets as a basis for renegotiating more favorable terms with its existing lenders.

♦ An issuer may have to alter its corporate governance policies or take other action in order to list its securities on a U.S. securities exchange or to improve the marketability of its securities. For example, many non-U.S. businesses offering securities for the first time are managed by a board of directors that includes no independent, or nonmanagement, directors. In cases in which the issuer is listing its securities on a U.S. securities exchange, the issuer will need to consider the appointment of independent directors now required by securities exchanges in the United States.

♦ It may be desirable for a business to enter into employment contracts with personnel that are crucial to the continued success of the business, could become significant competitors to the company, or both. It is common for securities firms to request such agreements to enable them to better market the securities of a business that was started and is currently being managed by one or more private entrepreneurs.

Because executive officers, directors, and the company itself potentially are liable when securities are offered in the United States, the company should take steps to protect its executive officers and directors from this liability to the extent permitted by the law of the issuer's jurisdiction. Possible sources of protection include an indemnity issued by the company and the purchase of directors' and officers' liability insurance.

Accounting Matters

A non-U.S. issuer that makes a registered public offering of its securities in the U.S. capital markets must provide investors with audited annual financial statements and interim financial statements that are appropriate to the type of offering involved. The SEC requires that financial statements of a non-U.S. issuer be prepared in accordance with, or be reconciled to, U.S. generally accepted accounting principles (GAAP). Most non-U.S. issuers choose the reconciliation alternative.

Although reconciliation seems a straightforward, if time-consuming, effort, deals have foundered after financial figures have been reconciled to U.S. standards. On a number of occasions, brokerage houses have been unable to market securities successfully in the U.S. capital markets or were forced to lower offering share prices because the non-U.S. issuer's financial condition and results of operation under its local GAAP and under U.S. GAAP differed so markedly.

For example, gains on the sale of real property are sometimes treated as ordinary income under non-U.S. GAAP but only as extraordinary income under U.S. GAAP. This difference has resulted in some non-U.S. issuers reporting substantially lower ordinary income under U.S. GAAP. Moreover, in many cases, revaluation of assets allowed under non-U.S. GAAP is not permitted under U.S.

GAAP. This has sometimes resulted in non-U.S. issuers having significantly lower, and sometimes negative, net worths when they prepare their financial statements in accordance with (or reconcile them to) U.S. GAAP.

Some non-U.S. issuers' accounts require substantial auditing and other work to meet U.S. market standards. In such cases, it is important that the securities firms and the accountants working on the transaction provide the non-U.S. issuer, and IR professionals, with a clear understanding of the financial statements that are necessary to market the equity or debt and comply with applicable accounting requirements.

Communications With Investors and the Public

In addition to the specific compliance requirements described above, the antifraud provisions of the U.S. federal securities laws and reporting requirements of the relevant U.S. securities exchanges give rise to a general obligation to report material events promptly to investors. In practice, issuers will need to establish adequate internal compliance procedures and, in particular, internal disclosure and financial reporting procedures to ensure compliance with applicable laws and exchange requirements.

Press Releases

Typically, the obligation to report material events to shareholders is satisfied through a press release. Press releases are generally distributed to the business wire services and other financial information channels and posted on company websites. Certain developments may be appropriate for public disclosure but not critical enough to require an immediate press release. These may be communicated in the issuer's interim reports.

Press releases must avoid material misstatements and omissions. They should be accurate, complete, and balanced between positive and negative factors. There is no room in financial disclosures for the degree of "puffing" that would be acceptable in general commercial advertising or other areas of commercial communication, and IR professionals must advise issuers accordingly.

Materiality Standards

Although there is no standard that can be applied with mechanical certainty, a fact will be considered "material" if there is a substantial likelihood that reasonable investors would consider it important, as part of the total mix of available information, in reaching their investment decisions. That is, information is material if investors would attach actual significance to it in making their deliberations. It is impossible to make a complete catalog of all material information, but typical examples include significant mergers or acquisitions, stock splits, adoption of a dividend policy or changes in dividends, major increases or decreases in revenues or profits, important new contracts or projects, and changes in senior corporate management or in basic corporate business policies.

In this connection, courts have treated the confirmation of a general market expectation as material information in some circumstances. For example, if an issuer confirms to one analyst the accuracy of its projection that it will achieve a specific level of earnings, this may trigger the obligation to make a general public announcement, even if outside analysts are arriving at the same projection based on their own analyses of published data.

Duty to Disclose

Good corporate practice generally calls for prompt public disclosure of material events. There has been some discussion among legal practitioners, however, concerning the extent to which the law requires such disclosure. Under the 1934 Act, a non-U.S. private issuer is required to report promptly on Form 6-K any information not contained in its latest Form 20-F that the non-U.S. private issuer (1) makes or is required to make public in its home country, or (2) files or is required to file with a non-U.S. stock exchange on which its securities are traded and that was made public by that exchange, or (3) distributes or is required to distribute to its security holders. The antifraud rules, such as Rule 10b-5 under the 1934 Act, prohibit material misstatements and omissions of facts that need to be known to prevent the statements that are issued from being misleading, given the circumstances under which they were made. The rules do not, however, deal directly with total silence.

An issuer with securities listed on a U.S. exchange is subject to an additional affirmative obligation to make timely public disclosure of material information.

Arguably, an issuer does not violate any legal requirements if, for good business reasons, it delays an announcement of important developments, absent special circumstances creating an affirmative duty to disclose. An affirmative duty to disclose may exist when there has been a leak of news or selective disclosure, when insider trading has occurred, when the issuer is acquiring its own equity securities, or when there is a rumor or a market report circulating for which the issuer had some responsibility.

Notwithstanding the foregoing, the SEC's enforcement policies, as well as the trend of the law as interpreted by the courts, favor full and fair disclosure. Accordingly, withholding material information is not recommended unless there is a countervailing bona fide and important business reason for doing so. In general, issuers subject to the U.S. federal securities laws should adopt a policy of disclosing material events on a timely basis. IR professionals can hardly overemphasize the importance of this policy.

Selective Disclosure

In 2000 the SEC adopted Regulation FD, which creates a reporting obligation for all public reporting companies (other than non-U.S. governmental issuers and non-U.S. private issuers), including closed-end investment companies but not other investment companies. In general, issuers subject to the new regulation must ensure that any material nonpublic information intentionally disclosed to specified persons outside the company is simultaneously disclosed to the public at large (in the case of a "non-intentional" disclosure, public disclosure must be made "promptly").

Although Regulation FD does not currently apply to non-U.S. governmental and non-U.S. private issuers, the SEC stated in the release adopting the new regulation that it intends to undertake a "comprehensive review of the reporting obligations of foreign private issuers" and, in the interim, reminded non-U.S. private issuers of their obligations to make timely disclosure of material information pursuant to applicable self-regulatory organization (SRO) rules and policies. It is possible that the SEC may in the future require non-U.S. governmental and non-U.S. private issuers to comply with the requirements of Regulation FD.

Antifraud Rules Under the 1934 Act

Section 10(b) of the 1934 Act and, within this section, Rule 10b-5 impose liability for fraud committed in connection with the purchase or sale of any security. Rule 10b-5 states that it is unlawful in connection with the purchase or sale of any security for any person to (1) employ any device, scheme, or artifice to defraud; (2) make any untrue statement of a material fact or omit to state a material fact necessary to prevent the statements made from being misleading, given the circumstances under which they were made; or (3) engage in any act, practice, or course of business that operates or would operate as a fraud or deceit upon any person. Rule 10b-5 has been construed to prohibit insiders from engaging in a purchase or sale while in possession of inside information.

Internal Controls

To effect a policy of timely disclosure, an issuer should, if it has not already done so, adopt internal procedures regarding disclosures to the financial community. The issuer should be certain that material information is disclosed on a timely basis when appropriate and that no leaks or inadvertent disclosures occur when the release of information is inappropriate. Usually, consultation with U.S. lawyers and IR professionals is needed to achieve this standard.

The issuer should establish clear internal lines of authority and responsibility and authorize a limited number of persons to deal with the financial community. These internal procedures should incorporate procedures for obtaining back-up certificates from various officers, managers, and personnel in positions of authority and responsibility to support officer certificates now required to be executed by chief executive officers and chief financial officers of issuers, confirming full and fair disclosure by the issuer of material information and adequacy of the issuer's internal disclosure controls. All employees should be alerted to the basic principles of disclosure, including the obligations to maintain the confidentiality of undisclosed material information and to refrain from trading while privy to such information. The person or persons authorized to deal with the financial community should be kept informed about material developments or should be instructed not to make comments until the accuracy of information regarding such developments is verified with more senior officials.

As a corollary to the foregoing, it is essential that all persons within the issuer, regardless of their title or position, strictly maintain the confidentiality of material information to which they have access. An issuer normally has some degree of discretion in determining when an event is ripe for public disclosure, assuming no leaks have occurred. A reasonable standard, consistently applied for affirmative as well as negative information, usually will avoid difficulties. Good practice, however, may require that an issuer disclose in certain circumstances—when there's been a leak of information, for example, or when rumors are circulating in the financial community. Care should be taken to prevent these circumstances from occurring.

13 | Investor Relations and Microcap Companies

RALPH A. RIEVES

Emerging Companies Research Institute

JOHN R. LEFEBVRE, JR.

Shareholder Relations

THE TERM *MICROCAP* refers to a public company with market capitalization of less than $250 million. The median market cap for microcap firms is about $70 million. The focus of this chapter is on only those microcap companies that are listed on Nasdaq or the American Stock Exchange (AMEX). Microcap companies seldom meet the listing requirements for the New York Stock Exchange (NYSE). Omitted from this discussion are over-the-counter bulletin board stocks (OTCBB). Also omitted are stocks of companies that inadvertently drop to microcap status; such entities can be characterized as reemerging companies. This chapter deals only with strategies for emerging companies, companies that are eight or fewer years out from their initial public offerings.

Attracting the Individual Investor

When conducting investor relations activities aimed at attracting individual investors, emerging companies need to stay aware of their company's inherent characteristics. Key among these are the following:

1. Microcap companies have small stock floats. That condition always impacts share value.
2. Typical risk/return characteristics make microcap stocks inappropriate for most individual investors.

3. Quantitative research indicates that returns from microcap stocks are proportionate to the risk incurred in owning them.

4. Research also indicates that returns from microcap stocks do co-vary (i.e., move in the opposite direction) with the returns of the largest capitalized stocks.

As a general rule, an emerging company's investor relations program directed to individuals should focus on investment advisers to high-net-worth individuals. What follows is a summary of research to support this recommendation.

What Do We Really Know About Microcap Risk and Return?

CEOs and directors of emerging growth companies need to consider their company's stock within the context of the capital markets. They must understand their company's appeal relative to other investments. There are many investment advisers who view emerging growth stocks as investment alternatives to higher capitalized stocks and high-grade bonds. Most investment advisers assign microcaps to the same high risk/return category as high-yield bonds and some types of hedge funds.

It bears repeating that this generally accepted characterization must always be considered when developing an IR strategy for an emerging growth corporation. Not every individual is an appropriate target for microcap IR programs. In fact, considerable research exists to support the case that the only viable, individual investor target for a microcap company is the high-net-worth individual (HNWI).

The Emerging Companies Research Institute (ECRI), using data from the Chicago research and consulting firm Ibbotson Associates and various websites, constructed the graph in *Figure 13-1,* which plots risk against return over the fourteen-year period ending December 31, 2000, for the four most common capitalization weights. The returns are annualized and expressed in percentages. The horizontal axis is risk measured by the commonly accepted computation of the standard deviation of returns. The apparent values in the graph clearly suggest that there is the likelihood of return proportionate to the risk incurred when investing in microcap stocks.

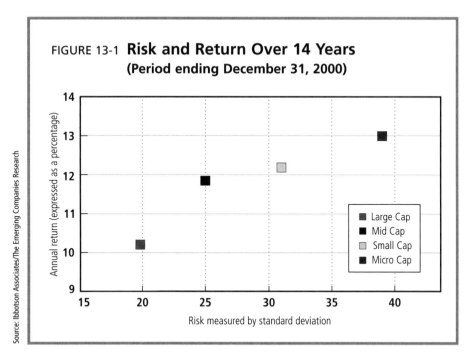

FIGURE 13-1 **Risk and Return Over 14 Years**
(Period ending December 31, 2000)

Source: Ibbotson Associates/The Emerging Companies Research

Does this mean that microcap stocks aren't risky? On the contrary, the graph shows that they are more than three times as risky as large-cap stocks. Thus, these stocks are not for widows and orphans or for persons at or nearing retirement age. Again, however, the point is that listed microcaps are relatively risky, but not speculative. They are an appropriate and reasonable asset class for people with discretionary investment dollars. Focus your IR activities on their advisers.

Microcap enthusiasts also argue that microcap stocks are appealing as so-called alternative investments, because they are inefficiently priced. Thus, they reason that this prevailing inefficiency provides real diversification in a strategy employing stocks of differing market capitalization. This presupposes some significant difference in market performance from the larger-cap stocks. Is there any evidence in support of this? If so, how valid is the evidence over several market cycles and macroeconomic cycles? And, in the spirit of prudent practice, does past performance guarantee the validity of projecting these attributes to this asset class?

Are Microcaps Diversification Plays?

The fact that almost no microcap company pays dividends simplifies the consideration of whether microcap stock returns co-vary with the returns of the largest cap stocks. What does not simplify this discussion is that transaction costs associated with microcap investing are very high.

Transaction costs and the related issue of small-float liquidity aggravate and complicate every microcap IR challenge. Those issues are there 24/7. If emerging growth companies ignore these omnipresent bugaboos in formulating share-price enhancing strategies, they may not survive as public companies. Let's review some research on how these issues affect portfolio returns relative to other equities.

In 1998 the Plexus Group, a Los Angeles consulting firm, completed an extensive study confirming that transaction costs involving the smallest cap stocks are much higher than the costs associated with trading the larger-cap stocks. The study also confirmed that investment style would influence transaction costs. Other than brokerage fees, what other transaction costs are there?

♦ **Market impact cost,** which is measured by taking the difference in the quoted price of the stock when the manager placed an order and when the order was executed.

♦ **Delay cost,** which occurs when the investor tries to wait for the "best price" to make a trade with someone who is monitoring the stock closely. The odds are about equal, even in engaging in a waiting game, that an experienced investor or trader will not get a better price. In the worst case, the order gets cancelled.

♦ **Opportunity cost,** which is a type of delay cost carried to its extreme. This is the cost of missing out on or only partially filling the order.

These costs, as they relate to market cap and style strategies, are summarized in *Figure 13-2* with the cost components expressed in basis points (0.01 percent).

Note the range of average transaction costs across investment styles. Not surprisingly, large-cap value managers (who, by definition,

FIGURE 13-2 **Cost Patterns by Manager Style**
Cost Components (in Basis Points)

Style	Delay (Manager Timing)	Delay (Trader Timing)	Market Impact	Commission	Opportunity (Missed Traders)	Total
Large cap value	1	13	8	15	28	65
Large cap growth	82	32	21	10	14	159
Index/passive	31	61	25	9	12	138
Small cap value	5	63	40	20	32	160
Small cap growth	136	72	57	18	29	312

Source: Plexus Group

are shoppers) enjoy a large trading-cost advantage. Investors in small-cap growth companies encounter higher transaction costs than other investors, and microcap growth investors face the highest cost of any investor. (Plexus Group has developed an inclusive transaction costs database and some benchmarks. Readers who desire extensive and refined data should visit www. plexusgroup.com to find out how this data can be obtained.)

The Size Effect

Relative-returns studies use the data compiled by the Center for Research in Securities Prices (CRSP) when making relative comparisons among stocks of different market caps. CRSP market-cap data are organized into deciles. Taking all of the New York Stock Exchange (NYSE) stocks (excluding REITs, ADRs, and closed-end funds) and dividing them into deciles by market capitalization create CRSP deciles. The Nasdaq and AMEX stocks are then added to the appropriate deciles. The largest cap stocks are in deciles 1 and 2. Microcaps are in deciles 9 and 10.

In the late 1970s, Rolf W. Banz at the University of Chicago began studying the returns of stocks based on their market capitalization. His research suggested that, even after adjusting for risk, small company stocks seemed to do better than the stocks of large companies. Banz and his colleague Marc R. Reinganum subsequently published papers arguing that stock in the smallest cap CRSP deciles generated returns more than 5 percent higher than the returns of the larger-cap stocks over the same periods. They construed this excess return as the risk premium for holding the smaller-capitalized stocks. This observation was discussed among academics in the context of the Capital Asset Pricing Model (CAPM) and became known as the size effect.

Enthusiasts for investing in smaller-cap companies (including microcaps) always cite these studies. Their critics have countered that transaction costs made the differences between absolute returns negligible.

What Risk Premium?

The debates over risk/return aspects of the size effect thus have focused on the actual costs of buying or selling the microcap stocks. Critics have argued that these inherent transaction costs cancel out much of the supposed risk premium. The subsequent Plexus research indicates that with respect to small-cap growth stocks, the risk premium is less than 2 percent (the Banz-Reinganum size effect of 5 percent minus the Plexus small-cap growth costs composite of 3.1 percent).

So, the net risk premium is low for microcap companies. As to relative cyclical performance, are there times when microcap returns vary significantly from the returns of the largest-cap stocks, deciles 1 and 2? Have there been periods when microcap stocks significantly outperformed the blue chips over and above any so-called risk premiums?

The answer is yes. The bad news is that risk and transaction costs, of course, remain intrinsic characteristics of microcap stocks. Yet the good news is that the returns have been proportionate to the risks and co-vary with the larger-cap stocks. Look at *Figure 13-3*.

When returns comparisons are broken down into manageable time segments, the argument in favor of cap size diversification holds up. True enough, the relative performance periods illustrated in *Figure 13-3* are of unequal length. This reflects the smoothing out of those periodic "bursts" and "busts" that occurred in the overall U.S. market from 1969 to 2000. Subsequent periods likewise would be configured for the systemic shocks sustained during the early years of

Source: The Emerging Companies Research Institute using data from The Center for Research in Securities Prices

FIGURE 13-3 **Comparison of Returns Between CRSP Deciles 1/2 and 9/10 Over Market Cycles From 1969–1999**

Time Period	Returns from 1/2 Return by	Returns from Deciles 9/10	The Better Deciles Percentage Points
1969–1974	-17%	-70%	Deciles 1/2 by 53%
1975–1983	+247.5%	+1,197.5%	Deciles 9/10 by 950%
1984–1990	+159%	-15%	Deciles 1/2 by 174%
1991–1994	+52%	+127.5%	Deciles 9/10 by 75.5%
1995–1999	+201%	+80%	Deciles 1/2 by 121%

this century. Nevertheless, the evidence illustrated in *Figure 13-3* is clear: Returns have co-varied.

Why? The nature of microcap stocks performance helps to explain the patterns. They are the last stocks to rally, because investors turn to microcaps when they suspect that the large caps are overvalued. They are the last stocks to be sold in a downturn, because investors are loath to sell their less liquid stocks in the face of a buyer's market.

With this capsule picture affirming the appropriateness of microcap stocks for a certain type of investor—namely, the high-net-worth individual—the next step is to outline the most effective means to reach that targeted class of individuals.

Targeting Advisers to High-Net-Worth Investors

A base of high-net-worth investors (HNWIs) is the needed ingredient to provide a microcap company's stocks with liquidity and a stable trading range. The time involved to cultivate and recruit the financial advisers of this investor group is a necessary investment. These stockbrokers or financial planners can be one of a company's best lines of defense when economic events or a poor quarter depresses stock prices. They provide a leveraged communications system, since they can provide interpretation of macro and microeconomics events for their customers.

The Retail Broker

Institutions drive the markets, but never discount the role of those brokers whose trade are individual investors. They provide the most cost-efficient way to tell your story to the high-net-worth individual market once, and then have it repeated scores of times. Moreover, a broker is a compliance shield. Brokers know securities law. They know what they can and cannot say. Brokers can insulate a company from disclosure problems.

Institutions make purchases in large share lots, but not with a high degree of frequency. Even though individuals trade stocks in smaller lots, they tend to be long-term holders. They are less likely to sell in the face of a small quarterly earnings decrease. If a stockbroker is convinced that a stock's price represents value, that broker will be encouraging its purchase every trading day. Retail brokers and their customers create daily volume for microcap stocks. Without this activity, the company is less likely to attract the attention of institutional investors.

Finding brokers who cater to high-net-worth individuals, essentially a task of elimination, is less daunting than most IR professionals think. One reason is the manner in which brokers from the major firms now conduct their business. Thirty-five percent of the brokers dealing with HNWIs don't earn commissions on stock transactions. Their compensation is based on fees earned on the amount of their clients, assets that they direct to investment managers and hedge funds. These professionals are commonly known as fee-based consultants or wrap-account brokers. This group is easily identified as candidates for your first cut.

You also can eliminate brokers who have had less than five years' experience working as a broker. At any given time, this is about 25 percent of the broker pool. They will not have earned the autonomy to make their own recommendations. Another 25 percent that should be eliminated are those brokers whose customers have low tolerance for risk, such as those nearing retirement. Customers over age sixty likely carry the overriding concern of capital preservation. This suggested winnowing leaves about 15 percent of the broker pool that represent stocks (not portfolios) to accredited or qualified investors. These are discretionary investors with annual incomes of more than $250,000 and liquid assets exceeding $1,000,000.

You can begin building your target broker list by asking the HNWIs you know for the names of their investment advisers. We also suggest perusing magazines that appeal to HNWIs. *Town and Country, Architectural Digest, Gourmet,* and *Medical Economics* are some of the periodicals that have run articles featuring stockbrokers. *Registered Representative,* the broker trade magazine, frequently features profiles of successful brokers with high-net-worth clients.

Brokers to Avoid

Microcap investor relations programs must dictate the shunning of brokers who cater to speculators and gamblers, those who flip stocks, and those who chase the hot money. This clientele represents impatient money and is gone within weeks.

The SEC explicitly prohibits any broker from accepting payment from a company in exchange for promoting a stock. In addition to this practice being illegal, there is another reason to decline any such arrangement. The risks of working with a broker with such bad judgment and questionable ethics as to make such a proposal are self-evident.

To summarize the benefits of individual investor-directed IR: Note that attracting a solid cadre of HNWIs will be evidence that a microcap company is a viable investment. These experienced individual investors are critical to enhancing shareholder value. They tend to hold shares for a longer time than institutions; therefore, they create the most stable portion of the stockholder base. They will be the first to buy more stock in the company, if it demonstrates its ability to grow shareholder value.

The most efficient way to attract HNWIs is through stockbrokers with years of experience in working with them. It can be time-consuming to build a target list of appropriate retail brokers. To facilitate this process, one approach may be to retain an IR consultant who has already compiled such a list.

Attracting Institutional Investors

The recent concerns of large mutual funds and investment management firms about operating with economies of scale have resulted in a number of corporate mergers. The resulting behemoths may be enjoying economies of scale, but their trading decisions have become more bureaucratic. They are not nimble.

Few of the mergers have involved microcap investment managers or microcap-focused mutual funds, however. Microcap investment managers remain a nimble group of competitors for large pools of money. They are ready buyers of emerging company stocks that meet their criteria.

The institutional microcap universe contains approximately sixty-five target portfolios, of which about forty are emerging growth mutual funds. The remaining fund pools are run by independent managers with core strategies reliant on the microcap component and by sector-style managers who hold some microcap companies.

Understanding the Microcap Investment Manager

All microcap managers seek superior returns, but their selection criteria and search patterns will differ. They all want a high rate of annual earnings growth (typically 20 percent plus), but they look at the earnings in the context of another operating measure. Some favor high rates of revenue growth, some will look for annual increases in free cash flow, and still others want a pattern of increasing operating margins. A company should never approach a portfolio manager until the company understands that manager's selection criteria. Read the manager's prospectus and sales literature. Search the Web for transcripts of interviews the media has conducted with the target manager.

About 15 percent of the microcap investment funds we follow use computer-based screening models to select stocks. Generally, the managers of these portfolios won't welcome contact with anyone from a company.

The Profit Challenge for Microcap Investment Managers

As has been noted, microcap investment managers bear high transaction costs, in fact, higher than those borne by any other type of specialist portfolio manager. What is the common factor that governs these costs? The size of the float. Name the three features of a stock that appeal to a portfolio manager? The answer is liquidity, liquidity, and liquidity.

Since institutional investors interested in microcap companies don't typically have a lot of liquidity, they have to outperform those using other styles of investing just to recover their costs. (See *Figure 13-2*). Since they cannot avoid incurring relatively high transaction costs, they work to attain other economic efficiencies. For instance, they do not delegate research.

It is therefore key that microcap IR practices be structured to make it easy for investment managers to get the information they need about the company (within the bounds of Regulation FD). The company needs to organize the IR team in a manner that permits the investment managers to reach someone in the company directly. If the investment manager's call is forwarded to voice mail, for example, make sure someone returns the call within the hour. These investors have huge demands on their time. There are only two staffing models for the microcap investor office: very lean and none.

It is a truism that no public company can have a credible shareholder constituency without some institutional investors. Attracting microcap growth portfolio managers requires understanding their risk management practices, as well as their selection criteria. Understanding the conditions under which they operate is critical to attracting their investments. Thin floats are the major impediments for an institutional investor taking a position in a microcap. Increasing the float is paramount, and a concern for stock dilution is unwarranted among directors of an emerging growth company. Availability of the stock is far more important than earnings per share. It's the quality of earnings that's important.

Benchmarking

Benchmarking is an important part of evaluating the effectiveness of an IR program. Investors will want to measure stock values against market cap peers, as well as against industry and sector peers. Recent research suggests that institutional investors prefer to benchmark microcaps against the S&P 600 rather than against the Russell 2000. New research also exists suggesting that any negative impact from being dropped from an index is short lived.

In connection with the float issue discussed previously, there is a sunny side to the fact that a microcap stock is almost always in relatively short supply. This fact, coupled with the rules governing microcap margin accounts, makes it unlikely that microcap companies will ever be targets of a short-selling bear raid. The shorts can get killed trying to cover on a run-up.

Where Are the Market Makers?

Another issue, the structure of the market for microcaps, compounds the transaction-cost challenge. The SEC issued a revised set of rules in 1997 that changed the way orders were handled by the Nasdaq system. The rules were intended to correct some practices that had been allegedly increasing investor's trading costs. Soon after those rules were in effect, decimal trading was introduced. The combined impact of the revised rules and the penny trades made it largely impossible to make any money trading the smallest-cap stocks. Microcap securities dealers subsequently shut down their trading operations and ceased making retail markets in the Nasdaq Small Cap Issues system.

A few large-capitalized dealer firms had been functioning as warehousing wholesalers to the smaller dealers. When the small dealers stopped making markets, these wholesalers became the only game in town. The new rules didn't permit those few large dealers to make any money on trades, either. They did, however, find a better way to make money from their well-capitalized advantage. They began to glean information from the flow of all those buy and sell orders that now came to them.

There is now an oligopoly structure standing astride the Nasdaq Small Cap Issues system that is not providing adequate liquidity for that system's listed stocks. Investment bankers who underwrite the small-cap issues are now arranging to have some of those stocks listed on the American Stock Exchange (AMEX). In some instances, companies have left the Small Cap System for the AMEX.

Conventional wisdom has held that the exchanges existed for the seasoned issues, and the negotiated markets accommodated the emerging companies. Such arrangements are no longer the case. Will the move toward trading qualified microcaps on the AMEX enhance their liquidity, and reduce transaction costs? How will the role of the Electronic Communications Networks (ECNs) evolve? Will another exchange decide to challenge the AMEX? In formulating microcap IR strategies, these questions are relevant, pertinent, and crucial.

The Cyberspace Aggravation

The Web offers unlimited creativity for renegade brokers and their associates. The problems associated with questionable activity are extensive. Internet insurgents may not always be investors or brokers out to profit from unfounded rumors. There have been hundreds of cases of malicious intent from former employees and the disgruntled still on the payroll. Another aggravating group might be composed of dissatisfied customers who have slipped through the company's customer-relations nets or its product warranty programs. Companies even may, heaven help them, be the target of some activist group.

IR professionals in microcap companies need to be especially vigilant. Emerging companies are the most susceptible to cyberspace scams, schemes, and rumors that do lasting harm. Constant vigilance and a well-reasoned countering plan are crucial aspects of an IR program. Sound internal policies and rapid responses are necessary preventive and countering tactics.

The SEC continues to become more adept at earlier identification and intervention in Internet fraud. However, bear in mind that the SEC's role is to protect investors, not companies. Instances exist in which investors who were victims of investment frauds have had some of their losses returned to them. However, there are no such instances when the courts or any agency has mandated the restoration of the market value of a stock diminished by fraudulent activity—or by the madness of crowds. IR professionals, beware.

Authors' Note

This article is based in part on ideas contained in our book, *Investor Relations for the Emerging Company,* published by John Wiley & Sons, Inc. Information for ordering that inclusive work on this subject can be found at www.wiley finance.com. Readers who want more information on the research discussed in this chapter can contact us at www.shareholder-relations.net.

14 | IR and the Credit-Ratings Process

CLIFFORD M. GRIEP
Standard & Poor's

C REDIT RATINGS ARE the common language of bonds and debt, both on Wall Street and in world financial markets. As global benchmarks of a company's relative capacity to meet its financial commitments, ratings can influence access to and pricing of capital. Moreover, more and more investors are turning to the recognized credit-rating agencies to serve as investment beacons.

Traditionally serving fixed-income markets, ratings have also gained utility in other risk-sensitive transaction markets, such as refinancings and mergers and acquisitions. In addition, vendors, financial journalists, equity analysts, and even potential employees might look at credit ratings in gauging a company's status. Consequently, ratings can influence the decisions of trade creditors, suppliers, rivals, and other business partners, especially in periods of economic stress when credit risk exposure receives greater attention. Because of the important role ratings play in financial markets, many businesses, especially those contemplating public debt issuance, will request a rating from one of the large, well-known, ratings agencies. It is the responsibility of investor relations professionals to make this request and to provide the information required to satisfy this request as skillfully as possible. Credit ratings, and especially "downgrades"—lowering of credit ratings—are now more closely watched than ever.

Role of Ratings Agencies

Ratings agencies play a unique role in the capital markets, both by tradition and, in some countries, because of regulation. In the United States, for example, some four ratings agencies are sanctioned as Nationally Recognized Statistical Rating Organizations (NRSROs) by the Securities Exchange Commission (SEC). This recognition was initiated in 1975 when ratings were first incorporated into the SEC's Net Capital Rule for broker dealers, and at the time simply reflected that the ratings of certain firms, Standard & Poor's, Moody's, and Fitch, were used nationally. Over the past thirty years however, the SEC and other regulators have increasingly used credit ratings to help monitor the risk of investments held by regulated entities.

In addition, many institutional and other bond investors hold portfolios limited by credit rating, such as "BBB– or better," in the case of funds which hold only investment-grade bonds. Other funds prefer the higher yield associated with bonds that are rated lower on the totem pole.

The unique role of credit-rating agencies was highlighted by the adoption in 2000 of SEC Regulation Fair Disclosure (Regulation FD). Although not widely noticed in the financial media, Regulation FD specifically exempts NRSROs, which routinely use nonpublic information in their analysis. This access to otherwise nonpublic information is one reason why credit-rating agency ratings are often taken more seriously than "buy" or "sell" recommendations from brokerage analysts. It is also worth noting that bond-rating analysts are free of the conflicts of interest which so infamously plague brokerage analysts.

A principal goal of IR professionals should be to establish an ongoing dialogue with one or more of the NRSROs and thus to build management creditability. A few warnings for IR professionals:

- ◆ The credit-rating agencies keep files and records, and what has been called "institutional memory" is elephantine.
- ◆ The rating process is iterative, providing a large platform to judge management's ability and a company's creditworthiness. For example, credit-rating agencies will evaluate management's ability to anticipate and respond to competitive devel-

opments, achieve budgeting goals, and measure and manage risk. They will also measure management's ability tell the truth, warts and all.

♦ IR professionals and management should not consider presentations to a credit-rating agency to be mere marketing. Hubris and deception will eventually be uncovered.

What is called for is open and timely communication between management and rating analysts. Given the importance that many market participants attach to ratings and rating changes, management needs to know the key factors and assumptions supporting the agencies' rating opinions and, more importantly, the factors that would cause that rating to be changed in a southerly direction.

Composition of the Ratings Analysis

Ratings are primarily based on publicly available information—although, as mentioned, NRSROs do have access to otherwise confidential information. They also require ongoing dialogue with management and IR professionals of rated companies. Public companies routinely disclose information to ratings agencies, such as budgets and related financial projections, internal reports on business unit performance, risk measurement and management, operational risks, liquidity and funding risks, and financial and operating policies. This information enhances the rating process, generally providing the ratings agency analytical team with a deeper understanding of the company. The greater the understanding, the greater the comfort. And, with each corporate meltdown, analysts are learning to ask more trenchant questions.

Quantitative and Qualitative Components

Ratings are based on fundamental credit analysis, including both quantitative and qualitative components. Company performance and balance sheet structure are evaluated relative to both peer companies within the same industry and absolute benchmarks. Ratio analysis encompasses comparative assessment of earnings, profitability, cash flow, financial leverage, liquidity, and funding profile.

Comparative financial analysis is, of course, reliant upon interpretation of financial statements. This interpretation process includes an effort to understand and evaluate the critical accounting policies that influence reported results.

It must be conceded that ratings agencies are *not* auditors and most rely on audited financial statements. Similar to investors and analysts, ratings agencies are held hostage to accurate audits. Still, adjustments are routinely made to the reported financial results to reflect the ratings agency's interpretation of the risks and the economic substance of the related business activities, or to facilitate comparison across countries with divergent accounting requirements. In the case of Standard & Poor's, these adjustments are transparent, covered in its published criteria. Partly in response to the increasing complexity of the accounting framework for some business activity such as derivatives and risk transfer activities and partly due to the increasing evidence of accounting abuse, Standard & Poor's has intensified its focus on accounting policies and their implications, as have other ratings agencies. Consistent with public disclosure requirements, Standard & Poor's expects management to fully disclose and discuss critical accounting issues, especially when the choice of accounting treatment can materially impact reported financial results. It is the job of the IR team of any public company to make sure that information flows easily and smoothly to the credit-rating agency. Detectives, news reporters, investors, and credit-rating agencies become suspicious when information is withheld, even unintentionally.

Supplementing the comparative financial statement analysis, qualitative assessment is also an important part of the process. This measure comprises review of the economic environment, including competitive dynamics and their implications; company-specific competitive position; competitive strategy, practices, and policies including financial and risk management practices; and—increasingly—aspects of corporate governance. Transparency counts for much, especially in recent years.

In addition to the relative performance of the company, dialogue and meetings between the IR team and the credit-rating agencies provide an incremental basis for judging management and are an integral part of the credit-rating process. The purpose of these meetings is to review in detail the company's key operating and financial plans, management policies, and other credit factors that have an impact on the rating.

Rating Assignment

The primary goal of the rating process is to assign a concrete rating—such as BB—that evaluates the operating and financial strategies and policies of the firm for the financial markets. A rating that anticipates and incorporates these strategies is likely to be relatively stable. Consequently, full and accurate disclosure during the rating process is key. Moreover, to the extent creditworthiness can be managed, company officers must determine the relative role and importance of creditworthiness in the context of their overall strategy. In other words, management must decide if it can live with, say, a noninvestment grade rating below "BBB," or if it behooves them—and more importantly, the board of directors—to take steps to upgrade the rating. *Figure 14-1* presents the range of credit quality assignments used by the three major ratings agencies.

If management decides to shoot for a higher rating, that fact should be telegraphed to the markets, investors, and ratings agencies, along with the plans to achieve the higher rating. Here the IR team has a vital role to play, perhaps in assuring certain debt holders that upgrades could be in the offing, and why.

On the other hand, sometimes in an overzealous quest for a better rating, too much growth capital is siphoned off into debt payments, or too many assets are sold. Without considering creditworthiness in a strategic context, management could mistakenly pursue a higher rating than necessary, imposing unrealistic operating or financial constraints. This situation requires especially astute IR. If the long-term risks from trying to achieve a higher rating seem to be too high, the IR team must relay to financial market participants why management is comfortable with a lower rating.

Request for a Rating

In response to a rating request, credit-rating agencies assign a team, usually of two to four members, which includes an industry analyst, who will handle day-to-day contact with the issuer and others familiar

FIGURE 14-1 **Credit Rating Assignments**

Credit Quality	S&P	Moody's	Fitch
Solid as a rock	AAA	Aaa	AAA
Very fine quality	AA+	Aa1	AA+
	AA	Aa2	AA
	AA-	Aa3	AA-
Strong capacity to pay	A+	A1	A+
	A	A2	A
	A-	A3	A-
	A	A	A
Adequate ability to pay;	BBB+	Baa1	BBB+
lowest investment grade	BBB	Baa2	BBB
for banks	BBB-	Baa3	BBB-
Somewhat speculative;	BB+	Ba1	BB+
risk exposure	BB	Ba2	BB
	BB-	Ba3	BB-
More speculative;	B+	B1	B+
risk exposure	B	B2	B
	B-	B3	B-
Major risk exposure;	CCC+	Caa1	CCC+
on verge of default	CCC	Caa2	CCC
	CCC-	Caa3	CCC-
Crucial risk exposure;	CC+	Ca1	CC+
may have defaulted	CC	Ca2	CC
on interest payments	CC-	Ca3	CC-
Default or Imminent Default	C	C	C
General default	D	D	D
No rating requested	NR	NR	NR

with the industry. Functional specialists may assist industry analysts. The company typically is represented by its chief financial officer. The chief executive officer usually participates when strategic issues are reviewed. Operating executives often present detailed information regarding business segments.

In general, IR professionals should anticipate the following:

Scheduling. Management meetings should be scheduled at least several weeks in advance, to ensure mutual availability of the appropriate participants and to allow adequate preparation time for the ratings analysts. In addition, if an initial rating is being sought for a pending issuance, it is to the issuer's advantage to allow at least three to four weeks following the meeting for the rating agency to complete its review process. More time may be needed in certain cases— if, for example, extensive review of documentation is necessary. However, where special circumstances exist and a quick turnaround is needed, credit-rating agencies will endeavor to meet the requirements of the marketplace.

Facility tours. Touring major facilities can be very helpful for a credit-rating agency in gaining an understanding of a company's business. However, this is generally not critical. Given the time constraints that typically arise in the initial rating exercise, arranging facility tours may not be feasible. However, as discussed below, such tours may well be a useful part of the subsequent surveillance process.

Preparing for meetings. Corporate management or IR professionals are usually well advised to contact their designated analysts for guidance in advance of the meeting. Standard & Poor's and other credit-rating agencies provide a rating methodology profile, also called a RAMP, which covers in detail the areas that should be discussed in management meetings. Credit-rating analysts are not shy or tricky; they will tell you what they want to see, and in what form. The details will vary from industry to industry and from company to company. Corporate Ratings Criteria as well as industry comments and articles on peer companies from *CreditWeek* may be helpful to management for understanding and appreciating the analytic perspective.

Well in advance of the meeting, the company should submit background materials (ideally, several sets), including

♦ five years of audited annual financial statements

♦ the last two years of interim financial statements, and key regulatory filings
♦ narrative descriptions of operations and products
♦ a draft registration statement or offering memorandum, or
equivalent information (if available)

Written presentations by management, while not mandatory,
often provide a valuable framework for the discussion. Such presentations typically mirror the format of the meeting discussions, as outlined below. When a written presentation is prepared, it is particularly
useful for a credit-rating agency's analytical team to be afforded the
opportunity to review this before the meeting.

If additional information to clarify points discussed in the meeting is not immediately available, it can be provided afterwards. In
any case, credit-rating agency analysts generally will have follow-up
questions that arise as the information covered at the management
meeting is further analyzed.

Confidentiality. A substantial portion of the information in company presentations is highly sensitive and is provided by the issuer to
the credit-rating agency solely for the purpose of arriving at a rating.
Such information is kept confidential by the ratings group. Even if
the assigned rating is subsequently made public, any rationales or
other information that NRSROs publish about the company will only
refer to publicly available corporate information. Confidential information is not used for any other purpose or by any third party.

Conduct of the Management Meeting

Management meetings with companies new to the rating process typically last two to four hours, although sometimes longer if the company's operations are particularly complex or if management and the
IR team try to substitute flash for substance. Short, formal presentations by management may be useful to introduce areas for discussion.
Standard & Poor's preference is for meetings to be largely informal,
with ample time allowed for questions and responses. At management
meetings, as well as at all other times, Standard & Poor's welcomes
questions regarding its procedures, methodology, and analytic criteria.

Typical Agenda

The following is an outline of the topics that credit-rating agencies typically expect issuers to address in a management meeting:

- ♦ The industry environment and prospects
- ♦ An overview of major business segments with reference to key operating statistics, including comparisons with competitors and industry norms
- ♦ Management's financial policies and financial performance goals
- ♦ Distinctive accounting practices

    A careful review of accounting methods has become more important in recent years. Obviously, much greater scrutiny will be given to unusual accounting procedures, and clarity, not opacity, will be rewarded. IR professionals should ask themselves, and pose the question also for management: If a team of credit-rating agency analysts finds itself puzzled trying to understand our business, then who else is going to understand our business? After all, very few money managers, and even brokerage industry analysts, can afford to spend the time deciphering a company's accounting, and no one else can get access to otherwise privileged information.

- ♦ Management's projections, including income and cash flow statements and balance sheets, together with the underlying market and operating assumptions

    In regard to management's projections, it should be understood that Standard & Poor's (and other credit-rating agencies') ratings are not based on the issuer's financial projections or its view of what the future may hold. Rather, ratings are based on Standard & Poor's own assessment of the firm's prospects. But management's financial projections are a valuable tool in the rating process, as they indicate management's plans, how management assesses the company's challenges, and how they intend to deal with problems. Projections also depict the company's financial strategy in terms of anticipated reliance on internal cash flow or outside funds, and they help articulate management's financial objectives and policies, capital spending plans, and financing alternatives and contingency plans.

The emphasis given to various risk factors may change over time, reflecting changes in the competitive or economic environment or changes in the business profile of the company. Occasionally, new risk factors emerge. For example, the rating analysis of U.S. banks emphasized asset liability management in the late 1970s and early 1980s as interest rates soared, while in subsequent recessions loan quality and capital received more attention.

When Capital Markets Tighten

IR professionals should note that whenever capital markets are tight, there is a heightened focus on liquidity for the corporate sector. Consequently, company presentations to a credit-rating agency need to provide detail on the company's management of liquidity and funding risks—including contingent commitments in debt, counterparty or operating agreements that would be triggered by changes in ratings, equity prices, or violation of financial covenants. IR professionals and company officials can expect credit agency analysts to ask about how the company will fare, in terms of liquidity, if sales should contract due to recessionary trends. Demonstrating adequate contingency plans for dealing with a challenging business environment, adverse or inhospitable markets, or conditional commitments serves to underscore management's preparedness and is supportive of sound financial policies and creditworthiness.

Debt holders and credit-rating agencies may have a different take on additional debt than shareholders. Tolerances for increasing debt leverage may be acceptable to, or even welcomed by, equity holders, whose upside—possible hefty returns—justifies the incremental risk. For debt holders or other creditors who hold only a fixed claim on company resources, incremental financial leverage may impair cash flow coverages. The ratings process recognizes that management must balance the needs of multiple constituencies and expects as much in the data management provides. IR professionals should not show one face to creditors and another to shareholders. Management builds credibility through the consistency of presentations on strategy and financial policy to all constituents; word tends to get around. Decide on a prudent course and sell that course to both creditors and shareholders.

Surveillance and Ongoing Maintenance Coverage

Credit ratings on publicly distributed issues are monitored for at least three years. Companies that have requested the rating have the option of surveillance, or being reviewed by the agency on what is termed a "point-in-time" basis. Surveillance is performed by the same credit analysts who work on the original rating assignment. To facilitate surveillance, companies are requested to put the primary analyst on mailing lists to receive interim and annual financial statements and press releases.

The primary analyst then remains in regular telephone contact with the company to discuss ongoing performance and developments. When these vary significantly from expectations, or when a major, new financing transaction is planned, scheduling of an update management meeting is appropriate. Also, Standard & Poor's encourages companies to discuss hypothetically—again, in strict confidence—transactions that are perhaps only being contemplated (e.g., acquisitions, new financings). Standard & Poor's, and the other credit-rating agencies, are generally frank about the potential ratings implications of such transactions.

In any event, management meetings are routinely scheduled at least annually. These meetings enable ratings agency analysts to keep abreast of management's view of current developments, to discuss businesses that have performed differently from original expectations, and to be apprised of changes in plans. As with initial management meetings, Standard & Poor's willingly provides guidance in advance regarding areas it believes warrant emphasis at the meeting. Typically, there is no need for management to dwell on the sort of basic information covered at the initial meeting. Apart from discussing revised projections, it is often helpful to revisit the prior projections and discuss how actual performance varied, and the reasons for this variance.

A significant proportion of the meetings with company officials take place on their own premises. This allows the credit-rating analysts to see members of management in their own environment, especially at the operating level. While no false fronts should be erected by IR professionals or anyone else, company officers should be well informed about the pending visit and be prepared. There have been unfortunate episodes in which well-run companies—perhaps because operating people were working hard—made terrible impressions on analysts. Key people have been "out in the field" leaving less-qualified underlings to handle questions or make presentations. One boss having a bad day on display can make a whole company suspect. IR professionals should be aware of any such pitfalls that can be avoided honestly.

Ratings agencies provide a recognized guide for a broad spectrum of participants in the financial markets. In reviewing and making pronouncements on an issuer's financial strength, they have become powerful players with whom IR professionals need to interact effectively to safeguard the interests of their constituency.

15 | The Information Investment Managers Want From Public Companies

CHRISTOPHER N. ORNDORFF, CFA
Payden & Rygel Investment Co.

W HY DO COMPANIES need to work on their relations with investors? In theory, if capital markets are efficient and if a company's information is quickly disseminated and understood by investors, investor relations should have little value. If we accept the efficient-market theory, a company could operate in isolation, and as long as its earnings were rising (and the price/earnings ratio is held constant), its stock price would follow the upward trajectory.

As any experienced Wall Streeter knows, however, that scenario is a fairy tale. The flow of information is not perfect. Nearly every real-world investment manager would say that the market for corporate securities—both stocks and bonds—is not perfectly efficient.

Imagine a grocery store aisle filled with more than ten thousand types of breakfast cereal. That would be a pretty daunting shopping experience, even for some children. To attract the consumer's attention, cereal manufacturers would launch different strategies to get shelf-space advantage. They would probably advertise, run promotions, and design competing, eye-catching cereal boxes—as they do anyway, even without ten thousand brands on the market.

There are some parallels with the stock market. On all U.S. stock exchanges combined, more than ten thousand securities are traded. This creates a difficult shopping experience for an investment manager. The old adage "time is money" rings especially true for money managers who must maintain portfolios of stocks and who have a fiduciary responsibility to keep abreast of their investments. In this context, investor relations is about how a company advertises itself to institutional investors, who are usually savvy but pressed for time.

Companies often pride themselves on how well they know the users of their product, thanks to extensive consumer surveys and anecdotal field information from salespeople. Senior managers are generally well versed in the preferences and needs of key clients. But those same managers often know little about the investors who purchase their companies' stock. These investors should also be considered customers.

Job One for IR is to enhance investor confidence in the company. Greater investor confidence in a company often increases the demand for the stock. The benefit is the potential for a higher P/E ratio and higher stock price.

Who are these institutional investors, why are they so important, and what do they want? And how does the recent jumble of regulations influence communications with institutional investors? The following pages provide guidance to IR professionals and senior management alike on the most effective ways to deal with an important customer, the institutional investor.

Institutional Investor Universe

Institutional investors—whether pension funds, mutual funds, insurance companies, or investment management firms generally comprise three functional categories: analysts, portfolio managers, and research departments. With some institutional investors, these functions overlap; with others, they are distinct and separate.

Functional Categories

A publicly traded company seeking to raise its profile with the institutional investment community will most often come into contact with the analyst. Analysts are usually charged with covering a specific industry and are responsible for tracking between ten and sixty companies. They are expected to have in-depth knowledge of their industry and of each of the most significant companies within it.

Consequently, analysts will typically ask very specific financial or business strategy questions. In some organizations, they play a significant role in the selection of a stock or its weighting in a portfolio. In other organizations, the analyst prepares a list of recommended stocks within an industry from which a portfolio manager makes the ultimate selections.

Portfolio managers are frequently in charge of selecting individual securities for inclusion in a portfolio and determining their weight in that portfolio. Some began their careers as analysts and may have in-depth knowledge of certain industries. The nature of the portfolio managers' jobs, however, requires that they be generalists. Consequently, they are likely not to ask specific questions but rather to seek to gain an intuitive feel for a company and its position in its industry. Their attention to financial statements will usually be limited to more significant items, such as revenue growth, operating margins, free cash flow, growth, and earnings per share. Portfolio managers frequently rely on analysts or their research departments to give opinions or to gather additional information.

Research departments typically focus on either general economic research or specific industry research. They are frequently training grounds for analysts. This does not imply, however, that an IR team should change its presentation if the audience is composed of research analysts. Poor presentations create lasting impressions, because today's junior analyst or researcher may be tomorrow's portfolio manager, able to influence the investment management company's decision to purchase a stock.

Strategy Orientation and Size

IR professionals should, of course, keep in mind that not all institutional investors are the same. Some investment managers follow a passive strategy, whose objective is to match the makeup of an index, such as the Standard & Poor's (S&P) 500 Index. Passive investors tend to hold a stock for as long as the issuing company is a member of the relevant index. A passive investor's purchases and sales of stock are usually driven by the purchases and redemptions of the investment manager's clients. Although every investment manager should certainly be taken seriously, index managers are obviously not the ones on which IR professionals should concentrate their efforts.

Most investment managers follow an active strategy. Actively managed portfolios usually do not mirror an index, so the managers have more discretion in what they purchase and how positions are weighted in the portfolio.

There are many different ways to categorize active managers, but for the purpose of this chapter, they are divided into "real money" investors and "momentum players" (see *Figure 15-1*). Real money investors tend to make decisions based on fundamental data and can be further subcategorized into long-term and medium-term investors. Long-term investors will hold a stock for two or more years. Medium-term investors will hold a stock for six months to two years. Real money investors typically do not employ leverage to purchase a company's stock. As "buy-and-hold" investors, they are a very important investing audience.

Momentum players are less interested in the fundamentals of a company. They are motivated by anticipated events that could affect a company's stock—for example, a future earnings announcement, a new business contract, a litigation outcome, a merger, or a management change. Some momentum investors rely on technical indicators based on the stock price movement. Momentum players typically have very short-term holding periods, which may range from several hours to six months. Some also employ leverage in their strategies, which can magnify the impact their actions have on a company's stock price. When a stock price suddenly declines 10 to 20 percent and no news has been released by the company or by any brokerage analyst that covers it, a reasonable conclusion is that the sudden decline is the result of the actions of one or more momentum players.

Another category of momentum players includes short sellers. Most short sellers are also event-driven, capitalizing on negative events and the resulting decline in a security's price. The exceptions are those investors who are selling short to hedge their purchases of a company's convertible debt.

Some publicly traded companies pay attention only to the largest institutional investors or to their largest shareholders. They may go so far as to allow only large institutional investors access to senior

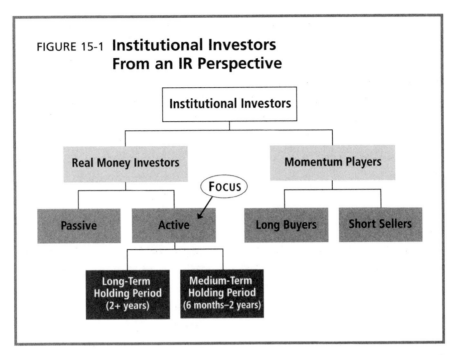

FIGURE 15-1 **Institutional Investors From an IR Perspective**

management. Some companies even screen out smaller institutional investors from asking questions on quarterly-earnings conference calls. This is a mistake for obvious reasons, many of which are detailed below, but the practice nevertheless continues.

The first reason for not ignoring smaller institutions is that they are still investors and can decide to sell. In soft markets, even modest selling can drive prices down. We may have entered a sustained period in which large institutions will not have more and more money each year to throw around. Think about the net outflows that the mutual fund industry has been experiencing month after month. If small institutions decide to sell, the big investors may not be there to sop up the shares. Indeed, they may be forced to be net sellers, too.

Second, analysts and portfolio managers tend to move from large firms to small ones, and vice versa. Large institutional investors may shrink, particularly if their investment performance is poor, and small institutional investors may grow. Hence it is important to treat all institutional investors equally.

Additionally, many companies mistakenly ignore fixed-income investors in favor of equity investors. In many institutional investment firms, the fixed-income analysts and equity analysts regularly discuss the companies they follow. The discussions may influence the investment firm's decision to purchase a stock and the weighting assigned to it in the portfolio. Moreover, should the company decide to access the public debt markets in the future, it will already by familiar to the investment community. This may pay off in the form of a well-subscribed debt offering at a commensurately lower interest rate cost.

Institutional Investor Information Needs

Institutional investors want access to information to help them make better decisions about the eventual purchase of a company's stock. Several years ago, companies spent a lot of money on slick, glossy investor relations kits that contained highly produced annual reports and supplementary documentation. Most institutional investors, however, are inundated with paper and, with the advent of broadband connections on the Internet, would prefer to receive company information in an electronic format.

Electronic Communication

Publicly traded companies interested in attracting and retaining investors should have well-designed websites that provide basic company information, access to SEC filings, press releases, and the most recent annual and quarterly reports in an easily readable format—for example, Adobe Acrobat. A company's website should also contain information about its products and strategy, attitude and culture, and professional biographies of key senior managers. In addition, it should include recent presentations that the company has made to institutional investors and at conferences or in one-on-one contexts. A good model is the website for Millipore Corp. (www.millipore.com), a Big Board–listed company that provides "separations technology" for the life science industry. Some companies are justifiably concerned about releasing information that could end up in competitors' hands. One solution is to require visitors to a website to register. In this way, the company can discern whether the person making an inquiry is a bona fide institutional investor.

The fact that information is released in electronic format is not a license to be oblique. Institutional investors want transparent financial disclosure. They want straightforward footnotes to financial statements and disclosure of items that may impact earnings in future reporting periods. Institutional investors generally prefer that companies adopt FASB (Financial Accounting Standards Board) rules earlier than the prescribed deadline. Early adoption reduces uncertainty about the effects of rule changes and demonstrates that the company is making a good-faith effort to fairly represent its operations in the financial statements.

Companies that earn a significant amount of revenue from licensing should perform additional disclosure. An excellent example of this practice is provided by Qualcomm. (www.qualcomm.com), a digital and wireless communications company that provides very good disclosure regarding its intellectual property and licensing revenue. Institutional investors appreciate companies that exhibit a spirit of transparency. It doesn't take long for most veteran investors to sense that a company is sitting on information.

Institutional investors like to receive e-mailed updates. Most company websites offer investors the opportunity to register for regular e-mail communications, which may disclose financial information as well as significant company announcements. Investment managers prefer portable e-mailed updates to paper updates sent via regular mail or fax. Such electronic information is more convenient. It can be received on mobile hand-held devices, categorized, and easily filed based on rules that are easily programmed into e-mail software. E-mail is also timelier than an announcement sent by regular mail.

Conference Calls

Institutional investors generally prefer at least quarterly conference calls with company management. Since the introduction of Regulation Fair Disclosure (FD), most conference calls have become highly scripted affairs, probably too much so, from the investor's perspective. Often, corporate legal counsel, fearful of inadvertently violating a regulation or being sued by a shareholder, guides senior management to a sometimes "*Dragnet*-like" recitation of the facts. However, such calls are still valuable. Most companies allow questions at the end of the company announcement, and the answers to these are often more important than the scripted part of the call. It is worth noting that the most interesting questions usually come from other institutional investors, not from brokerage analysts.

Despite that, some publicly traded companies allow only brokerage analysts or large shareholders to pass through the filter to ask questions on a conference call. This is a mistake. If a company has nothing to hide, why shouldn't it take on all comers? Investors can easily identify the planted questions and scripted answers, and this action merely serves to hurt the company's credibility.

Since many companies hold conference calls on the same days (and sometimes at the same time of day) during the earnings season, it is wise to have replays of the conference calls available online or at a toll-free number for at least one or two weeks following the original date of the call.

Face-to-Face Meetings

Institutional investors also value face-to-face meetings with senior management. These meetings, which may take the form of conferences, meetings in investment manager offices, analyst days, or even tours of company facilities, are important because they enable investors to personally assess senior managers rather than just read about them or hear them talk over the telephone. It's entirely possible that, on occasion, charisma carries more weight than facts: Surely, some managements have won the confidence of Wall Street without comprehensible business models but with a lot of attitude. Enron comes to mind. But clarity and earnestness are just as impressive, and more durable, to institutional investors.

Venues. Both analysts and portfolio managers will travel to visit a company. Usually, the institutional investor will want to speak with not one but various members of senior management. When arranging on-site face-to-face meetings a company should try to include a tour of the facility, the grounds, or the factory, if it is a manufacturer. A facility tour provides an opportunity to observe how work actually gets done and can create a lasting impression that may help the investor make a more informed decision.

Often, a company has a chance to make a presentation at a conference hosted by a brokerage house. These conferences may include hundreds or thousands of investors and several dozen companies. Company presentations typically are made to groups of 50 to 100 investors and often follow a strict format. A breakout session with a smaller group follows the presentation. The advantage of a conference is that a company can reach a relatively large number of investors in one or two hours. The disadvantage is that the company's message can get lost in the crowd, since investors are listening to up to six or more presentations in one day. In such sessions, it must be conceded that a little razzmatazz is in order, since it is necessary to stand out somehow in the crowd.

A common venue for face-to-face meetings is the investment manager's office. An investor relations firm or a brokerage firm often escorts client companies across the country to visit numerous institutional investors. These meetings are usually very efficient, because the investment manager typically has done some homework on the company before the visit. There is debate in the industry as to whether it is better to have an investor relations firm or a brokerage firm set up the meetings with institutional investors on a company's behalf. Although there are positives to both approaches, it can be argued that an introduction made by an IR firm provides the appearance of greater independence on the part of the company and may translate to a presentation that is more candid and free from conflict of interest. Institutional investors prefer to keep a copy of the company presentations in their files and refer to them on a regular basis.

Analyst days are much like exclusive conferences held at the company's site. These are often well worth attending if the investors are able to dedicate the time and make travel plans. The downside to analyst days is that they generally attract only analysts rather than portfolio managers or other investment professionals. Although this is not necessarily a negative, it means that the company has a limited audience. There is also the concern that most brokerage analysts are Trojan horses, in search of investment banking work. There may be a price to be paid for a "buy" recommendation.

Content. The content of face-to-face meetings should focus on the big picture, such as the firm's strategic direction, its efforts to cut costs, or its plans for a sustained share buyback program. It is better to tell a few big stories well than to delve into minutia that will be forgotten by the next day. A sensible business plan, which does not assume ideal circumstances or ninth-inning home runs, should be presented. Most investors will be familiar with a company's earnings growth and other financial numbers.

However, personal meetings need not be painted wholly in broad brush strokes. Such meetings are good opportunities for company management to explain important items that may be coming up in the next proxy vote or to review accounting policies that may be different from those found in other industries. Institutional investors like companies to make candid comments on their competitors. This reveals a depth of knowledge about the industry and a willingness to be frank. A victory over competitors or winning a market is a coup that warrants being brought up, as is "stealing away" a key employee or salesperson. When a smart individual who has spent much or all of his or her professional life in an industry places a bet on a company by moving there, it is bound to have an influence on investors.

Institutional investors use meetings with companies to gather the information they believe to be important. Unfortunately for IR teams at public companies, there are as many different investment styles as there are investors. Some institutional investors focus on qualitative factors, such as brand management and human resources. Others look at measures of financial performance. Still others try to get a sense of the leadership qualities of senior management. They may be asking themselves what it would be like to work for the person with whom they are meeting. Obviously, this is a personal judgment and hardly the determining factor in a decision to buy or sell a stock. Nevertheless, if they wouldn't like to work for this management, who would? Will the company have trouble retaining talented employees?

One question investors may ask managers is how they sell their company to potential hires. For example, if a company is in the biotechnology industry, how would they recruit a new doctorate-level research scientist? The motivation in asking the question is that happy employees are usually productive as well. Investors will get a sense of corporate culture during a personal visit. Again, company management and IR teams need not worry excessively that this is a matter of suave presentations, natty attire, or charisma. Investors will also want to find out if management regards itself as working for shareholders, rather than regarding shareholders as a group that must be tolerated, appeased, or handled. If the board, particularly the independent directors, are all a little too cozy, investors will want a good explanation why.

Know Your Stock and Its Place in the Universe

Stock is a product much like the product or service the company sells, except that, unlike consumers, shareholders own the company. Companies should understand their stock as well as they do their products or services. They should also learn something about the consumers who buy their stock. Knowing the indexes in which a stock is represented is a good place to start. The stock may be included in broad indices such as the S&P 500 or the Russell 2000 index of small-cap stocks. It may also be incorporated into a style index, such as the S&P/Barra Growth index or the Russell 2000 Growth index. The weighting a stock has in these indices is also important information.

There are more than six thousand investment advisers registered with the SEC. To help a publicly traded company narrow this universe, its investor relations staff should research the one hundred largest investment managers in the specific asset class in which its stock is represented. This may differ significantly from the one hundred largest investment managers overall. The IR staff should then ascertain the amount of money managed, both actively and passively, against the benchmark index of which the stock is a member. This will give the company a sense of the potential market for its stock. Obviously, if the stock is large-cap and included in the S&P 500 index, seeing a manager who specializes in small-cap stocks is not a good use of time.

The next step is to determine what would make particular managers purchase the stock or add to existing positions in it. This again depends on the type of investment strategy the managers follow. For some, the decision to purchase a new stock or beef up a position in an old one will depend on fundamental variables. Stable or increasing operating margins, increasing or stable revenues, and similar measures will entice these investors to buy a stock. If the company shows an ability to generate enough free cash flow to sustain a stock buyback program, this too creates an attraction among more fundamentals-oriented managers.

Managers who are more event-oriented will not purchase until, for example, a new product is released or a new senior executive is hired. Others focus mostly on technical indicators and will not buy until, say, the 50-day moving average of closing prices for a stock crosses above the 200-day moving average.

IR executives should also understand what would cause investors to sell a stock. Generally, the reasons are the inverse of those for purchasing it. But there may be other reasons, as well. Stock indices are rebalanced at different intervals. For example, the Russell stock indices are reconstituted once each year, in June. If a company's stock migrates from the Russell 2000 to the Russell 1000, the universe of buyers for that stock will change. This may cause selling from both passive and active investment managers. A logical inference is that the selling by small-cap investors should equal the purchases by large-cap investors. Recall, however, that stock indexes are capitalization-weighted: The larger the market capitalization, the greater the weight in the index. So, a stock will have a greater weight in the Russell 2000 small-cap stock than in the Russell 1000 large-cap stock index. Ironically, a company could be growing, migrating up to the Russell 1000 from the Russell 2000, and yet experience some selling pressure. A clever IR team might try to reach appropriate institutional shareholders and advise them of a pending potential buying opportunity.

IN THE FINAL ANALYSIS, a company's IR team, along with senior management, needs to focus on factors that can be controlled. There are also factors beyond their control that they must accept. Some investment managers are going to "rent" their stock and have high turnover. Some will sell the stock in a sloppy manner, causing the price to fall inexplicably. Some will short the stock. Others will buy or sell based solely on technical indicators, while others will buy or sell as the stock moves from one index to another. And some investment managers will never buy your stock, because it is a type they simply do not hold. Blue-chip managers, for example, generally eschew small cap stocks.

The IR team must accept these realities and concentrate its resources on those institutional investors who are making practical judgments about buying and selling stocks that are similar to the company's. The team should develop a rapport with institutional investors who are likely to buy and hold the company's stock. And remember, every such investor is important, not just those from large funds. The corporate culture should impress money managers in personal meetings. That almost always means showing respect for good corporate governance and shareholders.

Index

About Bloomberg

Bloomberg L.P., founded in 1981, is a global information services, news, and media company. Headquartered in New York, the company has nine sales offices, two data centers, and 87 news bureaus worldwide.

Bloomberg, serving customers in 126 countries around the world, holds a unique position within the financial services industry by providing an unparalleled range of features in a single package known as the BLOOMBERG PROFESSIONAL™ service. By addressing the demand for investment performance and efficiency through an exceptional combination of information, analytic, electronic trading, and Straight Through Processing tools, Bloomberg has built a worldwide customer base of corporations, issuers, financial intermediaries, and institutional investors.

BLOOMBERG NEWS®, founded in 1990, provides stories and columns on business, general news, politics, and sports to leading newspapers and magazines throughout the world. BLOOMBERG TELEVISION®, a 24-hour business and financial news network, is produced and distributed globally in seven different languages. BLOOMBERG RADIO℠ is an international radio network anchored by flagship station BLOOMBERG® 1130 (WBBR-AM) in New York.

In addition to the BLOOMBERG PRESS® line of books, Bloomberg publishes BLOOMBERG MARKETS™ and BLOOMBERG WEALTH MANAGER®. To learn more about Bloomberg, call a sales representative at:

Frankfurt:	49-69-92041-0	São Paulo:	55-11-3048-4500
Hong Kong:	852-2977-6900	Singapore:	65-6212-1000
London:	44-20-7330-7500	Sydney:	61-2-9777-8601
New York:	1-212-318-2200	Tokyo:	81-3-3201-8900
San Francisco:	1-415-318-2970		

FOR IN-DEPTH MARKET INFORMATION and news, visit the Bloomberg website at www.bloomberg.com, which draws from the news and power of the BLOOMBERG PROFESSIONAL® service and Bloomberg's host of media products to provide high-quality news and information in multiple languages on stocks, bonds, currencies, and commodities.

About the Editor

Benjamin Mark Cole has been a financial journalist for more than two decades, starting as a researcher-reporter with *U.S. News & World Report* in Washington, D.C., in 1980. After four years with *U.S. News,* covering federal budget issues, securities, and the economy, Cole returned to his native Los Angeles to help launch *Investor's Daily* (now *Investor's Business Daily*), the financial newspaper. Cole then joined the staff of *The Los Angeles Herald Examiner* as a reporter on the daily paper's "Money" section. In 1986, his investigation of insurance industry practices was cited by the Heart newspaper group as "the best business story of the year" for the entire, nationwide chain. Later that year Cole joined the *Los Angeles Business Journal,* covering the securities industry and general economic news. In 1997, Cole won the Best Feature Story of the Year from the Association of Area Business Journals in a national competition of more than fifty regional business publications. Cole also authored the popular "Wall Street West" column for the *Business Journal,* from 1997 through 2003. In addition, Cole has written weekly national columns on the securities industry for Knight-Ridder and for Bridge Information Systems. In 2001, Bloomberg Press published Cole's book, *The Pied Pipers of Wall Street: How Analysts Sell You Down the River.* Cole testified before Congressional hearings on brokerage industry analyst abuse that same year. Cole is a graduate of the University of California at Berkeley and obtained a master's degree from the University of Texas at Austin's Lyndon B. Johnson School of Public Affairs.